Not by Bread Alone

Not by Bread Alone

Social Support in the New Russia

Melissa L. Caldwell

UNIVERSITY OF CALIFORNIA PRESS

Berkeley / Los Angeles / London

University of California Press
Berkeley and Los Angeles, California

University of California Press, Ltd.
London, England

© 2004 by the Regents of the University of California

Chapter 6 was adapted from an article previously published as "The Social Economy of Food Poverty in Russia," in *Culture and Economy: Contemporary Perspectives,* edited by Ullrich Kockel (Aldershot, England: Ashgate Publishing [2002]).

All photographs by the author, William H. Caldwell, and Sandra L. Caldwell.

Manufactured in the United States of America

13   12   11   10   09   08   07   06   05   04
10   9   8   7   6   5   4   3   2   1

The paper used in this publication meets the minimum requirements of ANSI/NISO Z39.48–1992 (R 1997) (*Permanence of Paper*).

Contents

Illustrations

Note on Transliteration

I have followed the U.S. Library of Congress system of transliteration in this book, except in cases where spellings for certain proper names and other words have become more familiar to North American readers (for instance, Anya instead of Ania).

Preface

As so often happens with field research, this project emerged from a series of coincidences and tangents. During the late summer and early fall of 1997, shortly before I left the United States to begin my fieldwork on changing consumer practices in Moscow, I began encountering on a fairly regular basis newspaper and television articles about severe food shortages and food aid programs in Russia. Journalists and policy makers alike warned that with the coming winter, the Russian population was facing imminent hunger and in some cases outright starvation. While domestic and international soup kitchens were gearing up to meet the expected increase in demand, American and other foreign organizations were actively soliciting donations of money and supplies that they would send to Russia. A frequent stylistic strategy that the authors used to make these reports more compelling was to juxtapose images of hardship and fanciful tales about Russia's nouveaux riches, the so-called New Russians, who were allegedly idling their days away in their châteaus in the south of France, buying expensive luxury cars, and providing the clientele base for a growing niche of high-end restaurants and food boutiques in Russia.

As I monitored these reports I became convinced that I had found a topical angle to incorporate into my initial, and perhaps intellectually drier, project about post-Soviet consumption changes. If I were to study those who were exercising their capacities to consume, I reasoned, I must necessarily also address the conditions of those Muscovites whose consumption practices were severely constrained by economic circumstances. I thus envisioned that my project would be transformed into a comparative examination of two seemingly disparate groups of Moscow consumers: those with the resources to make consumer choices and those without.

Through several fortuitous connections in the United States and in Moscow, I was put in touch with the Christian Church of Moscow, an international Protestant congregation that runs a soup kitchen program in the city. Although it was not my original intent to focus on this community exclusively, I quickly found myself caught up in the lives and networks of the people who belonged to this group. I also discovered that the soup kitchens provided a valuable vantage point from which to approach and understand the larger social changes that have been taking place in Russia, particularly that distinctions between "haves" and "have-nots" do not accurately reflect the realities of a society in which informal support networks take precedence over money and other resources. Thus, I did not abandon my original project entirely, but rather reworked the focus to accommodate research in one of the soup kitchens. Through the writing process, however, I realized that the soup kitchen was an intriguing and complex site worthy of investigation in its own right. Consequently, I have decided to focus in this book primarily on issues of everyday survival and explore aspects of consumption more fully elsewhere (Caldwell 1998, 1999, 2002).

Although this book begins with life in a soup kitchen, it is not explicitly about the material conditions of poverty and hardship in Russia today, even though the recipients in this program are among the poorest people in the city. Nor is it strictly an account of the elderly in Russia, even though most immediate members of the soup kitchen are pensioners and veterans. Instead I use the themes of scarcity and hardship as points of departure for an examination of Muscovites' everyday survival practices. Specifically I am interested in understanding how Muscovites "make do": How do individuals create alternative forms of security when the official economy is unable to meet their material needs? How do individuals elaborate complex cultural and social lives through the skillful manipulation of scarce resources? What is the importance of social relations in these activities? What do these activities say about the relationship between economy and society in Russia today? How well does the capacity to improvise help individuals make sense of the rapid changes that are taking place in Russian society? And finally, what does it mean to talk about social support and "social security"?

Because much of this book is about social networks and collective activities, it is only appropriate that I acknowledge that the research project on which it is based is in fact a collaborative product. I have benefited from the assistance of many individuals, but I am especially grateful to the members of the Christian Church of Moscow congregation and soup kitchens. Members of this community helped me in ways great and small, ranging from responding to requests for data about the program's day-to-day operations and taking the time to sit down for formal interviews, to helping me navigate the bureaucratic quagmires of Russian official-dom and offering treasured friendships and gentle companionship. People graciously opened their homes and their lives to me, and I feel honored to have been given such a dear gift. While I cannot possibly thank each person sufficiently, or even individually in most cases, I hope that perhaps with this book I can repay some of the great debts I owe them and reassure them that they are always close in my thoughts.

My Moscow experiences have also benefited from the assistance of many friends and colleagues who have given their time, encouragement, advice, and in some cases, a way to recuperate by inviting me to visit them at their summer cottages, where they pampered me. I am especially in-debted to Konstantin, Oktiabrina, and Ekaterina Cherëmovskii; Valentina, Yurii, and Ekaterina Gribov; Habib Khazali; Sofia Alekseevna Komorova; Dora Lindenbaum; Olga and Anton Nosov; Chang Nyikako; Igor Osipov; Valentina Osipova; Olga Pestunenko; Michael Roseman; Twila Schock; Bill Swanson; members of the Russian Red Cross; and members of the International Red Cross. Maria Tarasova of the Moscow office of the Davis Center for Russian and Eurasian Studies at Harvard University arranged for my housing and visa invitation dur-ing my extended fieldwork. Oona Schreiner has gone beyond the bounds of friendship in helping me with visas and housing problems during sub-sequent visits to Moscow.

Funding was provided by the U.S. Department of Education (Title VI), the Mellon Foundation, and several small travel grants from the de-partment of anthropology and the Kathryn W. and Shelby Cullom Davis Center for Russian and Eurasian Studies at Harvard University. The Davis Center has also provided institutional support, both in Moscow and in Cambridge, and opportunities for me to present work-in-progress for critical evaluation. Harvard University provided a write-up fellowship through the Cora Du Bois Fellowship Program. Lastly, the Committee on Degrees in Social Studies at Harvard University provided additional research funds between 2000 and 2002.

Academic colleagues both in Russia and in the United States have of-fered valuable suggestions on various stages of the project and the written work. Nikolai Ssorin-Chaikov graciously arranged two opportunities for me to present my work in Moscow, one of which was through his friend and colleague Leokadia Drobizheva, head of the Institute on Poverty and Wealth at the Institute of Ethnography, Russian Academy of Sciences. Her comments and suggestions, and those of her colleagues in the institute, helped me sharpen my focus and introduced me to certain techniques of "making do." I am grateful to Julie Hemment, Nancy Ries, and Valentina Uspenskaia for their critical advice and support on all things anthropological "in the field." Other friends and colleagues have talked through ideas with me and have read drafts of this work at various stages of its development. For their valuable criticisms, suggestions, and assistance, I thank Manduhai Buyandelgeryin, Jennifer Cash, Chao Chen, Erika Evasdottir, Maris Gillette, Tracey Heatherington, Natasha Hunter, Vladimir Kleyman, Eriberto Lozada, Thomas Malaby, Vasiliki Neofotistos, Jennifer Patico, Bernie Perley, Michele Rivkin-Fish, Rebecca Ruhlen, Kerry Sabbag, and Olga Shevchenko, as well as my colleagues and students in the Committee on Degrees in Social Studies at Harvard. Christine Kiernan did a phenomenal job transcribing audiotapes. Jeanne Moore deserves special commendation for coming up with the first part of the title of this book. As members of my dissertation committee, Rubie Watson and James Watson have guided the project and my development as an anthropologist through the rough terrain of both the postsocialist world and the academic world. I am fortunate to have had them on my side. I particularly appreciate Rubie's insistence that I think about the issue of "aloneness." That single piece of advice was a transformative moment in the way that I conceptualized the phenomenon of poverty in Russia. My greatest debt goes to Michael Herzfeld. Michael has been an unflagging supporter, critical advocate, and dear friend. He has taught me more about anthropology and the joys of ethnographic research than he probably will ever realize, and for that I thank him.

At the University of California Press, I have been fortunate to work with Stan Holwitz, who has been exceedingly generous in his support and encouragement of this project, and Randy Heyman and Lynn Meinhardt, who have cheerfully answered my many questions. In their capacity as reviewers, Darra Goldstein and Matti Bunzl offered both critical feedback and wonderful suggestions for ways to improve this text. I deeply appreciate their assistance. I am also grateful to Robin Whitaker for her careful editing of the manuscript.

Finally, I am fortunate to have had the support of many friends and family members who have offered necessary words of advice and have always helped me find both humor and pleasure in my academic pursuits. I would like to thank Pat and Cliff Baker, Sharon Cohen, Jane Huber, Kristin Caldwell Peto, Joe Peto, Amy Troutman, and Kathleen Wage. I am grateful to my parents, Bill and Sandy Caldwell, who inspired in me the joys of learning and of being curious, and who shared several of my Russian adventures. Finally, none of this would have been possible without the love, encouragement, patience, and good humor of my husband, Andrew Baker. He has willingly read drafts, talked through ideas with me, and supported my academic choices, even when they have taken me across continents. This book is for him.

CHAPTER 1

Transnational Soup

No matter the time of year, mornings are busy in Moscow. From the center to the outskirts of the city, subways and buses are crammed with jostling passengers on their way to work, school, and the markets. Although there is a certain homogeneity to the morning commute all across Moscow, the specific stories that are related in this book converge at the Park Kul'tury (Culture Park) metro station (figure 1), centrally located just a few stops from the Kremlin, the Bolshoi Theater, and Moscow State University. During rush hour, the train cars that arrive at Park Kul'tury are packed so tightly that it is impossible to hang on to the railings; commuters are kept upright simply because there is no room to move. When the train stops, the doors open, expelling an anonymous mass of bodies. The crowd moves as one, along the platform and up the long, packed escalators to the single set of exit doors that lead to the street. Just outside, young women hover expectantly, thrusting flyers describing offerings such as English lessons, fur coats, and trips to Greece and Egypt into the faces of commuters. Finally, the crowd dissipates as Muscovites break away and head toward their respective destinations.

Along the sidewalks and underground walkways that tunnel beneath the busy Moscow streets at Park Kul'tury, store clerks busily open their shop doors. Vendors unroll the flaps of their stalls, unload wares off the backs of trucks, and unpack goods from battered boxes and bags. The aromas of freshly baked bread, roasting pork, and recently picked garlic and dill mingle with exhaust fumes and the smell of stale beer. Even before nine o'clock, customers have already lined up in front of kiosks that offer bread, sausage and other meats, fresh fruit, beer and snacks, ice

FIGURE 1. The Park Kul'tury metro station is a busy site as Muscovites stop to shop and visit.

cream, lottery tickets, transportation passes, flowers, newspapers, and shoe repair. Under the supervision of imposing security guards, clerks at currency exchange booths post the day's exchange rate between the ruble and the U.S. dollar. Policemen armed with heavy weapons watch pedestrians walk by and occasionally stop young men to ask them for their documents. During the day it is not unusual to glimpse workers from the nearby circus exercising camels and horses along the side streets. Pedestrians in an underground crosswalk may have to step around paramedics tending to a homeless person who has passed away during the night.

In this historic district of Moscow, a neighborhood whose residents have included famous writers, dancers, and politicians and whose landmarks have included military academies, artists' unions, foreign embassies, and the Park Kul'tury, for which the metro is named, a steady stream of students, faculty, and other visitors make their way from the metro station and bus stops to the Moscow Scientific Institute (a pseudonym).[1] This university, one of the most prestigious centers of higher education in Russia, is located in a squat historic building just blocks away from the Kremlin. Immediately beyond the main doors, two uniformed guards stand duty at a rusty set of turnstiles. They occasionally break from their animated conversation to glance at those who come inside, check entry passes, and answer questions. Inside the hallway that opens off this entry, students huddle in small groups and review their notes, chat with friends, inspect pencil choices at the school supply kiosk, and queue for the automated bank machine in the corner. Posters and flyers announcing upcoming lectures, study trips abroad, and organizational meetings are scattered on the walls, adding touches of color to the otherwise institutional brown that pervades the building. The scents of boiled cabbage, sausage, fresh bread, and coffee waft through the corridors. A scruffy cat darts through the crowd and then disappears down a long hallway. Those who have time before their first class wander toward the cafeteria, stopping along the way to browse at tables covered with books, cosmetics, and (today) slippers that are for sale.

Mingling with these fashionably attired and coiffed young people and conservatively dressed faculty are members of another group of Moscow residents. The composition of this group is more mixed, reflecting the vast experiential diversity that both separates and unites them. Most of these people move slowly and tentatively, and the entry guards barely look at them as they pass by, much less question their destinations. Many are stooped from age and decades of hard labor. Some juggle bags filled with thermoses, pots, and jars or struggle with shopping carts and small children. When they reach the cafeteria, unlike the students and faculty who go directly to the counter to collect food and pay for it, these Muscovites stand patiently in the narrow hallway outside the dining area and chat with one another while they wait to be called inside (figure 2).

There is another distinct group of people gathering at the cafeteria, noticeable for their energy and youth. Some are distinguished by their casual attire: blue jeans and expensive athletic gear. These individuals are white, middle-class, primarily middle-aged North Americans and Europeans. Others are more conspicuous for the color of their skin; they are young African university students and refugees who live in Moscow and come to the cafeteria between classes and part-time jobs elsewhere in the city. After greeting the Muscovites waiting in the hallway, the members of this group walk directly into the cafeteria, shed their coats, and begin their volunteer work. Against a backdrop of posters advertising American soft drinks and contests sponsored by international candy companies; display cases full of bread, pastries, tins of caviar, boxes of juice, and elegant

FIGURE 2. Christian Church of Moscow soup kitchen recipients wait in this hallway before they are invited into the dining area.

salads; and warming pans full of meat, fish, and potato dishes, they arm themselves with trays and cleaning rags. The people still waiting in the hallway are called inside, where they present registration cards to a young man who dispenses meal tickets. They seat themselves at four-person tables in the dining area and wait for volunteers to serve them food.

Together these individuals, Russians and non-Russians, the elderly and the young, make up the Christian Church of Moscow (CCM) soup kitchen community. From Monday to Friday, between 9 A.M. and 12 P.M., members of this community come together in four sites in the greater Moscow area, including the one here in the main cafeteria at the Moscow Scientific Institute. In all, fifteen hundred Muscovite pensioners are registered to receive free meals at four CCM soup kitchens. Approximately one hundred African, North American, and European volunteers rotate among the four sites, serving meals, clearing tables, and soliciting support for the program. After ten years of continuous operation, an uncommon feat in today's Moscow, where aid programs are at the mercy of capricious donors and fluctuating legal codes, the CCM's soup kitchen ministry has established itself as a responsible and well-respected social welfare provider in Moscow. Recipients advise their friends to get on the registration list, and volunteers enlist their friends and coworkers to help in various ways. Local welfare officials and regional politicians publicly praise the efforts of CCM staff and volunteers to assist local residents and to promote international cooperation and understanding.

The Social Economy of Poverty in Russia

This book is an ethnography about everyday life in Moscow, rendered through an intimate look at the lives and experiences of the members of the Christian Church of Moscow soup kitchen community, an international food aid program in Moscow. My intent in this account is to grapple with the concept of scarcity in Moscow society and to unravel the mythologies of hunger, poverty, and community that percolate through recent depictions of Russian social life. To do so, I focus on the survival strategies that members of the CCM community patch together and implement on a daily basis as they manage to "make do" with limited material resources and strict bureaucratic regulations. Ultimately, I am interested in the forms of social organization that emerge from these endeavors.

By chronicling the ways in which people who live in a society undergoing profound political and economic transformations scramble to make ends meet, I interrogate a central set of questions: Why do Muscovites who have limited financial resources and receive food assistance refuse to identify themselves as poor and instead see themselves as possessing sufficient social capital to guarantee their everyday survival? Why do Muscovites who receive food and other forms of aid divert those commodities to relatives and friends? What are the practical techniques by which individuals who worry that their incomes cannot sufficiently cover the costs of feeding a family, much less pay for other expenses, support themselves? How are ideologies of cooperation, assistance, entitlement, and social responsibility that were cultivated as critical components of Russian society—and especially so during the Soviet period—being reconfigured in the present moment? As the Russian state has ceded its role as primary provider of welfare services, how are domestic and international charities defining their roles and their clientele? How are "needs" being defined and contested by aid workers and recipients? How are Russians negotiating these spheres and expectations? And finally, to what extent do the renewed need for aid and the use of welfare programs represent either a departure from or a continuation of a socialist worldview?

By considering the phenomenon of poverty in Russia today, I investigate how Muscovites translate their apprehensions about material scarcity into concerns about the durability and productivity of their relationships with relatives, friends, neighbors, and other members of their community. In contrast to conventional policy interpretations of poverty, and of the circumstances of Russian poverty more specifically, Muscovites conceptualize material shortages as evidence of insufficient social resources and identify social isolation, not financial limitations, as the primary cause of scarcity in Russia today. Accordingly, they actively invest time and energy in personal relationships with other people as forms of social security, a practice that anthropologists and sociologists have documented among other social groups facing limited material resources (Allahyari 2000; Desjarlais 1996; Dordick 1997; Glasser 1988; Myerhoff 1978; Newman 1999; Stevens 1997). Although members of the CCM soup kitchen community are potentially marginalized from the greater Russian society by virtue of their ages, incomes, and nationalities, especially in the case of foreign volunteers, they approach their interactions through the soup kitchen as opportunities to create constructive social relations through which they have access to material support. Even more important, however, is their access to the social life that this interaction provides: opportunities to celebrate birthdays and holidays, form friendships, and create networks of pseudorelatives—what one regional welfare official described as making these people feel "human."

I suggest that an exploration of these questions about strategic social practice requires a rethinking of the relationship between economic and social practices. Rather than approaching social and economic resources as distinct phenomena that possess unique characteristics and belong to different spheres in everyday life (e.g., Bourdieu 1977; Burawoy, Krotov, and Lytkina 2000), I propose to investigate the ways in which they are mutually constituted and interdependent. Specifically, I want to suggest that the everyday events and interactions in the CCM soup kitchen provide a lens for examining how Muscovites employ social relations and social status as economic currency that can be exchanged, invested, and withdrawn. Processes of community building thus serve a dual purpose as aspects of a "social poetics" (Herzfeld 1985) of economic practice, whereby "social security" alludes to both the material resources and the social relations from which they are generated that sustain Muscovites in their daily lives.

Poverty, Public Assistance, and the Post-Soviet Welfare State

Clarification of this relationship between the social and the economic is especially relevant for rethinking the phenomena of poverty and welfare in the former Soviet Union and Eastern Europe. In the twentieth century, and particularly in the reform period of the postsocialist "transition," social scientists have typically treated issues of poverty and welfare in the socialist world according to two overlapping paradigms. In the first model, welfare programs have been held up as evidence of the totalitarian nature of the Soviet regime: the state controlled its citizens by making them dependent on state-distributed aid (Siegelbaum 1998). In the second model, which is often posited as the logical outcome of the first, aspects of poverty such as homelessness, alcoholism, high mortality rates, substandard health care, rising crime levels, and declining living standards have been interpreted as irrefutable indications of the instability of the Soviet—and now post-Soviet—political economy (Field 2000; Hollander 1991; Kornai, Haggard, and Kaufman 2001; Twigg 2000).[2] At the heart of these two models are assumptions that the post-Soviet state is flawed and that what is needed to fix it are reforms that shift the balance of political and economic power away from the state and to citizens who have been given autonomy to act as individuals with free choice (Kornai 2001:183).

This perspective resonates with models more familiar in liberal democratic societies, where expectations are placed on individual citizens to provide for themselves. In these types of social systems, public assistance and social defense measures such as soup kitchens, food packages, and community service centers are treated as extraordinary institutional responses to moments of crisis and social disorder (Poppendieck 1998). Circumstances such as climatic disaster, economic uncertainty, political instability, and even personal incapacity or irresponsibility lead to anomalous conditions of material shortage that require relief. Because the individuals who are most affected by these conditions are generally those with limited material resources, these problems are seen as belonging to the realm of "poverty," and the corresponding programs are lumped into the category of "welfare." Emphasis on state-initiated relief measures as correctives for a system in disarray reveals a subtle privileging of a notion of the individual who is distinct from the state and acts independently. Moreover, inequalities among the population, while unfortunate, nonetheless offer "proof" of the autonomy of the individual. Intrusions of the state occur rarely, and only in situations of extreme disorder and danger.

In the more extreme logic of neoliberal economic theories, the presence of the state at any point, even in exceptional circumstances, disrupts the stability of the economic system (Hayek 1984). This stance has attracted considerable support among social scientists and policy advisers who have been critical of the close relationships between state and citizen in the former Soviet Union and Eastern Europe. Perhaps the most notable proponent of this perspective has been Hungarian economist János Kornai. In his recent recommendations for health care and welfare reform in postsocialist Europe, Kornai (2001) has consistently called for the removal of the state from its efforts to manage the personal welfare of its constituents. Instead, individual citizens must be made responsible for their own well-being. Similarly, in another study, Kornai and Eggleston have argued that reformers must develop a "new ethos that places the sovereignty and responsibility of the individual to the fore" (2001:17). Nevertheless, as Mark Field and his colleagues have persuasively argued, these neoliberal policies are themselves catalysts for alarming declines in Russia's public welfare (Field, Kotz, and Bukhman 2000).

Unfortunately, approaches that locate poverty and welfare solely within economic and political discourses, and especially those that privilege the sovereign individual, neglect the long and rich relationship between economy and society in the history of poverty and welfare in Russian social life. More important, these perspectives overlook the ways in which welfare programs are in fact beneficial to society because they foster social cohesion (Pine and Bridger 1998:12). In many ways, poverty occupies a place of honor in Russian discourse as a form of expression about one's experience with state and society. As Nancy Ries (1997) and Dale Pesmen (2000) have described, themes of poverty, scarcity, and assistance are the tropes around which Russians' sense of self and social solidarity are formed.[3] The roots of these trends lie in Imperial Russia, where the economic and the social were intertwined when both private and public welfare-oriented institutions such as poorhouses, work relief programs, soup kitchens, and other charities emerged to care specifically for the economically, physically, and socially disadvantaged (Kaiser 1988; Lindenmeyr 1996).[4] The Russian Orthodox Church was an especially influential element. With its theological emphasis on benevolence as a simultaneously personal and social necessity, the Church nurtured permissive attitudes toward begging and an enduring "culture of giving" that insinuated itself in the popular imagination as a distinctively Russian trait (Lindenmeyr 1996).

After the Russian Revolution in 1917, private welfare services were gradually replaced by state welfare agencies. Although the sponsors behind welfare services changed with the creation of the Soviet Union, the connections between the economic and the social did not. More precisely, the concept of social welfare as it was envisioned during the Soviet period expanded the realm of needs and services so that they were applicable to all members of society, not just the disadvantaged minority. In particular, welfare services were part of an extensive project of social engineering to promote and achieve the Soviet regime's Utopian visions of a new "Soviet" person, *Homo sovieticus* (Zinoviev 1985), as well as scientific and technological progress, productive labor, and social equality.[5] At the same time that citizens provided the necessary labor to support the state, the state would provide the necessary resources to sustain and reward the people's efforts. For instance, in order to sustain its commitment to gender equality, as well as to bulk up the work force with female labor, Soviet leaders reduced women's dual burden of domestic and work responsibilities by granting maternity leave, guaranteeing that women could return to their original jobs after maternity leave, and establishing daily and overnight child care facilities. Additional forms of support were realized in the allocation of low-cost housing; subsidized utilities, food, and medical care; paid vacations and therapeutic visits to health spas; cultural programs; education; and other forms of professional training.

One of the most innovative projects in the Soviet Union's welfare system was the attempt to move food practices out of the private sphere and into the realm of the public. In his history of communal dining in the Soviet Union, Mauricio Borrero (1997) notes that immediately following the October 1917 Revolution, members of the Bolshevik government capitalized on the prevailing food shortages at the time to promote their visions of ideal communism. Although soup kitchens were initially introduced to solve temporary problems with food scarcities (see also Moine 2000), the subsequent replacement of family kitchens and private restaurants with communal kitchens, state-owned cafeterias and food shops, workplace canteens, and cafeterias run by consumers' societies offered precious opportunities to instill socialist values in the population.[6] The aim of public dining was to reinforce the ideals of social equality through a communal eating experience. Corollary goals included further gender emancipation, which was to be accomplished by freeing women from their obligations in the kitchen (Goldstein 1996; Rothstein and Rothstein 1997). The growth of industrial food complexes, automated cafeterias, and nutritional research institutes also corresponded to an overall push for industrialization and scientific rationalization in Soviet society (Rothstein and Rothstein 1997). Finally, policy makers anticipated that the visible benefits of socialist egalitarian distribution would prevail over the wastage of capitalist consumption and excess. Ultimately, however, despite the optimistic objectives embodied in these programs, public dining never achieved its full potential, and Soviet citizens reclaimed their homes as sites of primary food preparation and consumption (Glants and Toomre 1997; Goldstein 1996).[7]

Moreover, coinciding with the official rhetoric of food management as a means to create a productive society was the reality that through the regulated allocation of food and other resources, state officials monitored and controlled the routines, events, practices, and relationships of Soviet citizens' daily lives (Fitzpatrick 1999). The extent of this management of the most mundane aspects of social life was heightened during the periodic shortages that plagued the Soviet era. Through welfare programs of redistribution, such as rationing, closed shops (that is, shops open only to members of a particular group), workplace stores, and emergency aid programs, the state carefully regulated the amount of food that citizens could consume. These practices produced a paradoxical situation whereby individuals counted on the state to provide certain goods and services, even as they recognized the limitations and unpredictability of the state and consequently created alternative means to satisfy those needs. Nevertheless, there remained an expectation that the state was responsible for taking care of its citizens, even if in symbolic gesture only, and that citizens were "entitled" to this care.[8]

Today the recent transitional period in Russia has complicated the relationship between state and citizen in terms of the nature of the welfare state and its responsibilities to Russian citizens. Strapped by cash-flow problems, illegal diversions of domestic funds and foreign aid to private accounts, and demands to repay international loans, federal authorities have been unable (or unwilling) to release money from the federal reserve to increase the pensions and salaries of civil servants or to subsidize public assistance programs. Although assistance programs remain in place from the Soviet system, regional welfare authorities express their frustrations at lacking sufficient funds to support the programs adequately, much less to expand services to more clients. Western observers have interpreted these economic constraints as evidence that the survival of Russians and of Russian society—and of civil society, in particular—is doomed. In response, foreign governments and private agencies have flooded Russia with loans, development experts, and community assistance programs. Feeding programs such as soup kitchens, food packages, and airlifts of grain and other products have been particularly popular forms of assistance.

Contrary to the pessimistic rhetoric used in international development and philanthropic literature, however, Muscovites do not see their participation within a feeding program as the only factor determining their everyday survival. Instead Muscovites approach soup kitchens and food packages as yet one more variable in a diverse repertoire of everyday survival strategies. This perspective was supported by comments that I encountered in conversations with people outside established food aid programs in Moscow and elsewhere in Russia. Respondents argued that soup kitchens and food packages were neither novel nor absolute solutions to more sweeping problems of an unpredictable market and a potential scarcity of resources. Food aid programs complemented a range of other tactics but did not replace them; Muscovites seemed always to be ready with contingency plans in case their original efforts proved unsuccessful.

Furthermore, despite the long history of public assistance programs in Russia, international aid projects have been problematic for many Russians who perceive ulterior motives wrapped up in packages of dried milk and tins of fish. As Marta Bruno notes, international aid to Russia during the 1990s was envisioned by its senders as a means to foster democratic market economies at the same time that it was "to reinforce the victory of capitalism over socialism" (1998:172–173). This perspective was not merely Russian paranoia but was, in fact, openly proposed by advisers to the U.S. government, a key source of aid to Russia. In a hearing before the Senate Foreign Relations Committee in 1999, Senator Gordon Smith (R-Oreg.) questioned two researchers who were testifying about the feasibility of giving aid to Russia. Thomas Graham Jr., from the Carnegie Endowment for International Peace, advised the committee, "We need to do a much better job of selling America and our values to Russia" (Senate 1999). At various points during the 1990s, Russian citizens responded to American aid with both moral outrage and an ironically capitalist move—by boycotting American products. In a debate over food aid that appeared in a Russian studies list-serve, Leonid Bershidsky, editor of Russia's *Kapital Weekly,* reminded readers that in 1991 and 1992, Russians threw away food aid they had received from the United States because they did not appreciate the political symbolism embodied by the food (Bershidsky 1998). American frozen chicken legs became a volatile rallying point for these tensions: Russians nicknamed them "Bush Legs" to protest President George Bush's imperialist attitudes toward Russia and boycotted them. Early in 2002, Russian officials were still debating whether to allow American chicken legs to be imported to Russia, albeit under the rubric of whether American food products met Russian health standards. Even more problematic for foreign donors, however, is that Russians have reworked these aid programs in ways that defy the objectives and needs envisioned by project coordinators (Bruno 1998). Recipients redistribute or resell food aid, or they use development agencies as opportunities to further personal agendas (Wedel 1998a).

It is within this political context of poverty and food assistance that the CCM program is situated. Yet the CCM program enjoys a level of success and respect that is unmatched by its fellow international agencies. This is primarily because CCM staff have carefully modeled their program after its Russian counterparts. By working closely with Moscow politicians and welfare officials and following their guidance on presenting services that are not only responsive but also familiar to Muscovites, CCM staff have successfully created a program that is fully integrated into the local welfare community. Ultimately the key to this success is that, just like its Russian partners, the CCM soup kitchen programs offer recipients a range of benefits that far exceed the value of material assistance alone—namely, a sense of social solidarity. In the rest of this book, I will explore the ways in which social aspects are correlated with material resources and how these components are satisfied in the CCM soup kitchens.[9]

Moscow: A City in Motion

Most of the research on which this project is based comes from ethnographic fieldwork conducted in Moscow between November 1997 and October 1998, and between May and August in 1999. A preliminary trip in the summer of 1995 and subsequent visits in the summers of 2000 and 2001 enabled me to continue the project at the same time as I was writing about it. The return visits have been particularly valuable for giving me insight into how quickly "the field" changes. As I describe throughout the book, the soup kitchen community is a dynamic one, and it has been important for me to be able to document these changes, even as this has posed challenges to the creation of a finite written work.

Although the process of fieldwork is always challenging, conducting research in Moscow is further complicated by two factors: its urban setting and the postsocialist context. In terms of the first constraint, the physical and demographic scale of cities complicates ethnographers' efforts to locate bounded and manageable social groups that retain sufficient commonalities to enable the researcher to say something useful about both particularities and generalities. Neighborhoods that consist of high-rise apartment buildings with locked entrances, such as those that exist in Moscow and other Russian cities, or secluded suburbs with private homes set behind fences impede researchers' attempts to do the kind of "drop-in-unannounced" fieldwork that is conventionally associated with village ethnography. Reliance on public transportation also increases the amount of time that one spends traveling to and through the field, thereby affecting the amount of time available with informants— or even the settings in which one conducts research, as trips on the subway become transformed into impromptu interviews. These are not insurmountable obstacles, however; and urban ethnographers have responded with a variety of strategies. More-or-less-finite communities based on social relations still exist in urban spaces, even as their contours are tied less to territory and geography than they are to common interests or transactions such as those generated in the workplace (Kondo 1990; Zabusky 1995), educational programs (Patico 2001a), markets (Bestor 1999), political interest groups (Aretxaga 1997), and health programs (Jackson 2000), among others. Telephones and the Internet also offer valuable tools for making fieldwork more manageable and intimate in urban environments (Berdahl 2000b; Erwin 2000).

The practical setting in which this ethnography is situated, my "home base," begins and concludes in the community that radiates from the CCM soup kitchen program. In many ways, working through the networks that intersected in the CCM community was an ideal means to conduct fieldwork. Within a cityscape of roughly twelve million people (unofficial estimates put Moscow's population closer to fifteen million), the eighteen hundred individuals who compose the CCM congregation and soup kitchen program form a relatively bounded and consistent social group with common interests, goals, activities, and routines. Nevertheless, despite the fact that this project originated in the soup kitchens, the story that I am telling is not exclusively about the CCM community, nor is it solely about the state of poverty and food assistance in Russia today. At the same time that the four soup kitchens within the CCM community are critical elements in this narrative, they are also individual nodes within a much larger system of assistance networks and transactions that span Moscow, Russia, and beyond. As I will further elaborate below, my intent has been to follow members of this community from the soup kitchens and into the other domains that shape their daily lives, stories, and practices.

From both methodological and theoretical perspectives, however, it is probably the postsocialist context of this project that has been the most challenging and intellectually engaging. Despite anthropology's long history of "in the field" ethnography, this type of research methodology is a relatively recent phenomenon in Eurasian communities. On the one hand, although anthropology has a long history in Russian scholarly research, Russian ethnographers' efforts were generally devoted to projects of collecting and preserving the customs of minority groups living in the former Soviet Union. Fieldwork was conducted in short periods, often dependent on funding and state interests. On the other hand, North American and Western European research in the broader discipline of Soviet and East European studies was done at a distance, through the use of materials deposited in North American libraries, interviews with émigrés, and analyses of information collected by government agencies enmeshed in objectives and ideologies powered by the Cold War.

Foreign researchers who were fortunate to be given access to "the field" were typically restricted to working in archives or were placed under the strict supervision of local officials and scholars, who defined acceptable research topics and monitored their methodologies, movements, and contact with ordinary people (Ries 1997; Verdery 1996). For nonanthropologists, the practical consequences of these constraints included an overreliance on intellectuals and other elites as valid sources of authentic everyday life (Barker 1999b) and a dearth of knowledge of what life was like for the nonelites who composed the vast majority of the population. A very small group of fieldworking anthropologists successfully navigated these challenges in their quests to explore ordinary life "behind the Iron Curtain" (e.g., Creed 1997; Dragadze 1988; Humphrey 1983; Kideckel 1993; Ries 1997; Wedel 1986; Verdery 1983). The costs of these projects were high, however, especially in terms of the consequences faced by villagers and other friends with whom ethnographers came into contact. For instance, David Kideckel reported (1993) that his Romanian contacts were interrogated and fined for interacting with him. It is only in the aftermath of the fall of the Berlin Wall in 1989 and the dissolution of the Soviet Union in 1991 that sustained ethnography has been possible in these regions. This research has been invaluable for challenging the privileged authority previously held by political scientists and economists.

More than simply providing information to fill in the gaps in our knowledge of the former Soviet Union and Eastern Europe, however, ethnographers in these regions have found themselves in the remarkable position of being able to comment on the ways in which social life moves and changes. Most notably, a consistent observation in their accounts is that events and circumstances in these spaces change with dazzling speed and often have unpredictable consequences (Platz 2000; Szemere 2000). Political and economic systems can be transformed suddenly (during my fieldwork, Russian president Boris Yeltsin sacked three prime ministers), and the markers that seem to give some sense of stability to our communities disappear and reappear in new guises. Street signs and shops change overnight (literally), and informants increasingly move through our field sites on their journeys to new opportunities elsewhere. As will become clear, this sense of rapid movement spills over into the everyday lives of the members of the community depicted here.

As the capital of Russia, Moscow represents an extreme case of this disorientation.[10] Moscow is a city where the textures of daily life have long been epitomized by paradoxes, incongruous pairings, irony, and the unexpected. Founded in A.D. 1147, it is both the historical center of Russia and the heart of its industrial and technological future. Today the glittering high fashion boutiques, elegant coffee shops and Internet cafés, and glamorous restaurants and nightclubs that line Tverskaia Ulitsa, the main street that picks up from the highway from St. Petersburg and leads directly to Red Square and the Kremlin, depart sharply from the images of elderly women hawking their shoes, silverware, and old photographs along the sidewalks. Politicians who pledge to reform the economy and ease the material constraints facing their constituents funnel federal and international funds to their offshore bank accounts in order to support and protect their lavish lifestyles. The golden domes, marble tiled floors, and professionally landscaped gardens of the recently reerected Cathedral of Christ the Savior present an image of religiosity in sharp contrast to a nearby monastery whose wooden chapel is in danger of rotting from the ground up and whose yard is mostly dirt with the occasional clump of overgrown weeds.[11] While some priests take vows of poverty, others fortify themselves with luxury cars and armed entourages. Beyond the archways of what otherwise appear to be nondescript blocks of massive apartment and office buildings, the knowledgeable and the curious can stumble onto forgotten museums filled with historical artifacts, priceless art treasures, and elegant theaters.

These competing portraits of Moscow may, on the one hand, be read as evidence for an inherent duality in Russian life that has continued into the post-Soviet transitional moment: communism versus capitalist democracy; rich versus poor; secrecy versus openness; insider versus outsider. In many ways, this book is about these contrasts. But rather than examining social phenomena as if they belong exclusively to one category or the other, or as if spatial and temporal sites of social experience are in tension with each other (Fabian 1983; Herzfeld 1991), I follow the cues given by my Muscovite informants, who engage with these contrasts on a daily basis and live in the realities that simultaneously link and separate them.

At the same time, when one is in the midst of frenetic changes and contradictions such as those present in Russian life today, it becomes tempting to look for "stable" topics that allow one to complete a research project before the parameters shift and the questions and topic lose their viability and relevance. As Daphne Berdahl has noted, however, these intermediary moments "are often fields of heightened consciousness that demand articulation or identification" (1999b:7). Thus the danger in searching out neatly defined spatial and temporal environments is that we lose the unique opportunity to engage directly with systemic and social change in meaningful theoretical and ethnographic ways (cf. Bourdieu 1977). Interesting and productive questions emerge when one considers what it is like to live through change. How do ordinary people navigate transformation? What are the means by which they create order from disorder, and to what extent can uncertainty carry its own sense of stability (Malaby 2003)? This ethnography is a record of the ways in which everyday life in Moscow is constituted and experienced in these interstices, where the past meets the present, the local meets the foreign, and the economic meets the social.

To engage with the dynamism of life in today's Moscow, and to give a glimpse into the ways in which Muscovites cope with the flexible contours of life in a society undergoing rapid transformation, I started my project in the Christian Church of Moscow soup kitchen program.[12] CCM congregants initially established their food aid program in the early 1990s in response to the severe consumer shortages and economic uncertainties that existed at that time. Their first project was a food package program for their student members. Several members were Russian students, but most were African students who had been brought to study in the Soviet Union as a part of the government's efforts to facilitate the development of socialist movements in sympathetic African countries. All were on scholarships, and at that time their stipends barely covered daily necessities. One young Russian woman recalled the creative ways she and her friends prepared potatoes every day, because that was all they could afford to buy. Shortly afterward, political developments in Africa prompted an additional influx of refugees, and CCM members expanded the food package program to include these persons as well. Eventually a United Nations organization took over the refugee food aid program, and the congregation decided to open a soup kitchen to help Russian pensioners who were similarly constrained.[13] Between 1993 and 2000, the CCM soup kitchen program expanded to four soup kitchens that served fifteen hundred people, five days a week, fifty-two weeks a year.[14] The food package program remains an important source of support for student members of the CCM congregation and several other Russian members.

Social workers in three regional welfare offices work with local residents to compile a list of eligible pensioners. Applicants submit documents certifying their legal residence, income, and benefit status as a pensioner, military veteran, laborer, single parent with many children, or disabled person. Social workers submit lists of names and telephone numbers to CCM staff, who add people to the soup kitchen rosters as spaces become available. Every September, CCM recipients must attend their respective soup kitchens to be "registered," a process that involves presenting their documents, verifying that all personal information remains correct, and receiving a new "membership card" with identification number. This yearly process enables CCM staff to purge their roster of people who are no longer attending the soup kitchens and to add new people to the program. Despite the advanced age of most recipients, only a few spaces open up every year, and competition to be included is fierce among applicants.

Initially I saw working with the CCM community as a strategic way to gain access to what seemed to be a finite community of recipients and volunteers. I quickly discovered, however, that the CCM community was anything but static and predictable.[15] The CCM group is dynamic and fluid, both in terms of membership attendance and in the places where it comes together, but it is not in danger of declining through natural attrition (cf. Myerhoff 1978). As recipients pass away or move into apartments with adult children who do not live near the soup kitchens, clients on a waiting list fill empty slots as soon as they become available. ·Recipients attend when they are able; most come every day, but some may miss days or weeks at a time for reasons such as bad weather, illness, or travel. Similarly, the volunteer pool is always changing to reflect the rhythms of the educational system and market fluctuations. The beginning of each term brings an influx of new student assistants, while such events as graduation and summer holidays see departures of volunteers. During the year, although a regular cohort of student volunteers attend several days a week around their class schedules, between-term and holiday breaks are often marked by a significant increase of African helpers who are unable to travel elsewhere. The majority of the remaining volunteers are the spouses of expatriate North American and European businesspeople in Moscow. Most have incorporated weekly participation at the soup kitchens into personal schedules that include volunteer work at other charitable programs, social luncheons, reading groups, Bible studies, and their children's activities at the Anglo-American school. Turnover among this group generally occurs when their spouses' contracts for foreign duty are finished.

The members of the CCM community include individuals from a diversity of life experiences. Recipients include military veterans, retired schoolteachers, professors, geologists, journalists, electricians, musicians, gymnasts, ballerinas, soldiers, historians, and even, if rumors are to be believed, a cosmonaut, as well as middle-aged mothers with large families, disabled soldiers, and mentally challenged adults and their children. Their relatives and friends, who are members of the extended CCM community, represent successful members of the new middle-class, staunch supporters of the Communist Party, university students, and political and economic elites. The children or grandchildren of a number of recipients have emigrated to the United States, Germany, and Israel. Among the volunteers are practicing journalists, diplomats, lawyers, scientists, corporate executives, and graduate students in such disciplines as veterinary medicine, international law, business management, aeronautical engineering, and education.

The primary places where CCM recipients and volunteers gather are the soup kitchens themselves. On several occasions recipients and volunteers from different soup kitchens have been brought together when one cafeteria has closed temporarily. Other interactions occur in the social welfare offices, the offices of regional authorities, and within the context of CCM spiritual events. Approximately 250 church members gather weekly for religious services; a majority of the volunteers belongs to this congregation and attends worship services on a regular basis. Church members meet every Sunday morning for worship and fellowship hour; smaller interest groups from the congregation meet weekly or biweekly for Bible study or social activities. Several soup kitchen recipients frequently attend worship services and are actively involved in other church activities of the CCM. Throughout the year, congregants sponsor churchwide fellowship events and outings in which the offerings are earmarked for the soup kitchen program. Other special events benefiting the food aid ministry attract other supporters and guests. Within the congregation two subgroups meet on a monthly basis to discuss soup kitchen affairs. One subgroup is the fund-raising committee, charged with publicizing the CCM food aid program in the international community, soliciting donations, and overseeing the purchase of special gifts to recipients on important holidays. The other is the soup kitchen coordinators' committee, a select group of the nine men and women who are the official representatives and administrators in the soup kitchens. Most of these individuals have held their positions for several years and will continue to do so for as long as they live in Moscow.

These individuals formed nodes within the larger community that emerged from the soup kitchens, church services, and welfare offices and spread across the city and across the globe (from my home in Boston I conducted telephone interviews with people in other parts of the United States), ultimately reaching into unexpected corners (for instance, on a number of occasions I visited seemingly unrelated sites in Moscow only to encounter CCM recipients and volunteers, a surprising situation given the size of the city and the population). In an odd twist on the more usual position of ethnographer as interloper, during the course of my research I was one of the more stable and continuous elements.

Thus instead of relying on an arbitrary community created through the artificial confines of geographic location, membership rosters, and meal times, I found it more useful to follow members of this community out into their daily lives and into the social networks that were important to them. Through this strategy I was introduced to Muscovites at different economic levels and experiences, including pensioners, government bureaucrats, politicians, academics, middle-class workers, and New Russians. This, I believe, gave me access to a deeper understanding of the routines and practices of these persons' daily lives, because for them, the soup kitchen was simply one locus within a complex of relations. In addition, an analysis of Muscovites' social networks and transactions restores the "face-to-face" interactions that are seen to be lacking in symbolic communities such as those formed through the Internet and diaspora groups.[16] Hence I am not suggesting that transactional communities are more anonymous or utilitarian than symbolic social movements based on shared sentiment and experience (Anderson 1983). Rather, I propose that Muscovites blur these distinctions by setting up economic exchanges as personal relations. This approach demonstrates that imagined communities may be mapped onto transactional communities but that the two do not necessarily align completely.

At the soup kitchens, most recipients attend either every day or every other day; many appear regularly at the same time every day, often joining the same friends and relatives. Among the volunteers, the majority tend to serve on specific days during the week: for example, Abraham and Mary, who are students at the university at which most African CCM members are enrolled, work every Monday morning before their classes; Sheila and Donna, two British women who have accompanied their working spouses to Moscow, serve every Tuesday before joining their bridge group; Sally, Louise, and Holly, also nonworking spouses of foreign businessmen, attend faithfully on Wednesdays and then leave together for the Women's Club meeting. Fridays are the domain of the North American students at a foreign missionary institute, a religious program that combines service projects with theological training. Approximately twenty African volunteers provide a more constant presence by working four or five times a week.

Before beginning my project, I discussed my interests and methodological aims with the two CCM ministers and Dr. Steve, the Sudanese staff director in charge of the CCM's feeding and clothing distribution programs. Fortunately, they were sympathetic to my research plans and graciously offered assistance in many forms, including allowing me to participate in church meetings and explaining to recipients, volunteers, and congregants why I had appeared in their midst. They also allowed me to look at letters they had received from grateful recipients and at statistics about attendance records, and they answered numerous questions about the program, both in terms of local operations and international fund-raising. In addition, because the soup kitchens are so closely connected with the CCM congregation, I attended worship services and all other congregation events that focused on soup kitchen activities.

Ironically colleagues in other disciplines have raised concerns that my participation in CCM activities has compromised my objectivity about the soup kitchens. In response, I would argue that had I ignored this aspect, I would have overlooked the threads and tensions that bring these two communities into a larger network. An even more compelling reason to include the CCM congregation in my research is that most African volunteers and several Russian recipients also attend CCM worship services; and many CCM worship activities center around the soup kitchen program. Consequently, a comprehensive study of the CCM soup kitchens can be completed only within an understanding of the moral rhetoric for action that guides congregants and volunteers (Allahyari 2000). I am also quite certain that my involvement in church activities of the CCM facilitated my personal relationships with members of this community. My role was not that of a formally distant observer but that of an observant participant.[17] Moreover, I consider myself fortunate to have been able to conduct research among a group of people whose expressions of generosity and concern went far beyond offers of professional courtesy and became displays of friendship and affection. For this I am deeply grateful. Thus, I have no regrets about having followed the piece of advice that James Watson frequently gives his graduate students: "In fieldwork you live where people live, you do what people do, and you go where people go" (1997:viii). For me, that included going to church.

By attending the soup kitchens on an almost daily basis, I, too, became incorporated into the everyday rhythms, rituals, and politics of this community. Between fall 1997 and fall 1998, I based myself in the soup kitchen at the Moscow Scientific Institute. As the largest of the CCM soup kitchens and the one with the longest serving time, this site afforded me the greatest access to both recipients and volunteers. For the first several months I worked primarily as a volunteer, serving meals and clearing tables. As a fellow student and expatriate, I was quickly accepted into the ranks of the volunteers and was able to ask questions about their experiences with the program. Gradually, as recipients came to see me as a regular presence and, perhaps more important, as someone with whom they could communicate in Russian (most non-African volunteers did not speak more than a few words of basic Russian), they allowed me to participate in their conversations and activities at the soup kitchens. Most important, they brought me into their lives outside the soup kitchens and introduced me to their friends and relatives. At their invitation I accompanied recipients and members of their extended networks on their visits to shops, markets, church, government offices, other assistance programs, and their summer cottages. We attended concerts, plays, and other events together; and they invited me to join them for formal dinners as well as informal chats over tea and dessert. I was also fortunate to celebrate such special occasions as birthdays, International Women's Day, and death remembrances with them. It is from this mixture of large, small, personal, and public events that I draw my observations and analyses.

I conducted both formal and informal interviews with people, depending on the setting, mood of the informant, and type of material that

I hoped to gather. Sessions with busy officials were most productive when they were presented in structured interview format, while interactions with friends and acquaintances generally took place over meals or during informal visits. Informal conversations spontaneously took place on park benches, around kitchen tables, and on public transportation. Although public officials generally responded willingly, or at least neutrally, to my requests to use a tape recorder in our conversations, the vast majority of recipients and volunteers adamantly refused my requests to back up my notes with an audio version, although most were comfortable with my use of written transcriptions.

In the soup kitchens, however, my efforts to take notes quickly met with angry suspicion. The CCM ministers and director had initially given me permission to write down my observations, but after a number of worried recipients voiced their concerns that I was a spy working for a government agency, they asked me to put away my notebook while in the soup kitchen. Although anthropologists have long faced suspicions of engaging in undercover work, my position was further complicated by the unfamiliarity of most people with North American and British traditions of sociocultural anthropology that emphasize ethnography, the extended observation and analysis of the everyday lives of ordinary people. In Russia, ethnography belongs to the disciplines of history and political science, and researchers work with statistics and archival materials and take short-term expeditions to record folk customs in remote villages. As a researcher who did not work in the archives but was instead based for a long period of time in a contemporary, urban setting, I was an anomaly. To allay recipients' fears, I found spaces outside the soup kitchens to make my notes: hallways, bathrooms, secluded tables in the sections reserved for paying customers, and an office off the kitchen in one cafeteria that CCM staff generously offered for my use.

My efforts to follow in the tracks of informants led me to a variety of other communities. I became a regular participant in the monthly meetings of the CCM soup kitchen coordinators and the CCM fund-raising committee. I also visited other state-funded soup kitchens and food packet programs for senior citizens; private feeding programs for homeless and other disadvantaged persons; the United Way agency; a Russian Red Cross after-school soup kitchen and activity program for children (figure 3); and the International Red Cross headquarters and winter appeal press conference (figure 4). Contacts with colleagues in Russia gave me access to researchers who were interested in related topics, as well as glimpses of different types of nongovernmental organizations in regions outside Moscow.

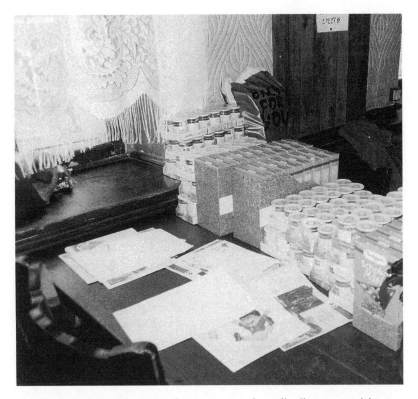

FIGURE 3. Packages of cereal and yogurt are ready to distribute to participants in a children's soup kitchen.

The transnational aspect of my research offered a number of intriguing methodological and personal challenges. Language was a particularly important issue and highlighted subtle power relations between interviewer and interviewee. In most cases, conversations with Russians were conducted in Russian, while conversations with North American and European informants were conducted in English. Communication with CCM coordinators and other bilingual persons, however, alternated between Russian and English. (In several cases, I was forced to dust off my very rusty French, and even rustier German, skills.) In general, however, I allowed my interlocutors to choose the linguistic medium of our interactions, and most conversations were in Russian. In presenting the words and views of my informants here, I have used direct quotations only for instances in which I was able to record an informant's words verbatim. I have used reported speech for all other cases when I was able to

FIGURE 4. Displays at the 1998 International Red Cross winter appeal draw attention to the agency's programs throughout the former Soviet Union.

capture the meaning and an approximation of a statement but was unable to write down an informant's words exactly as they were spoken. All translations in the text are mine.

The issue of money presents another complication. Although rubles are Russia's legal currency, American dollars and, less frequently, other foreign currencies (British pounds, German deutschmarks and, now, Euros) are the media through which much of Russia's informal economy operates. Unofficial economic transactions, such as those for rent, tutoring, and other jobs, are typically paid in dollars; and automated bank machines spit out both rubles and dollars. When I present monetary amounts in this book, I will either indicate the specific currency or indicate that the amount given is an equivalence.

Finally, issues of race and nationality presented special dilemmas for my informants in their daily lives and for me in my writing. Both Russians and Africans have had to confront the legacy of the Soviet Union's colonizing activities in Africa. Black Africans in Russia are citizens of countries that have received aid from the Soviet Union in the past, a factor that is identifiable in many Russians' attitudes toward Africans today. Some people, including many CCM recipients, express their discomfort with receiving aid from Africans. Others articulate their convictions that blacks and other foreigners are taking aid resources that should be reserved for Russians. Although these attitudes about Africans are borne out through sometimes slight but unmistakable acts of discrimination, which occasionally occur in CCM soup kitchens, they are also manifested in more violent acts. Most African members of the CCM community have experienced physical harassment of greater or lesser degrees of severity. All members of the CCM community have had to confront these challenges on a daily basis in their efforts to create a productive and cohesive community. In my writing, I have been forced to think carefully about how I deal with the issue of race as it plays out in CCM activities. Although race is not an overt or constant feature of interactions among recipients and volunteers, it nevertheless is an important aspect that colors how members of this community understand one another. Hence I have chosen not to omit racially charged moments from this book, but I have tried to present them as objectively as possible.

Two events significantly influenced my research. The first took place at the midpoint of my year-long fieldwork stint, when I was introduced to Aleksandra Petrovna Korchagina. Aleksandra Petrovna had been an active volunteer in veterans' and pensioners' affairs in her district for many years and was one of the very first CCM soup kitchen recipients. Since then, she has contributed greatly to the CCM program, most notably by helping CCM staff expand their operations and mediating their relations with local officials. Through her volunteer work, she has become acquainted with politicians, social workers, and businesspeople throughout the city; and she calls on these contacts—and holds them accountable—to help the CCM program. Aleksandra Petrovna generously took me under her wing and introduced me to people at all levels of the CCM community, from officials to recipients. And it was Aleksandra Petrovna who inadvertently solved the problem of my identity in the soup kitchen. When I explained that I was writing a book on the soup kitchen, she understood that I was a journalist and subsequently, despite my repeated corrections, introduced me to everyone as "our American journalist."

The second turning point was the series of events that transpired with the opening of the fourth CCM soup kitchen in summer 1999. I had just returned to Moscow for several additional months of research and was able to observe closely the negotiations surrounding this event, from the collapse of the initial arrangements to the alternatives hastily proposed and put into action by Aleksandra Petrovna, Dr. Steve, and the district welfare director. The first days at the new soup kitchen were chaotic, and I was quickly enlisted to help register recipients and instruct them and the new volunteers and supervisors as to the proper procedures. Although I had previously worked intensively for a year in the other CCM soup kitchens and had established close working relationships and friendships with many individuals, it was not until this series of events that I became completely enmeshed in the tensions and political machinations that underlay public welfare programs and the ordinary interactions of friends and neighbors. Because of my knowledge of the CCM program and my language abilities, I was frequently asked to mediate and translate conversations and disputes among recipients, volunteers, cafeteria staff, and CCM staff. This, as well as my friendship with Aleksandra Petrovna, inserted me directly into the center of a simmering personal feud that eventually split the soup kitchen into two sides. The fortunate confluence of these events enriched my previous observations and data in ways that I had never anticipated. I discuss the feud in chapter 3 and the events of the registration period in chapter 5.

Although there may initially appear to be a gendered component to this project, it does not reflect a deliberate methodological strategy on my part. The fact that most recipients are elderly women and most volunteers are young African males accurately represents the composition of the community around the CCM program, as well as Russian society as a whole. Demographically, most pensioners are elderly women (Shkolnikov, Field, and Andreev 2001), primarily because of the enormous loss of young male soldiers during World War II. A combination of secondary factors such as alcoholism, violence, and military service has subsequently decreased the life expectancy of Russian men in general, thereby further increasing the disparity between the number of males and females in Russia. Of the younger women who receive food through assistance programs, most are single mothers, a circumstance that says much about local gendered expectations regarding responsibilities to dependent children. As for the composition of volunteers, most African students who are sponsored to study in Russia are male. They are also more likely to be targets of racially motivated attacks than are African women, and many of them turn to the CCM congregation and volunteer ranks to find both social and material support.

In keeping with standard ethnographic practices aimed at protecting the identities of informants, I have created pseudonyms for the CCM congregation and the members of the soup kitchen community, and I have attempted to disguise features of the organization such as the precise locations of its programs. Nevertheless, I have retained the form of people's names as I used them. In Russia, people may be addressed by their first name and patronymic (i.e., middle name), by first name alone, or by nickname. The first form is used as a marker of respect or unfamiliarity; the last two as signs of close intimacy between friends or relatives. These cues will indicate the degree of intimacy between my informants and me. The one exception is that of Aleksandra Petrovna. Although we were very close to each other and used very intimate terms to address each other, I have preferred to identify her by first name and patronymic as a small token of the very deep respect I feel for her. Although people who are familiar with Moscow's food aid community will undoubtedly recognize the program, these precautions are particularly necessary because of recent governmental and popular views about foreign "intervention" in Russia.[18] Although local welfare authorities and politicians publicly praise the CCM congregation and actively support its aid programs, the community has recently come under scrutiny from officials at higher levels in both the city and state government who are concerned that the CCM congregation is directly competing with "traditional" Russian religious beliefs and practices.

Recent legislation in Russia has given legal recognition only to religious groups that were registered with the government before 1982. The first draft of the law technically granted full legal rights only to the Russian Orthodox Church, Islam, Judaism, and Buddhism, although its amended version has given leeway to Catholicism and several "mainstream" Protestant denominations (Kornblatt 1999:431 n.1).[19] Leaders in the Orthodox Church in particular have lobbied the federal government to restrict competing expressions of religion, especially proselytizing and charismatic movements introduced by foreign congregations. Religious communities must apply for official recognition as social groups and provide proof of sponsorship from local organizations. Unofficial preventative measures include harassment of missionaries at the immigrations and customs checkpoints upon arrival to Russia, surveillance by the police and tax authorities during services, raids on aid programs and the confiscation of volunteers' passports, and social pressure on congregants. One young Muscovite woman who attends a long-established Protestant church in Moscow stated that the Orthodox priest in her neighborhood pressured her and her husband not to baptize their new baby outside Orthodoxy by claiming that such a baptism would be un-Russian. Staff persons at various churches in Moscow, including the CCM congregation, have reported being followed and having their telephones tapped and mail opened.

Consequently, the CCM congregation is in a precarious position in Russia. Despite the affiliation of the CCM with the foreign diplomatic community in Moscow and its legal authorization to exist in Russia, the willingness of the sponsoring embassies to continue their support of the congregation has waned as the congregation has expanded in the last two decades from serving primarily North American and European diplomats to including professionals, students, and refugees from Asia, Africa, and even Russia. To comply with federal regulations governing religious expression, CCM staff have agreed not to proselytize to Russian citizens. Primarily this means that CCM staff guarantee that the soup kitchens are removed from any spiritual connotations: staff and volunteers cannot offer prayers or hand out religious texts, crosses, or other items. It also means that CCM members are forbidden to use Russian in services or church texts. For their part, CCM staff encourage Russian congregants not to register themselves officially on the church roster.

Ironically, if this ban was meant to discourage opportunities for social interaction between Russians and non-Russians, it has only prompted creative circumventions and liaisons. Not all Russian and African members of the congregation are fluent in English, and many North American and European members have limited Russian abilities. Congregants thus rely on each other to translate through a variety of languages (Russian, English, French, and Swahili, among others) the informal conversations that emerge outside official worship services. It is through these creative interactions and the strategic negotiation of practical communication (Habermas 1987) that the CCM community is constituted and maintained.

The Art of Russianness: Making Sense of "Making Do"

One summer evening during my fieldwork, I was visiting a friend when several other friends dropped by unexpectedly. My hostess's pantry was low on supplies, but she had an assortment of vegetables and spices that I quickly tossed together as a makeshift curry dish for our supper. Our visitors had never experienced Asian cuisine before and praised the dish and asked me for the recipe. When I confessed that I had simply added all the leftover vegetables to the sauce, they laughed and informed me that I had just made a meal *po-russki,* or Russian-style. By way of further explanation, one woman volunteered that Russian pizza was simply the resulting combination of whatever one found in the refrigerator. For my Muscovite informants, the ability to improvise, to patch together a random assortment of goods and circumstances, is a distinctively Russian trait, an activity often referred to as doing something in the Russian style.[20]

The organizing theme for this book is "making do" (de Certeau 1984; Reed-Danahay 1996), the repertoires of social and economic strategies that Muscovites use in their everyday lives to cope with economic and material uncertainties by creatively manipulating the resources that are available. More than this, however, these tactics are intricately caught up with perceptions and processes of sociality. The underlying needs of material provisioning are products of society: the need to offer hospitality or assistance occurs only when one is already located within a social milieu laced with responsibilities, interests, and affections. Thus, the successful navigation of the rules and structures of society is both possible and necessary only through cooperative assistance and shared knowledge. At the same time, social relations are themselves uncertain, and agents must successfully navigate the rules and potentialities of friendship. The provisional tactics of Muscovite *bricoleurs* are always simultaneously economic and social, utilitarian and symbolic.

In each chapter I explore a different style and arena in which these tactics of coping with uncertainty are played out, and I describe how social support operates as a practical metaphor for accommodating economic security. In chapter 2 I introduce the idea of making do by looking at the various ways Muscovites have combined material and social provisioning efforts during the twentieth century. Consumers' everyday experiences with the Soviet shortage economy produced unique social behaviors such as queuing, hoarding, informal and semilegal exchange systems, ironic anecdotes, and ideologies of mutual assistance. As the economic circumstances in Russia have changed from a market in which goods were scarce to one in which shortages of money are the primary constraint, Muscovites have created new strategies to consolidate social assets and convert them into economic resources.

Chapter 3 describes the informal economies of exchange through which Muscovites circulate resources when the official economy is incapable of maintaining regular distribution and access. Social scientists typically categorize these types of exchange practices as belonging either to the black market or to *blat,* a specific relationship corresponding to hierarchies of influence. I suggest that another type of exchange network exists, less dependent on power than on local ideas about mutual assistance and generalized reciprocity within the collective, and I explore the tensions that emerge in the soup kitchen between foreign volunteers and donors who coopt these informal exchange relations into systems of charity on the one hand and recipients who attempt to restore balance through reciprocity on the other.

This theme of mutual assistance is continued in chapter 4, where I investigate how summer gardens and forests create a space where material and social resources merge. Originally intended to supplement the ability of the state to provide for its citizens, personal agriculture is today conceived as a necessary alternative to reliance on bureaucratic support. Aid recipients frequently forgo their guaranteed meals in favor of natural produce gathered at family cottages outside the city. At the same time that recipients process personal agricultural products for long-term storage against future uncertainties, they also cultivate social networks through exchanges of these products and related services.

Chapter 5 explores the use of stereotypes as productive security strategies. Bureaucratic identity categories were initially imposed during the Soviet period to regulate social equality through compensations for disabilities, wartime contributions, and the attainment of high labor standards. Today, Muscovites continue to participate actively in the reduction of selfhood to generalized labels—first, to locate themselves within communities of people with similar experiences and, second, to procure goods and services available to those specific groups of beneficiaries. This chapter examines the types of categories that Muscovites invoke and the conditions under which they use them as strategies for securing social and economic resources.

In chapter 6, I continue with the theme of identity classifications and look specifically at the social phenomenon of "hunger." Russian recipients at soup kitchens and other food aid programs receive their eligibility precisely because their material circumstances severely restrict their abilities to buy sufficient food. Yet within the larger aid community, recipients and aid workers invoke images of hunger as a commentary not on material resources but rather on social resources. Contrary to Western emphases on individualism, Muscovites conceptualize the state of being an individual as an exclusion from social groups and the support that circulates through the collective. Recipients not only approach the soup kitchen as a site of communal support but also turn it back as a reflection on the socially marginal and potentially dangerous status of persons who are outside the CCM community.

Finally, in chapter 7, I examine the themes of collective identity and mutual assistance in the context of the developing economic system in Russia. A significant feature of market capitalism is the differentiation of consumers into socioeconomic classes. In Moscow, because every consumer has potential access to all resources, social distinction varies according to the ability of consumers to manipulate their social networks and to distribute resources to others. In this conclusion I hold up Muscovites' mutual assistance practices as a commentary on the ineffectiveness of outside efforts to "reform" Russia, and I argue for a more balanced perspective on the efficacy and appropriateness of Western models for understanding Russian selfhood, poverty, and the need for charitable assistance.

CHAPTER 2

Making Do

Everyday Survival in a Shortage Society

What is long and green and smells like sausage?
An intercity train leaving Moscow.

Joke heard in Moscow

Within a rich tradition of joking and storytelling, riddles such as the one shown in the epigraph poke fun at the naïveté and backwardness of rural Russians who visit the city and desperately load up with food products and other commodities.[1] At a deeper level, however, the numerous quips and anecdotes that circulate in Russians' conversations have been important forms of social and political commentary, both for the state and for its citizens. During the Soviet period, forms of satire, such as those found in the popular journal *Krokodil* or in circus acts, became vehicles for cultivating national values.[2] At the same time, within a context where dissent was carefully managed and kept in check through tactics of surveillance and redirection, Soviet citizens became masters at creating and deciphering metaphors and subtexts as alternative means to express themselves. In this vein, humor became an especially powerful medium for articulating personal opinions that were at odds with or that commented on official rhetoric and policies. As Anna Krylova has noted, jokes are powerful because they represent the insider's view of life as it is actually experienced (1999:247). Similarly, an acquaintance in Moscow reflected that *anekdoty* were powerful during Soviet days precisely because they protected the realities of everyday life from official—and often corrected—versions.

Although political events and leaders offered particularly vulnerable targets for jokes and anecdotes, everyday survival provided another popular theme. Many jokes, such as the one in the epigraph, drew ironic attention to the important place that consumer goods occupied in people's lives, the lengths to which people went to acquire them, and people's frustrations with the state's inability to produce and distribute goods adequately. In a conversation about shopping in Russia, a friend asked if I had heard about the "In principle" stores. In response to my negative answer, she related the following anecdote: Back in the Soviet days, a young man from the provinces prepared to travel to Moscow. He and his neighbors in the village had heard stories that the stores in Moscow were teeming with goods, unlike in the provinces, where store shelves were bare. Before the young man left on his trip, his relatives and neighbors asked him to buy certain things that were unavailable in the village. When the man arrived in the city and attempted to make his purchases, he visited the first store, only to find the shelves bare. He asked a fellow customer, "Is it possible to buy shoes?" The other person responded, "In principle, yes." The man went to a second store and discovered that it too was bare. He asked another person, "Is it possible to buy shoes?" That person also responded, "In principle, yes." The young man made several more attempts with the same results. Finally, in frustration, he stopped yet another customer and asked, "Where is this store, 'In principle'?" Svetlana Boym relates a similar joke about shortages from the Brezhnev era: "A man asks the salesgirl: 'Don't you have meat?' 'You must be in the wrong store,' she answers. 'Here we don't have fish. Across the street is where they don't have meat' " (Boym 1994:227).

As these examples illustrate, humor became an important, and collective, coping mechanism for dealing with the peculiarities of an economic system that was consistently challenged by low incomes, delayed wages, high prices, shortages, and the unequal distribution of goods (Krylova 1999; Ries 1997). In reply to my inquiry about how people have responded to shortages and other consumer inconveniences, one Muscovite told me, "We relate with humor. That's how we survive." Yet humor is only one strategy among many that Muscovites have devised for managing the unpredictability of Russia's social and political economy. In this chapter, I discuss Muscovites' survival strategies as forms of improvisation, or "making do"; and I suggest that through collective efforts to manipulate the system, Muscovites graft social relations onto economic interests.

The Tactics of Improvisation

In Moscow, a common response to the ever-present changes and sense of uncertainty that colored daily life during my fieldwork was a shrug of the shoulders and the statement, "We do not know what tomorrow will bring" *(My ne znaem, chto budet zavtra)*. This sense of uncertainty is not unique to the post-Soviet moment, however. Nor has it been perceived as an insurmountable obstacle. Despite the ambiguities that mark the world around them, Muscovites assert that they will *perezhivat'*—that is, endure, or live through—these circumstances. The unique circumstances of state socialism as it was produced and experienced in the former Soviet Union and Eastern Europe have engendered a series of cultural practices in which the creative capacity to make do is a valuable and critical strategy for navigating daily life. In this sense, Russian society closely resembles what Steven Sampson has described for the case of another socialist state, Romania: "a society where all things were possible and nothing was certain" (1995:162).

Two of the most paradigmatic features of the Soviet system of state socialism were its chronic shortages (Kornai 1997) and queues. These resulted largely from the Soviet state's efforts to control and manage all aspects of the economy, including supply, production, and distribution (Verdery 1996). Unlike market capitalist economies, in which supplies are generated in response to market demands (Smith 1981), the Soviet economy was artificially directed by state officials who determined public interests and established target plans to satisfy those interests. The primary consequence of this system was that the emphasis on production encouraged hoarding of labor and resources at all levels, what János Kornai has called an "insatiable investment hunger" (1997:19), which led to scarcities of both raw materials and manufactured goods (Verdery 1996). Irregular distribution practices, as well as exceptional circumstances caused by war and poor harvests, further limited the equitable supply of goods to the Soviet population.

These conditions of scarcity fostered a unique set of cultural dispositions and expectations, so that Soviet daily life was not simply an economy of shortages but rather a society of shortages.[3] In an observation reminiscent of Bourdieu's (1977) notion of the habitus, János Kornai remarked, "People became used to the shortages around them, and this was built into their expectations and behaviour, which further enhanced the shortage. Shortage breeds shortage" (1997:30).[4] Although I would disagree with Kornai's negative assessment of this self-generating system, I believe the habitus analogy is fitting, because socialism was a total social fact that shaped every aspect of daily life. Accordingly, both the state and its citizens built an elaborate cultural system to accommodate and make sense of it. For its part, the Soviet government introduced various methods of redistribution such as special stores linked to citizens' workplaces or party status; social welfare programs; and even rationing, in more extreme circumstances. Soviet citizens, meanwhile, generated their own strategies for accessing scarce goods, ranging from hoarding, pilfering from workplaces, and counterfeiting ration cards, to reselling manufactured goods and personal property in flea markets and bartering (Fitzpatrick 1999; Hessler 1996; Osokina 2001; Verdery 1996).[5]

Since perestroika and the advent of a capitalist-style consumer market in the 1990s, the commercial landscape has been transformed in Russia and elsewhere in the former Soviet Union and Eastern Europe (Barker 1999c; Berdahl 1999b; Patico and Caldwell 2002). Imported food products and consumer goods compete for shelf space with domestic commodities. Privately owned restaurants, cafés, pubs, and supermarkets offer festive, brightly lit, and sometimes even air-conditioned alternatives to state-owned enterprises. Increasingly, post-Soviet consumers are generating practices of consumption that include evaluating products and exercising choice (Caldwell 1999; Patico 2001a).[6] Nevertheless, the general constraints facing consumers have persisted. Whereas in the past, shoppers had money but there were few goods to buy, today consumers complain that there are stores full of products but no money for their purchase (figure 5).

Russian consumers have felt this monetary shortage in both absolute and relative terms. Inflationary trends in the early 1990s resulted in prices that were calculated in the thousands of rubles (a loaf of bread, for instance, cost on average three thousand rubles). Consequently, large-denomination bills were the norm, while smaller coins, kopecks in particular, became scarcer. During my fieldwork, it was not uncommon to observe vendors refusing to sell any of their goods because they did not have enough coins with which to make change for customers.[7] At the same time, Russians have been affected by severe financial constraints in the form of wage delays, reduced salaries, layoffs, an unstable domestic currency, and a volatile economy. To compensate for shortages such as these, Muscovites have availed themselves of a familiar repertoire of survival strategies reminiscent of the Soviet era, a practice noted by other ethnographers who have worked in the former Soviet Union (Grant 1995; Ledeneva 1998; Ries 1997; Walker 1998).

FIGURE 5. The beautiful GUM department store is now a testament to changes that have taken place in Russia's commercial sphere.

The skill of evaluating and making the best of the circumstances offered by the Soviet—and today Russian—state for one's personal benefit approximates what Reed-Danahay has termed the art of "making do" *(debrouiller)* (1996:61–62). The unique combination produced by the fluid and fluent manipulation of opportunities, contingencies, and expectations is what gives a culture its particular form and substance (Bourdieu 1980; de Certeau 1984). These practices are aimed not only at producing a version of social reality by selectively reworking and refitting the possibilities and constraints within the system but also at producing the meaning of that reality. Practical activity is thus a way of relating to and through the world (Bourdieu 1980:52).[8]

In the rationality of practical activity, improvisation is embedded within the very structures that it seeks to manipulate (Bourdieu 1977, 1980). Yet analysts disagree over the implications of these structural constraints. In contrast to Bourdieu's insistence that the creativity of making do is realized in the paradox of "a world of already realized ends" (1980:53) is the perspective that agents are active participants in the production of those ends and their expression (Herzfeld 1985; Reed-Danahay 1996). Yet even this acknowledgment of social actors as agents relies on a zero-sum assessment of the power relations at work in the control of resources. This is the essence of de Certeau's distinction between "strategies" and "tactics" (1984:34–38). Strategic action belongs to those institutions that possess both will and power and that establish first their place within the social order and the precise arrangements of the structures and resources of that system. Tactics, on the other hand, are the "weapons of the weak" (Scott 1985), whose attempts to play with the available resources are ultimately efforts to resist and subvert the system (de Certeau 1984; Crowley and Reid 2000; Desjarlais 1996).

I want to depart from this approach by suggesting that attention to the social context in which these activities occur reveals a more balanced negotiation among participants. The institutions and structures to which Bourdieu and de Certeau ascribe power are not, in fact, monolithic, autonomous structures, but rather associations composed of independent individuals with the ability to act in their own self-interest. In this sense, not only is improvisation not possible outside the realm of social relations, but the potential for its expression is also the result of the careful coordination of the interests of all participants. Creativity must be collectively and socially negotiated, performed, and understood (Herzfeld 1985). Even though Habermas is analyzing linguistic improvisation, his point about "repair work" as a collectively constituted project is applicable here: "The actors have to draw upon the means of strategic action, with an orientation toward coming to a mutual understanding, so as to bring about a common definition of the situation or to negotiate one directly" (Habermas 1987:121). For the successful articulation of survival strategies, the sense of collectivity is crucial. Practices of making do are possible only through cooperation and are at the same time beneficial to the collective.

In the case of Russia, because even the persons who compose institutions operate according to notions of poaching and posturing, private citizens and bureaucratic structures alike are complicit partners in the system. Together these agents do not aim to resist or overthrow the system but rather aim to accommodate and refashion both its strengths and weaknesses in order to make it productive. In a sense, the coherence and order of Russian society depend on continual acts of internal readjustment. Drawing from this approach, I break from analyses that posit Russia as an entity in crisis or chaos and instead suggest that Russia's stability and social cohesion derive precisely from the capacity of its citizens to manage change and uncertainty. Moreover, acts of making do in Russian affairs are not indications of sneaky or subversive practices but are instead rational expressions of everyday social life.[9] These practices make up a system of habituated values and dispositions that are more constant and continuous than the analytical and temporal categories of "Soviet" and "post-Soviet" suggest. Although these practices respond to immediately felt material needs, their constancy is the product of more deeply held cultural values about social relations. In the remainder of this chapter I will elaborate on a number of these improvisational tactics in their post-Soviet reformulation before moving on in the rest of the book to an exploration of the importance of social relations in Muscovites' practices of making do.

Just in Case: Practices of Everyday Life

In a carryover practice from the Soviet period, an essential staple in people's purses and briefcases—and the sign of a prepared shopper—is the "just-in-case" bag (Fitzpatrick 1999:41) that can be used for unexpected purchases.[10] More than once when fellow commuters have opened their briefcases to fish out a newspaper or book, I have been afforded a quick glimpse inside and have seen a case empty except for a tote bag or plastic sack. CCM soup kitchen recipients commonly bring extra bags in case unannounced "extras" are dispensed. On occasions when unpackaged items such as beans or rice are available, people who have forgotten to bring an extra bag desperately try to find someone who has a bag or container to share. Periodically volunteers bring in used plastic containers and glass jars that they can no longer use, and recipients eagerly sort through them, looking for items of particular sizes and shapes that will be useful for transporting food home, as well as for storing homemade pickles or preserves later. On one such occasion, when I went into the hallway off the cafeteria at the Moscow Scientific Institute, I met a recipient who was standing at the table where extra containers were left and carefully comparing the various plastic tubs that were available against the tubs that she already had in her bag. When she had made her selection, she turned to me and explained that she was trying to find a container in a size that would complement those she already owned. In a similarly revealing instance, shortly before I left Moscow at the end of my fieldwork, my next-door neighbor met me in the stairwell of our apartment building while I was carrying trash outside to the dumpster. Noticing that I had bagged my garbage before carrying it outside, he scolded me for wasting bags. Later when I returned to the dumpster with a second load of trash, I discovered that someone had carefully untied the plastic bags containing my garbage, dumped the contents into the dumpster, and removed the bags.

More general recycling practices include looking through dumpsters for discarded items such as containers and pieces of wood, leather, and metal that can be reused for various tasks at home, in the car, or at the cottage. One CCM recipient repairs discarded items that he has found in garbage bins and along the streets. Another works part-time as a janitor in an apartment building and brings home articles of clothing that she finds, washes and irons them, and then resells them. One enterprising gentleman collects free concert tickets and attempts to sell them just outside the concert hall's box office. As hospitals become increasingly strapped for funds, doctors repeatedly wash out single-use rubber gloves and hypodermic needles. When I gave a physician friend a package of twenty disposable rubber gloves that my husband had collected at a trade show, the woman's daughter excitedly remarked that her mother would never need to buy gloves again. By the same token, car owners frequently carry informal tool kits of odds and ends in their cars. It is not uncommon for drivers to stop and help a disabled motorist along the side of the road. Similarly, several CCM recipients who assist a regional pensioners' welfare program helped their organization put advertisements on television asking Muscovites who have purchased new televisions, refrigerators, or other appliances to donate their used models to the program. Volunteers repair the items and then distribute them to needy pensioners.[11]

Although environmental recycling movements have been slow to develop in Moscow, collecting empty bottles is an important source of secondary revenue for many Muscovites, pensioners in particular. People find empty bottles along the street, left in buses, or tossed into refuse bins and stash them in their purses, briefcases, and tote bags. They then redeem the bottles for one ruble, thirty kopecks (as of 2000) at one of several redemption centers located around the city. An elderly woman who was collecting bottles inside Gorky Park explained that her pension was very meager and that she had to pay for gas, lights, medicine, and food.

She counted the bottles she had already placed in her bag (about ten) and said they would provide a little money toward these expenses. The value of recycling is recognized by other Muscovites who generously place their empty beer bottles near, but not inside, the rubbish bins in their hallways, so that they are readily apparent to neighbors who collect them. While several friends and I strolled through a park one summer evening, an elderly man patiently followed us as we talked and sipped our beers. When we finished our drinks, the daughter of one friend carried the bottles back to the elderly man.

Recycling practices such as these complicate relationships between consumer and commodity, because Muscovite bricoleurs appreciate goods not for the social lives that they have accrued through previous uses (Appadurai 1986; Herrmann 1997), but rather for their future potentialities. By disassociating secondhand goods from their original purposes, Muscovites can create new uses and new symbolic meanings for them. These acts of recycling occasionally have ironic consequences, however, a feature that emerges most clearly in the use of plastic containers by CCM recipients. Most containers that are donated to the soup kitchens come from North American and European volunteers, many of whom shop primarily in the Western supermarkets in Moscow. These individuals are more likely to buy higher-priced, and generally imported, foods that come in high-quality plastic containers, glass jars, and metal canisters with securely fitting lids. Even though these items serve necessary utilitarian purposes for those who acquire them secondhand, it is nonetheless jarring to see elderly Russians spooning their meals into containers marked by labels for expensive, transnational brands.

Just-in-case tactics extend to hoarding practices as well. During the chronic shortages that plagued the Soviet period, consumers became accustomed to buying up goods when they were available and holding on to them until they were needed or could be exchanged for another item or service. When word of the impending ruble devaluation hit Moscow streets in August 1998, shoppers quickly went to the stores and stocked up on staples such as flour, rice, sugar, tea, coffee, and sausage—and to automated banking machines and currency exchange counters to stock up on money, hard currency in particular. One woman, an official with a regional welfare program, explained that hoarding was a common practice: "It is not like you have in America, where there's only one egg lying in the refrigerator for breakfast." In Russia, the common perception is that Americans eat only prepackaged and take-out foods and no one cooks, so kitchens would never be well-stocked with basic staples. This view contrasts sharply with what the official identified as a particularly Russian practice: "For us, we're used to the fact that at any moment we need to support the government. Therefore, every person has a reserve supply. . . . At one point even I bought up [things]. At home I have grains, macaroni. I still have that."

In the CCM soup kitchens, recipients prepare for long weekends and holiday breaks by asking for extra servings of foods that can be preserved and stretched to last longer. Hearty soups with vegetables can be watered down to last for several meals, unlike meat and potatoes; and more use can be gained from tea bags than from already prepared hot tea. Recipients who have enough food at home, such as during the summer when friends and relatives are more likely to give away extras from their gardens, often save their meal tickets for a future time when their personal resources have been depleted.[12] Bread occupies an especially important role in the hoarding activities of CCM members.[13] Recipients are entitled to exchange portions of their meals for extra slices of bread or their entire meal for two loaves of bread. Bread can then be stored in the freezer or dried into croutons until it is needed later. Recipients acknowledge that bread is one of the most valuable resources at their disposal to protect themselves against uncertainty. At the end of the month, when their pensions have been depleted, recipients bring out the extra meal tickets that they have tucked away and redeem them for bread.

Muscovites prepare in advance for social encounters as well. Hostesses may purchase extra bed linens, slippers, or robes for an occasion when a guest might come to visit; and small souvenir gifts can be tucked away until a later time. Shortly after I had arrived at the home of a friend's mother for the first time, the woman presented me with a small wooden bowl and set of nesting dolls *(matrëshki)*. When I fussed that she should not have gone to any trouble to buy me a present, she laughed and replied that she had tucked away the items long before in case such an opportunity presented itself.[14]

Consuming on the Side

In an environment where one never knows which goods will be available at the store or at what price, Muscovites watch carefully for opportunities and potentialities on which they can capitalize, and they identify a sense of pride and accomplishment in successfully scoring a bargain or unexpected purchase.[15] The importance of acquisition is evident in the language that Muscovites use to describe their shopping achievements. Just as in the Soviet period (Fitzpatrick 1999:40), people talk not about "buying" items but about "finding" *(naiti)* or, more commonly, "obtaining" *(dostat')* goods; and narratives of "heroic shopping" (Ries 1997) provide dramatic insight into the travails associated with consumption.[16] In summer 1999, my landlady spent most late evenings calling her friends, exchanging news with them about current prices for various foods and other items, and rejoicing in a successful trip to the market. During an informal interview at Aleksandra Petrovna's apartment with Valentina Fëdorovna, one of Aleksandra Petrovna's close friends and a fellow activist for the elderly in their region, the two women moved from a general conversation about the material constraints facing pensioners to specific benefits and opportunities that were available to people in their district. Valentina Fëdorovna mentioned a discount store that was run by the local police and was stocked with items that had been seized in raids. The goods ranged from dishes and appliances to clothing, books, and car parts and were resold at lower-than-original prices, with the proceeds going back to the police department to support its programs. Aleksandra Petrovna interrupted her to tell us that she had purchased a handbag at the store several days before. She brought out the bag for us to inspect, and the two women compared notes about other bargains they had found at the store. After the interview, the two women organized an excursion to the store so that I could see for myself the bargains that were available.[17]

For people who have the financial means but not the capability to go shopping—for instance, individuals who are confined to home or the hospital—close friends are entrusted with money to buy goods while doing their own shopping. Shopping as a collective practice has long been an important tactic for Muscovite consumers (figure 6). Elena, the middle-aged neighbor of a soup kitchen recipient, reminisced about how she and a friend shopped together during Soviet times. She and her friend arrived at the store before it opened, and each person stood in front of a different entrance. Although most stores, restaurants, theaters, and other public buildings have multiple doors, usually only one is open at any given time; this causes a certain amount of chaotic pushing and shoving when large numbers of people attempt to make their way through at once. When the shop clerks randomly selected one door to open, either Elena or her friend was able to enter with the first group of customers. After both women were inside, they divided the store into two halves, and each person investigated what was for sale and at what price in her assigned section. Each woman then made purchases from her section,

FIGURE 6. Two women consult while shopping in a Moscow market.

both for herself and for the other. Elena remarked that an intelligent, experienced person could quickly scan a store, know immediately what goods were for sale and at what price, purchase the items, and leave. Hence, shopping cooperatively with a skilled friend was a productive strategy, because it decreased the time Elena spent shopping and increased the number of products she and her friend could access. Similarly, several times a week my landlady went shopping with a close friend so that they could help each other manage their shopping bags and seek each other's advice and reassurance before making a purchase.[18]

Russian consumers have also relied on more secretive means to get needed goods and services. Since the Soviet period, professional speculators and private citizens alike who have goods to sell or are in search of goods can make careful inquiries or offers through discreet acquaintances or even directly to strangers on the street. Signs propped up on cars outside train stations and along the Old Arbat shopping district announce that Muscovites can sell their gold and silver jewelry, as well as old coins and other antiques, for cash. At various times in the past, currency exchanges frequently occurred on street corners rather than in official banking institutions, particularly during periods when possession of for-

FIGURE 7. Enterprising Muscovites line a city sidewalk and offer produce and personal items for sale.

eign currency was illegal. Dealing with unauthorized exchangers is risky, however; one risks being handed a roll of counterfeit bills or other paper filler. In summer 2001, notices warning about the dangers of informal, hand-to-hand money exchanges appeared at currency exchange points throughout Moscow. Other vendors carefully hawk items ranging from fresh flowers and pickles to bandages, books, and batteries along sidewalks and on busy subway cars, ready to stash their wares into bags at the first sight of the police (figure 7).[19]

One of the most recognizable forms of alternative consumption that originated in the Soviet period was the mobilization of personal networks and inside information. Customers with connections *(sviazi)* to employees in shops and other offices could invoke their personal relations in order to bypass the ever-present queues and to access goods that were not available to the general public. Kostya, a middle-aged businessman in Moscow, reflected that life was different during shortage periods *(defitsitom)*: "Then you had to get everything through the back door" *(dostat' chto-to cherez 'zadnee kryl'tso')*. If a person had a friend or relative at a particular shop, he explained, one would know to go to a particular side hallway to get items that were not available to the general public. More to the point, however, these side channels implied transactions that took place out of the public view.

These alternative channels are closely related to *blat,* a form of informal exchange that I will discuss more fully in chapter 3. In this form of access, which was used extensively during the Soviet era, consumers manipulated personal connections and obligations, as well as rhetorical invocations of "friendship," in order to access goods and services to which they might not otherwise be entitled.[20] As Kostya recalled when describing the everyday techniques of socialist consumption, blat was a means to get something better than what was available, such as a better cut of meat, or more than what one had been allotted. He elaborated that if he were a customer with the proper connections he could make a secretive request of a contact (he pretended to whisper behind his hands), who might find him a pair of boots, and then he would pay and hurry off with them. Kostya's wife, Anya, entered the conversation at this point in the discussion and mimed the way she might clutch boots to her chest in such a scenario. Anya added that consumers could also use blat when there were clothes or shoes in the stores but they were identical *(odinakovye).* A customer who wanted something different, perhaps in a different color, she explained, could go through blat *(po blatu)* so as not to be the same as everyone else.

At the same time that attempts to bypass official channels gave consumers a means to access scarce material goods, it also enabled them to exert control over another resource that was in short supply: time. In the Soviet Union and Eastern Europe, shoppers spent hours (literally, in some cases) every day going between stores and standing in lines (Verdery 1996). Although the necessity of moving among stores was partly the product of scarcities, it was also a consequence of the way in which Soviet shopping was structured. Many stores specialized in a single type or category of goods—for instance, dairy products, bread, produce, shoes, and so on—thereby forcing consumers to visit multiple shops in order to complete their shopping. Valentina, the neighbor of a soup kitchen recipient, recalled that during perestroika, she often spent the greater part of the day running *(begat')* from one store to another. People who could not get to the stores in time were in real trouble, she finished. Personal connections and cooperative shopping practices were thus exceedingly useful and valuable strategies that allowed consumers to reclaim at least a portion of their time away from the market.

In recent years, the markets *(rynki;* sing., *rynok)* that have popped up throughout Moscow and elsewhere in Russia (often near train stations) have offered shoppers the conveniences of one-stop shopping (figure 8).[21] Typically one can buy produce, meat, dairy products, personal care products, housewares, clothing, tools, and almost anything else imaginable at one of the large outdoor markets in Moscow. Consumers, however, often view markets with a mixture of appreciation and frustration. Although prices are generally lower than in the stores and goods are plentiful, Muscovites complain about the amount of time required to navigate the many aisles and throngs of people and to decide which seller has the best goods at the most reasonable prices. In 1995, despite my best efforts to accompany my landlady on her shopping trips, she refused to take me to the market with her. Although she was forty years older than I was, she claimed that I would not be able to keep up with her (and would undoubtedly cost her precious time). A friend confided that she preferred to send her husband to the market, because he could save time by driving his car.

Transportation is a useful example for understanding the ways in which social context both facilitates the means by which people manipulate the system and defines the conditions under which these practices are locally acceptable. Ethics of cooperation and collective responsibility characterize public transportation in Moscow and elsewhere in Russia. Buses, trams, and trolleys operate on the honor system for payment. Riders can buy monthly passes or single tickets in advance at counters in the metro stations, at booths located throughout the city, or directly from drivers. Technically, once riders board the vehicle, they have until the next stop to purchase a ticket and then void it at one of the punch machines located in the vehicle. Frequently, however, vehicles are so crowded that passengers cannot approach the driver's booth. Instead, they pass their money to other passengers, who in turn pass it all the way to the front, where the rider closest to the driver buys the tickets, collects the change, and passes both all the way back down the line. It is not uncommon for several such orders to be passed up simultaneously. Riders also pass their tickets to passengers who are seated closest to the punch machines to have them voided. When transportation inspectors make spot checks, passengers must present either their voided tickets or monthly passes. As each vehicle's punch machines have a unique pattern, inspectors can tell if a ticket has been validated on that particular bus or trolley. Alaina Lemon (2000) has described how some riders feel the constraints of this system so acutely that pass holders, who do not have to "prove" their tickets by visibly using a ticket machine, nevertheless insist on publicly announcing that they possess a transport pass.

FIGURE 8. Moscow markets are always bustling with shoppers.

Despite social coercion to demonstrate that one is conforming with the official system, there are often even greater pressures to buck the system by riding "like a hare" *(zaitsem),* that is, without paying. Although the penalties for being caught without a valid ticket are either paying a ten-ruble fine on the spot to the inspector or being tossed off the vehicle, some commuters see this tactic as a risk worth taking. The most common explanation that I encountered was that the chances of being caught and fined were so low that one could actually save money by taking the gamble. One afternoon while I was traveling with one of the CCM pensioners to a soup kitchen event, the other woman refused to let me punch my bus ticket. She argued that as a student, I was as poor as she was and that I should not have to give up my earnings to the government. Friends have described the elaborate ruses they have employed in order to get around paying for tickets: some compare notes with friends to determine which routes are most likely to be checked by inspectors and at what times of the day. Others keep a pocket full of used tickets with different punch patterns that they can present to inspectors as they make a show of trying to find the correct one. As was the case with one friend, who did in fact have a legitimate ticket but could not locate it in the mix of other tickets in her wallet, inspectors become impatient and move on to another passenger without asking for payment. Meanwhile, through informal connections passengers can buy counterfeit subway passes or multiride tickets that have been doctored to fool the machines at the entryways. In summer 1998, when new, magnetic cards replaced the tokens used for subways, stories circulated throughout Moscow about ways to modify the passes in order to trick the machines into miscounting the number of times one went through.[22]

The Illusion of Pretense: The Post-Soviet Experience with Work and Income

Although Soviet ideology privileged labor as a fundamental component in the project of socialist modernity, the realities of the workplace meant that guarantees of employment, the hoarding of labor to meet target plans, and worker resentment over the interference of Communist Party and labor union officials all contributed to an "oppositional cult of non-work" (Verdery 1996:23).[23] These conditions of labor under state socialism were nicely captured in the widely circulated ironic comment, "As long as they pretend to pay us, we'll pretend to work" *(Oni delaiut vid, chto nam platiat, a my delaem vid, chto rabotaem)*. Despite these allusions to work as a pretense, Russians in fact invest considerable time and energy into piecing together various forms of employment as responses to their financial circumstances. Moreover, at the same time that formal employment constrains workers by restricting their time and income, the resources to be mined from colleagues and the workplace enlarge the realm of alternative possibilities for making do.

Many people work multiple jobs—sometimes as many as three or four—at one time, a practice that Michael Walker (1998) has observed for the comparable case of post-Soviet Ukraine. In Moscow, researchers supplement their work in state-funded institutes by translating for foreign journals and newspapers, interpreting, organizing conferences and business trips, and consulting for private firms. Many teachers and professors tutor students privately. English-language instructors can easily earn twenty dollars an hour for private instruction, a substantial contribution to their official monthly salaries. One young man, a respected scholar in his early thirties, reportedly works five such jobs to support his wife and small child. A professor at one of Moscow's largest universities argued that this multitasking, while necessary, is a serious problem among students in Moscow today. Although young people want to study, she said, they must work several jobs and so have neither the time nor the energy to complete their assignments. Much to the disappointment of not a few parents, many students perceive the potential financial and other rewards to be gained through successful employment opportunities as exceeding the benefits of education itself. Misha, the roommate of a friend's son, worked several office jobs while he was still a university student in Moscow. He claimed that he did not worry about the state of his grades, because the money that he earned was more important. A thriving underground business in counterfeit diplomas and grade records, for both Russian and foreign universities, and in false documentation of work histories, further provides means for enterprising individuals to make claims to better jobs and financial ventures that bypass the formal education system.

A common second job for men is a position as a security guard or night watchman. Both men and women also find positions supervising the entrances and floors of hotels, apartment buildings, and dormitories. Older adults who are already minding grandchildren at home often watch other children in informal day care situations. A single mother in her early twenties took a job as a live-in nanny so that she could save the expenses of renting a room for her and her six-year-old daughter. Nannies can earn as much as $250 per month (or even more), a sum that caused a CCM soup kitchen coordinator to resign her position because she could not find a sitter for her son at a price that she could afford. A CCM recipient who had heard of the young woman's dilemma lamented that if only she were younger and more energetic, she could have offered her services as a nanny for a much lower price.

Although many Muscovites work multiple jobs sequentially, moving from one workplace to another over the course of a day or week, a more common strategy is to stay put in one workplace and use the resources that are available there—things such as telephone, fax machine, computers, electronic mail and Internet access, and stationery—for other jobs. Physicians offer private surgery hours and extend their routine services to include massage therapy, chiropractic, and other forms of holistic healing. In a more unusual turn, one CCM congregant, a young teacher of English who travels several hours by train every day between her students who are based in Moscow and those who live in an industrial town outside Moscow, also markets herself as a "healer" and combines language lessons with exorcisms and channeling sessions.

A pervasive practice both in Moscow and elsewhere is for individual drivers to operate as private or rogue taxis. Men who work as personal drivers frequently run private errands for company employees and provide transportation for employees' personal guests. Many of these private jobs involve inconvenience, such as having to make the forty-five-minute drive to the airport in the wee hours of the morning or spending time waiting for a client to finish with a meeting or other personal business. For many, however, the inconvenience of waiting or having to forgo sleep is outweighed by the benefits of making as much as fifty dollars for a single trip. On one occasion a friend had arranged for the driver from her office to take me to the airport at 4 A.M. My driver casually informed me that he had already made one such run and that after he dropped me off he was going to the other side of the city to deliver some packages for another customer. He confided that he had been a successful entrepreneur until the 1998 financial crisis, when he had lost everything. He was confident that by supplementing his two part-time jobs as a personal driver with running errands, making deliveries, and driving people to the airport, he would be able to regain his former affluence.

Even more informal is the practice of offering rides to strangers for a small fee. Although Russia is crossed by an extensive transportation system, commuters who are in a hurry or have multiple bags to juggle can stick out their arms on the street. Within minutes—or even seconds—a car will stop, and negotiations begin with the driver as to distance and price. Drivers often refuse a trip because the destination is out of their way, but others willingly accommodate requests that are in the opposite direction of where they are headed. Some people advise agreeing on a price with the driver before getting into the car, but it is not uncommon for the driver simply to shrug and tell the pedestrian to hop in and they will negotiate later. One driver laughingly responded to my inquiry as to the cost with the phrase, "The more, the better." Once when a friend and I were trying to hail a ride, we were picked up by two young male security guards, who were wearing their uniforms and driving the company car at the time. During the conversation that accompanied our ride, the two men admitted that they were technically on duty. Ambulance and truck drivers also stop to pick up fares while on duty. Friends noted that typically it was only Muscovites with old or Russian-made cars who stopped to collect fares. By contrast, they pointed out, people who drove luxury cars rarely stopped, and when they did, they tended to ask higher prices and were less willing to haggle over the price.

Muscovites' views on hailing private "taxis" are mixed according to the different values that people place on time and money. Younger people tend to see the twenty or thirty rubles that one pays as reasonable expenses for traveling much more quickly and directly to one's destination. One CCM congregant calculated that taking a ride from another driver could save her thirty to forty-five minutes in travel time. Dr. Steve regularly hailed private cars when he was making his rounds among the four soup kitchens. Although the different cafeterias were in close proximity to each other, they were each located along a different subway line, which meant that travel between soup kitchens would have required first traveling to the center and then changing lines before heading back out of the city. Travel time by public transport between any two of the soup kitchens would easily take one hour, but by car, each trip could be made in ten to fifteen minutes. CCM recipients, however, focus on the cost of taxis and see them as expensive luxuries that should be avoided. For these Muscovites, money is more scarce than time. Except for a few fortunate recipients who live in apartment buildings next to their respective soup kitchens, most people are accustomed to spending one to one-and-a-half hours traveling to and from the soup kitchens. Several women frequently scold Dr. Steve for being impatient and wasting his money by taking taxis. When one woman suddenly became ill at the soup kitchen and volunteers discussed the possibility of finding a car to take her home, the recipient's friend insisted that they should not find a taxi, because there would not be anyone who could pay the fare. Even after another volunteer offered to drive the woman home (free of charge), the friend continued to voice her discomfort with that option in terms of the obligation that the woman might feel to pay something.

The tourism industry in Moscow offers another potentially lucrative source of income, particularly when tourists come from North America and Europe. Overtures of hospitality and promises to impart information can be parlayed into services that will be provided for a fee. Muscovites who speak English, particularly attractive young women, can often find additional work as translators, guides, and escorts for visiting businesspeople and tourists. Official Intourist tour guides and others with knowledge of Russia's cultural history wait outside popular tourist destinations, such as the Kremlin, Novodevichii Monastery and Cemetery, museums, and other historic sites, and offer tourists the opportunity for a guided tour with commentary for a fee plus the cost of admission for both visitors and guide. Lost tourists struggling with a map written in Russian can also be prime sources of revenue for a person who can offer directions in another language or even lead them directly to their destination. Foreigners who plan to stay in Moscow for a longer period of time are also approached for Russian-language lessons.

Offers such as these are generally not extended to persons who might otherwise be seen as friends, regardless of nationality or language background. Dale Pesmen (2000) notes that money-based, utilitarian transactions conflict with the ideology of *pomoshch'* (assistance) that characterizes relations of social intimacy. Between friends, such offers are veiled in terms of a mutually beneficial "exchange," whereby each person assists the other. A student in Moscow described how her mother, who earned a relatively good salary, "helped" a friend by buying stockings from the other woman and then giving them to her daughter and other relatives as gifts. Foreigners can provide help in such ways as mailing letters abroad or facilitating international academic exchanges (Ries 1997:14). When money does change hands, as in the case of a loan, it is often returned not in cash but in the form of a useful "gift" (Lemon 1998:48–49). I will elaborate further on the ideology of pomoshch' and local sensitivities about money in the next chapter.

Some Muscovites earn extra income by selling homemade food or other handicrafts along the sidewalks, inside underground pedestrian passages, or just outside the markets in Moscow. Those who do not have the skills or abilities to sell handmade goods resort to selling their personal belongings. Throughout Moscow, hopeful sellers spread blankets on the ground or erect makeshift tables from upturned boxes. On these they display used political buttons, clothing, books, porcelain, household items, fishing gear, tools, and many other items formerly a part of their personal lives.

Although much of the Russian economy is conducted through channels that are outside the realm of the mainstream, some additional opportunities are even more uncertain, and some are decidedly illegal. The one success story that I heard was told by a woman in her late twenties who revealed that she had made a small fortune working as an exotic dancer in Japan for three years. When she returned to Russia, she invested her money in a Mary Kay cosmetics franchise and was eventually able to buy her own apartment and an automobile and support her young husband through university. Not all are so fortunate, however. Investigative journalists have discovered that many of the advertisements that appear throughout the city offering workers promises of extraordinary opportunities and salaries are in fact fronts for international prostitution rings.

Despite Russians' general unfamiliarity with and distrust of banks, credit systems, investment practices, and insurance, gambling and other get-rich-quick schemes have become popular in Moscow. Large flashy casinos and small kiosks selling tickets for the Russian lottery have popped up across the city. In the early 1990s pyramid schemes such as the MMM program enticed thousands of Russians to invest—and eventually lose—their savings (Borenstein 1999a).[24] Similarly, while I was at home one afternoon, two young women came to my door with a consumer goods scheme: if I gave them a sum of around $150 as a deposit, they would give me the opportunity to test a stack of new appliances that included a toaster, blender, and steam iron, among others. Representatives of "security details," which can include local police authorities and members of organized crime groups, earn extra cash by collecting money from small business owners and vendors both for protection (*krysha*, lit., "roof") from other groups and for the right to occupy a specific patch of land.[25] The elderly are particularly vulnerable to acts of deception and pressure, and soup kitchen conversations are rife with stories about friends and neighbors who have allegedly been swindled by people posing as friends of relatives or as social workers. One recipient approached several volunteers for assistance in dealing with a renter who was trying to steal money and other belongings from her. Another woman asked a coordinator for suggestions on how to help a friend who had unknowingly allowed two thieves into her apartment. The two intruders had posed as caseworkers from the local social services office. While one woman asked the elderly woman seemingly genuine questions about her pension and expenses, the other woman carefully went through the apartment and looted several thousand dollars in cash that belonged to the live-in granddaughter of the elderly woman. Although the grandmother did not know of the existence of the money, when the granddaughter and her husband returned and discovered that it was missing, they allegedly beat the older woman and threatened her.

Exact figures about how much money is generated through the shadow economy are unknown, because few people report this supplemental income or invest it in the bank. Invalids and elderly pensioners who depend on government assistance deliberately underreport their earnings from undocumented work as house cleaners or dormitory security so as not to forfeit their pensions and other welfare privileges. Another common concern is that workers will be taxed on their extra incomes. Moreover, for individuals who are not legally registered in their apartments and routinely face harassment and extortion from the local policemen, public reporting of their supplemental resources could substantially increase the amount of money demanded by local authorities.

The pervasive use of barter further complicates evaluations of the Russian economy. For many employers, barter is a necessary alternative to payments in money. In factories that are short on cash, managers often pay workers in the specific goods that are produced in the company: these goods may range from porcelain and crystal to furniture. People then attempt to resell these items on the street or to friends, or recirculate them in transactions for other goods and services, including electricity (Woodruff 1999:86). When out walking with a CCM recipient one afternoon, we passed a woman who was minding an assortment of crystal glassware spread out on a blanket on the sidewalk. My friend shook her head sadly and commented that the factory obviously had stopped paying salaries in cash. Because wages are so often paid in kind, certain types of work are more advantageous than others. For instance, jobs in the food service industry have generally been seen as particularly advantageous, because workers have access to food goods that are otherwise in scarce supply to the general public (Shekshnia, Puffer, and McCarthy 2002). By contrast, during my fieldwork, a story circulated in Moscow that a coffin factory elsewhere in Russia had paid its workers with coffins. Muscovites speculated pessimistically on how successful those workers would be in their attempts to trade or resell their "wages" for other resources. Although the circuitous and secretive nature of Muscovites' efforts to generate income effectively conceals any objective evaluation of the monetary value of alternative employment, these activities are valuable markers of Muscovites' social worth and their ability to manipulate material and social resources. Both the necessity for additional income and the means through which these needs are realized are deeply embedded within a larger web of social relations, so that improvisation is possible only within the sphere of social relations (Habermas 1987).

Everyday Life in the CCM Community

Public assistance programs such as soup kitchens, senior citizens' centers, job training programs, and cultural events are still one more set of strategies nestled within this larger repertoire of everyday survival skills. In most cases, social welfare is not intended to replace other forms of income, assistance, and personal connections, but rather to supplement and enhance them. This is the perspective espoused by members of the CCM soup kitchen community. As such, the flexibility of soup kitchen interactions reflects the efforts of recipients, volunteers, and workers alike to make the best of changing opportunities. Yet the very ordinariness of programs such as the CCM soup kitchens belies the importance of the services that are available to recipients, particularly the sense of community and a collective social experience that emerges from the daily interactions among recipients, volunteers, and cafeteria employees. The actors who compose the CCM community represent a wide cross-section of Moscow's population in terms of age, nationality, occupation, class, race, and income. Accordingly, each person approaches the soup kitchen program with specific and unique interests and concerns. Together, these personalities and lifestyles combine to create a complex tapestry of social relations and material needs. To illustrate the diverse backgrounds and interests represented by the individuals who compose the CCM community, I will briefly introduce several different participants.

For Larissa Antonovna the soup kitchen is merely her first stop in a busy day of traveling around the city. A seventy-five-year-old retired historian, she arrives with her metal cart and canvas bags at the Moscow Scientific Institute around 10 A.M., having already spent an hour on public transportation from her apartment. After eating and socializing with friends at the soup kitchen, she makes her way to a city market on the opposite side of the city, where she carefully prices the merchandise and makes her selections. For the next several hours, she weaves her way through the city, visiting shops that she has frequented in the past and carefully noting the prices they are charging for bread, meat, and produce. In addition, Larissa Antonovna's true passion is listening to classical music, and she has a knack for finding free performances. In a typical week she manages to attend several such concerts. In the late afternoon or early evening, she makes her way home via the market near the Kievskaia train station, where prices are rumored to be the lowest in the city. She prefers to visit the market as late as possible, when vendors are likely to reduce their prices significantly in order to sell out their stock before going home. On weekends from April to October, she takes day trips to the countryside to gather wild herbs and mushrooms to supplement her food supplies. Although Larissa Antonovna's husband died almost ten years ago, she has a strong family network, with whom she keeps in close contact. Her son lives nearby with his family, and one of her sisters lives with her family in another neighborhood of Moscow. She has numerous other relatives and friends scattered throughout the city.

At fifty-eight, Mikhail Vassilievich is one of the youngest CCM recipients; the heart attack that he suffered five years ago has qualified him for participation. Most days he stops at the soup kitchen for a leisurely meal and lively debate with his friends. He enjoys teasing the female volunteers and often cajoles them into slipping him an extra bowl of soup or piece of bread. After finishing his meal, he heads down the street to the district senior citizens' services center, where he purchases yogurt, cheese, and meat at reduced prices. Then he goes home to rest before heading to the apartment of a relative or friend for a light meal. Mikhail Vassilievich's friend Igor Ivanovich participates in several different aid programs scattered across the city. He spends most of his day traveling from one cafeteria to another, eating and playing the piano for his various audiences. Meanwhile, Vladimir Andreevich proudly displays his registration card with the number 1, signifying that he was the first person in line when new registration cards were dispensed. Most days he is one of the first people to arrive and among the last to leave. He leisurely enjoys his meal and chats with other recipients and volunteers before heading home. Sergei Sergeevich is almost completely blind and eats at the soup kitchen because he lives alone and cannot see to light his stove. To get to and from the soup kitchen, he relies on the kindness of strangers who take his arm and guide him along the sidewalk.

Irina Mikhailovna uses the soup kitchens as opportunities to interact with volunteers and to peddle her homemade crafts and latest money-making schemes. Georgii Anatolievich is a retired cartoonist for *Krokodil;* he routinely asks new North American and European volunteers if they can help him arrange a lecture tour in their home countries for him to talk about his experiences. Aleksandra Petrovna, meanwhile, parlays her connections with local officials as well as recipients, volunteers, and staff at the soup kitchens into apartment rentals for neighbors, temporary jobs for volunteers, and information about where to find inexpensive food and other commodities. More important, over the years she has grown close to several volunteers and church staff, whom she trusts deeply. To supplement her income, she periodically sells off family heirlooms, such as the diamond earrings her father had given her mother or her grandmother's Fabergé tea set. She then asks these close friends to exchange the rubles she has received for the sales into dollars at a more favorable rate than that offered at the local currency exchanges.

For Svetlana Grigorievna, the director of one of the cafeterias contracted to provide food for the CCM program, the soup kitchen is an opportunity to make money. Not only does she get significant tax benefits for her business by providing a charitable service, but she increases the overall income of the cafeteria by demanding that her employees be given free meals as well. She has also parlayed her personal connections with

CCM staff and welfare officials into newspaper interviews and public appearances that have increased her political standing in the community. The former director of another cafeteria frequently employed more devious measures to increase her revenue by providing meals that cost well under the value for which she was compensated.

Roger has come to Russia from Sierra Leone to study mechanical engineering. He volunteers at the soup kitchens several times a week in order to visit with his fellow students and his surrogate grandparents, several elderly Russian women who fuss over him and bring him treats. Simon and Arthur, both refugees from Africa, see volunteering as a means to meet North Americans who might be able to help them with their immigration and employment applications. For Alan and other supervisors, the soup kitchens provide a steady salary and valuable managerial work experience.

Suzannah has moved between Moscow and Finland for several years as her husband's contract work takes them back and forth. Over time she has developed close friendships with several recipients and uses her volunteer days to visit with them. For Molly and Hilary, the wives of American businessmen stationed in Moscow, volunteering at the soup kitchen has given them valuable Russian language practice, an ease and familiarity with moving about the city and within confusing institutional settings, and submersion within a part of Moscow social life that many of their expatriate peers overlook. Tom, meanwhile, sees his time in the soup kitchens as a complement to his primary work as a spiritual adviser to a growing religious community.

Against a backdrop of bustling urban life, recipients and volunteers have carved out, within the conscripted spaces and operating times of the four CCM soup kitchens, a lively community that flexibly accommodates differences in age, nationality, race, religion, class, and occupation. Although volunteers and recipients move in and out of the community on daily, weekly, monthly, and seasonal schedules, relationships are constantly created and renewed but rarely ended. Through the mail, telephone calls, the Internet, and word of mouth, members stay in contact with each other across time and space. Within this environment, recipients and volunteers meet, discuss current events, trade recipes and homemade goods, organize outings and parties, and share their lives. Gossip, newspapers, and information about apartments circulate throughout the community. Friendships and marriages have been initiated, and formal and informal business partnerships created and subsequently dissolved.

The CCM operates a secondary feeding program as well. Less publicized, this program is directed toward student and refugee members of the congregation whose monthly stipends barely cover the necessities of everyday student life: food, winter clothing, and school supplies. Food packages containing staples such as flour, sugar, oil, butter, and rice are distributed after the monthly meetings of the student fellowship group. Periodically throughout the year these distributions are combined with distributions of used clothing. Student and refugee members of the CCM congregation admit that this assistance is the primary enticement for many people to join the church program. Yet even though this program is more directly part of an internal church project, it is intimately connected with the soup kitchen. Although people in desperate need of assistance are rarely turned away, priority is given to those CCM members who have actively assisted with the soup kitchens. Student and refugee volunteers are encouraged to fill out forms that record the amount of time they have spent working in the soup kitchens. Those individuals who have demonstrated the most commitment to the soup kitchens, in terms of both time and genuine concern for the recipients, are further rewarded with extra benefits such as monthly transportation passes. All volunteers, regardless of nationality or financial circumstances, are entitled to a free lunch after their shift at the soup kitchens.

Other food aid programs in Moscow operate along similar lines and include a membership whose diversity resembles that of the CCM program. Individual Orthodox churches run soup kitchens that serve registered lists of recipients drawn from the same neighborhoods in which CCM participants live. One such enterprise shares space with a CCM soup kitchen and serves its meals immediately following the CCM serving time. Other churches distribute food packages, both on a regular basis and in cases of emergency. Synagogues offer senior citizen centers that include meals and other activities; and the Hare Krishna temple offers a weekly supper, to which members of the public are invited. The Russian Red Cross sponsors after-school activities and meals for children, youth centers that include drug rehabilitation and job training for teenagers, and mobile soup kitchens and food distributions. Other charitable organizations, both domestic and foreign, periodically disburse staples to the elderly and disabled or open temporary cafeterias. Several private charities run feeding programs for the homeless.

All of these programs are loosely connected through their staff and volunteers and occasionally through the recipients themselves. Two women's social clubs in Moscow work with the coordinators of the various programs to assign helpers where and when they are needed most.

Many of the students who serve in the different soup kitchens know each other from classes and the tightly knit African student community. Although recipients are discouraged from participating in more than one program—CCM staff will remove recipients from their registration list if they discover that individuals are attending more than one soup kitchen—several have successfully circumvented this restriction. Others have children, grandchildren, siblings, or friends who attend other programs. The grandchildren of several CCM recipients attend a Red Cross children's soup kitchen that meets in the same cafeteria in which the CCM program meets.

Through these overlapping spaces and memberships, participants in the larger food aid network in Moscow have successfully carved out a set of shared experiences, connections, and resources within an otherwise sprawling and impersonal urban landscape. More important, they have found ways to incorporate these resources—both social and material—into their routines of daily survival. Participation in assistance programs is thus not an indication that Muscovites cannot fend for themselves or a sign that they have "given up," but rather evidence that they are deeply embedded within a network of potentialities and that they can work this system knowledgeably and successfully. In the next chapter, I take up this theme of networks and look at how Muscovites parlay exchange activities into both economic and social resources.

CHAPTER 3

From Hand to Hand

Informal Networks

Sveta and Sasha,
Beautiful girls,
Little white doves,
You fill up our dishes,
With warm soup.
You have a cutlet ready
For each of us.
Cereal and potatoes, too,
At least a spoonful each,
And sweet holiday juice
To refresh our elderly mouths,
As well as soft bread.
Thank you for the meal.

> *Excerpt from a poem of appreciation written by soup
> kitchen recipients of the charity Nash Dolg (Our Duty)
> and given to the cafeteria employees*

During my fieldwork in 1997–1998, I became close with Vera, a seventy-five-year-old retired artist who had been a recipient at the soup kitchen since the program's inception. For the first several months of my research, Vera and I had chatted briefly and formally about the weather or the quality of the food when I delivered her meal. It was not until my parents came to Moscow in September that our relationship blossomed. During my parents' visit I brought them to the soup kitchen and introduced them to the volunteers and recipients. The soup kitchen was festively chaotic that day: several volunteers and recipients had organized a party for another recipient. Upon her arrival, Vera greeted me and then asked what kind of special occasion had prompted such a holiday atmosphere. I first mentioned the birthday party and then indicated my parents, adding that they were *my* special occasion. In response to this news, Vera waved my mother and father over to her table and welcomed them warmly. Then she insisted that the three of us come to her house for tea. An hour later, over the kitchen table that filled most of Vera's kitchen, the four of us became acquainted with each other, sharing personal stories and nibbling Vera's homemade pastries. That spontaneous invitation proved to be the beginning of a warm relationship with Vera, her sister, and her sister's son. After that day Vera and I frequently chatted during lunches at the soup kitchen, and several days before I left Moscow at the end of my fieldwork, she presented me with several jars of homemade fruit preserves and pastries.

Despite my promises to write from the United States, I discovered that I had misplaced Vera's address during the several moves that accompanied my return home from fieldwork. When I arrived back in Moscow in May 1999, the first thing I did after settling into my rented room was to visit the soup kitchen and attempt to locate Vera and other friends whom I had not seen since the previous fall. Fortunately, Vera was among the first to arrive that morning, and we greeted each other tearfully in front of the ticket table. Brushing aside my apologies for failing to write, Vera immediately invited me to her home for lunch so that we could catch up on everything that had happened in each other's lives during the previous year.

Over a lunch of soup, salad, salted fish, tea, and cake that she magically whisked together from the odds and ends in her refrigerator, Vera first showed me the new hot water pipes and kitchen sink that city authorities had installed in a recent wave of city-funded capital repairs, and then related the news of her family. From there our conversation segued into a discussion about how Russia had changed over the past year. Vera described the difficulties she faced in surviving on a pension of six hundred rubles a month (approximately twenty-five dollars at that time). Prices had gone up after the August 1998 financial crisis, but pension amounts had remained basically the same. In addition, Vera was currently supporting her middle-aged nephew, who frequently came to Moscow to earn extra money for his wife and daughter, who lived in a small town several hours away. As I was collecting my things to leave, she shyly asked if I wanted to see her new washing machine. Intrigued, particularly after her comments about the pitiful pension she received, I followed her into the tiny bathroom that led off the foyer. Pushing back the shower curtain, Vera proudly pointed to the brand-new German washing machine that sat on the back of the bathtub and said that it had been a gift. By way of explanation, she first reminded me that she occasionally stuffed envelopes for an international company in Moscow—a job that she had secured two years earlier when CCM soup kitchen supervisors had recommended her to a company representative who was looking for two reliable and needy pensioners to do occasional jobs. The other woman who stuffed envelopes with Vera had recently become unable to continue her work, and Vera had recommended a neighbor who also lived alone and was surviving on a tiny pension to fill her position. When the neighbor received the job and the opportunity to earn an additional twenty to twenty-five dollars a month, her relatives "found" a washing machine to express their gratitude for Vera's generosity and assistance.

Vera's story is important because it reveals the value that Muscovites place on personal relationships as means to access goods and services, as well as to circulate information, show friendship, and support one another. In a setting where a majority of the population faces paltry *(mizernye)* pensions and wages, informal networks permeate Muscovites' daily lives as an important coping strategy. Just as in the Soviet period, when goods were in short supply *(defitsit)*, today, when it is often money or knowledge of the market that is in short supply, Muscovites continue to help each other find necessary items and then redistribute them through their connections. Conversations in the soup kitchen often included intense discussions about the prices for various items, where to find sale merchandise, and how to receive extra welfare benefits. Several concerned recipients regularly inquired about the shops I had frequented and the prices I had paid for certain products, and then methodically told me where I could buy each item for substantially less. One woman included me in the group of people to whom she brought advertisements from the newspaper, and her friend thoughtfully provided detailed directions on how to reach particular stores.

This chapter examines the ways in which Muscovites mobilize informal exchange networks to circulate scarce resources. I describe how Muscovites patch together commodity and gift relationships so that exchanges are always simultaneously personal and impersonal. The improvisational nature of these tactics is regulated by moral "rules" that are codified through practice and ideology. Individuals rely on these tactics as good faith markers of trust and legitimacy for their relationships with other people. Through these activities, Muscovites not only distribute resources but also create distinct communities of mutual support by mapping personal affections onto utilitarian concerns. Tensions and disputes that emerge from the misrecognition of exchange transactions provide important cues for understanding the ways in which the social and the economic are mutually constituting and interdependent.

Circles of Life: Exchange and Personal Survival

Social scientists who examine the personal strategies that citizens in socialist and postsocialist societies employ for everyday survival have focused primarily on what Wedel (1998a:90) has called the necessary "wheeling and dealing" of everyday life. These negotiations primarily make up informal exchange negotiations such as "under the table" transactions, barter, and speculation that are outside the scope of institutionalized economic practices of production, distribution, and consumption and divert capital from the official economy to personal channels. Typically labeled the second economy or the gray economy (Katseneliboigen 1978), or in some cases labeled more simply as corruption, this system coexists with the state's official economy (see also Shlapentokh 1989). Russian citizens were not the only ones to employ these tactics, however. To a great extent, the survival of the socialist state itself depended on these practices to meet production targets and to maintain control over the economy (Verdery 1996). Thus, both the state and its citizens were partners—albeit uncomfortably—in this sphere.

During the Soviet period, one of the most recognizable forms of this second economy was the black market. Enterprising individuals could earn extra income by procuring goods either from freight trucks and factories or through connections with business partners elsewhere and then selling these items from the backs of trucks and cars, out of their apartments, or from within briefcases or bags surreptitiously opened to potential customers. Areas around train stations and bus depots were bustling centers for black market transactions as traders moved from town to town. Caroline Humphrey has noted that in the Soviet Union the black market existed somewhere in every town: "In the old days it was fed largely from the depots (*baza*) of imported goods, where employees regularly stole whatever they could for distribution to traders" (1995:62). It was through this alternative distribution system that many foreign consumer goods entered the Soviet market and became accessible for nonelites who lacked access to foreign travel or to special hard currency shops where both foreign and domestic goods were available (see Boym 1994:65; Humphrey 1995:62–63). Even cultural trends such as Western music among St. Petersburg musicians were disseminated through the black market (Cushman 1995:48). More recently, the proliferation of petty trading in Russia (Humphrey 1999) and elsewhere in Eastern Europe (Konstantinov 1996) has greatly facilitated the transfer of goods across regional and international borders. Ironically these diversions of items from official channels contributed to consumer shortages in shops even as they provided a necessary strategy for coping with those scarcities.

Survival strategies such as the black market, trading, and barter were grounded within complicated and overlapping networks of informal exchanges among relatives, friends, coworkers, and acquaintances. Probably the most important means to resolve the problems of everyday life under state socialism, these connections crossed generations as well as local, national, and international boundaries. Through these informal social networks, people throughout the Soviet Union and Eastern Europe engaged in acts of mutual assistance by circulating goods, information, job contacts, and even leads on apartments. The successful enactment of exchange practices contributed significantly to the economic *and* the social well-being of one's household (Kideckel 1993).[1]

Today, although Russia's increasing openness to the outside has fostered a burgeoning consumer market where goods of every type conceivable are available, the current economic climate continues to be marked by uncertainty and by shortages of both consumer goods and money. Despite the introduction of Western capitalist models to rehabilitate and "modernize" the Russian economy, the exchange value of the Russian ruble remains unstable (when I began my fieldwork in November 1997, the exchange rate was approximately six rubles to one U.S. dollar; in August 1998, fifteen rubles to one dollar; in June 1999, twenty-four rubles; in June 2001, thirty rubles); and Russian banks have defaulted on foreign loans. Millions of dollars of development aid from private corporations and foreign investors, as well as from the World Bank and the International Monetary Fund, have been concentrated in the hands of a few and have never reached their intended beneficiaries (Wedel 1998a). At times the state has dispersed wages and pensions erratically, and both public and private enterprises have resorted to salary and staff reductions to stay solvent. In some cases, employees returned portions of their earnings as temporary loans to their companies. In other cases, workers endured repeated layoffs; one friend found herself looking for a new job every several months.

The situation became more severe in the aftermath of the August 1998 financial crisis, when the Federal Bank devalued the ruble by releasing it from its fixed rate of exchange with the U.S. dollar in order for it to be determined by the international market. Because of the rapidly changing value of the ruble, Russian banks could not guarantee that the value of the funds invested by their clients would remain stable. Because the Russian economy was officially calculated in rubles, and thus all official transactions had to be recorded in ruble amounts, deposits made in hard currency were credited to investors' accounts at the corresponding ruble equivalent. In the days immediately following the devaluation, the value of the ruble dropped to approximately fifteen rubles to one dollar. An investor who had originally deposited a hundred dollars at the equivalent of six hundred rubles suddenly found the deposit worth only forty dollars. Muscovites formed long lines in front of banks and automated banking machines, attempting to recover some small portion of their investments or to change rubles into dollars and other currencies before the exchange rate plummeted further. In response, many banks and exchange points allowed customers only to invest money or to change dollars for rubles. Ultimately many banks declared bankruptcy and closed. Owing to longstanding popular distrust of banks, many Muscovites were fortunate to have previously changed their salaries and pensions into dollars that they had hidden at home for safekeeping. One CCM recipient could scarcely believe her luck at having sold some property and changing the money she had received into dollars just days before the crisis. Nevertheless, not everyone in Moscow was so fortunate. Many people lost their entire savings. A friend described how a colleague had saved for years to buy an apartment just a few weeks before the crisis. The woman had exhausted her savings and then borrowed a significant amount of money to cover the forty thousand dollar price of the flat; just days after the crisis, the value of real estate had depreciated so significantly that the apartment was worth only a fraction of its original cost. Nonetheless, with her savings gone and her salary cut severely, she was still responsible for paying back her debts in full at their original amount.

This monetary scarcity was compounded by price inflation. Although the prices of some products—notably food staples such as bread, milk, flour, and sugar—were more or less regulated by federal standards, the prices of other goods were determined by their value in the international market. Many foreign companies, particularly those whose income in Russia was in rubles but whose expenses were paid in hard currency, incurred huge losses because they could not compensate for differences in the exchange rates. Some companies halted production in Russia, and others recalled shipments of goods to Russia out of fears that they would not receive payment. These shortages and expenses contributed to higher prices. In the months following the crisis, the Russian economy suffered further by the exodus of foreign workers and companies from Russia. The CCM congregation shrank considerably when many North American and European members were sent home. Despite the rising cost of living during and after the crisis, however, wage and pension amounts either remained the same or, in some cases, decreased significantly for many Russian workers.

Yet even as people complain about insufficient funds, they have not stopped consuming. Although overall spending on more expensive goods, particularly imports, has decreased in the last several years, Russians continue to spend money on electronics, large appliances (Shevchenko 2002), automobiles, and trips abroad, as well as on more modest and oftentimes necessary products and services such as new work clothes or specialized training to renew or earn professional certificates. As one friend, a young teacher who barely survives on her tiny salary, told me, if she wants to buy something badly enough (in this case, an expensive outfit), she will find a way to come up with the funds.

To explain these apparent paradoxes, Muscovites point to the cooperative assistance of their friends, relatives, coworkers, and acquaintances.[2] In moments of hardship, family and friends are the most reliable source of help and provide the most immediately exploitable set of resources, factors that Bourdieu has called "practical kinship" (1977:33–36; Yan 1996:116). Throughout Russia it is not uncommon for several generations of a single family to live together in one apartment, pooling their incomes and savings and sharing expenses (see also Ries, n.d.). When salaries are delayed, workers who receive their wages distribute the money to those who have not yet been so lucky, or they buy the necessary items, such as food or clothing, directly for those individuals. One woman divulged that her father's pension kept the family afloat, because he received two times more than she did every month and his income was generally paid on time. The elderly mother of another friend sold her apartment and gave the money to her grandson as a wedding present so that he could set up his own household. Meanwhile, several CCM recipients pooled their resources to help buy school supplies for their grandchildren and the grandchildren of equally destitute friends.

Grandparents are particularly valuable sources of capital, not just for their pensions, but also for the contributions they make to household chores such as shopping, cooking, cleaning, and babysitting the small children of working adults. Parents who have the opportunity to earn more money by working in a different city or abroad leave children in the care of their grandparents for extended periods of time. Several children whom I interviewed in a small town outside Moscow said that they saw their parents only for short periods of time over the weekends and holidays, when their parents returned home from working in the city. A close friend regularly left her daughter with her mother in a small town eight hours outside Moscow so that she could look for work in Moscow, and the college-aged roommate of another friend had not seen his mother for several months because she was working in a research institute in Western Europe.

Friends, relatives, coworkers, and other acquaintances may be approached with requests for many kinds of assistance: small financial loans; rides; vehicle loans, for moving belongings from one apartment to another; moving services, perhaps to transport large appliances or to haul tools and produce to and from summer gardens; or even temporary housing. One friend spent almost a year living with her family in apartments that were borrowed from other friends who were either out of town or had moved in with their own relatives. Several Muscovites reported asking coworkers and employees to help them with jobs ranging from moving construction materials to assisting with apartment renovations. When Lidiia Konstantinovna, a retired professor, organized a trip back home to Moscow from her summer cottage, she made plans to maximize her time in the city by asking various contacts to find specific items for her in advance. At the same time, she phoned other friends to find out if she could be of assistance to them. She called one friend who had recently been released from the hospital and asked for a list of groceries that the other woman needed. In response to the friend's apparent hesitation, Lidiia Konstantinovna sharply responded, "If you want it, I'll buy it for you." Similarly, when a young Muscovite who volunteers at the CCM soup kitchens returned from a holiday in America, she parceled out to various friends the clothes, baby shoes, and electronics equipment she had purchased for them while abroad.

During my first visit to the home of Irina, a widowed, middle-aged doctor, I was fortunate to catch one such exchange cycle in action. Irina's friend Valya called and reported that she had found cheap eggs and meat at her factory store. Irina placed an order and then called her friend Lena to inform her that she would be receiving meat and eggs as well. Lena replied that she had purchased tomatoes and would bring those to Irina. When Irina finally hung up the phone after multiple back-and-forth negotiations, she explained that even though both meat and eggs were readily and cheaply available in the stores at that time, she still preferred to work through personal contacts. In another example, Aleksandra Petrovna appealed to owners of a neighborhood bakery to offer bread to pensioners at reduced prices. As part of her negotiating strategy, she convinced the bakery owners that in exchange for these discounts, the bakery would benefit from increased business from a reliable consumer base of appreciative pensioners and their friends and relatives.

Aid programs such as the CCM community provide an important arena for these transactions, both as spaces where they are enacted and as opportunities for partners to meet and organize. CCM recipients who find inexpensive food products at the market purchase extra supplies to share with friends and family, as well as with certain volunteers at the soup kitchen. Several women who are old friends frequently bring in empty jars and boxes and then meet at a back table at the soup kitchen to visit and distribute homemade foods and recipes. Other recipients also share food, ranging from staples such as sugar and flour to homemade goods such as jams and baked items, and, more rarely, money with their friends at the soup kitchen. Vera and other CCM recipients also occasionally offer to shop for favorite volunteers at the discount store run by the district welfare office. At the shop, registered pensioners can buy staples such as yogurt, milk, sausage, and cereal grains at significant reductions. During the summer season, Muscovites share produce from their summer gardens with friends and relatives, and especially with those who do not have their own gardens. As these examples illustrate, resources such as money or commodities are typically the first type of support that Muscovites identify as circulating through their exchange networks. By carefully positioning themselves within a multiplicity of social relations, Muscovites can maximize both the material and the social resources at their disposal.

Despite the spread of both domestic and foreign banks, Russia's economy remains largely cash-driven. The recurring instability of the banking sector and fluctuating currency values have generated widespread distrust among Russians. Investors who have lost their savings in bank failures often seek to safeguard their money by changing it into American dollars or British pounds (and now Euros) and then hoarding these denominations at home or investing them in commodities such as automobiles, large appliances, summer cottages, and apartments. Yet even as Muscovites seek to convert financial capital into permanent commodities, few people have sufficient funds to cover in full more expensive purchases such as apartments or vehicles. Credit, however, remains largely a private matter between friends and relatives. Although bank-sponsored credit cards were introduced in the early 1990s, most operated as debit cards and required a deposit to be activated; purchases were deducted from the amount available in the account. Muscovites typically bypass formal banking channels and turn to relatives, friends, and employers for loans to pay for both day-to-day necessities and more expensive purchases in full. Over time, they repay their debts, sometimes with interest but not necessarily so. In turn, the practice of informal loans creates a circulating system in which one's creditors know that they too can borrow money or other resources at another time. Small businesses also operate on this principle, and employees may occasionally lend their savings to the company to pay off outstanding debts or to meet payroll deadlines.

Muscovites like Andrei, a CCM congregant, prefer these informal credit associations precisely for the security they provide over formal banking transactions. Andrei and his wife bought both their car and their apartment with money borrowed from friends and family. As Andrei explained, if he and his wife lost their jobs or the economy was completely destroyed, they would still have a place to live. Unlike banks that would demand repayment regardless of one's financial situation and then seize ownership because of nonpayment, personally known lenders would be understanding and not call in the debts.

Despite the immediate importance of money, however, it nonetheless complicates exchanges among friends. As a socially disruptive force, money refocuses the ethic of relationships from that of mutual assistance and altruistic friendship to that of a more commercial, impersonal, and individualistic transaction (Frisby 1998; Lemon 1998; Pesmen 2000). To avoid the depersonalizing force of money-based interactions, social intimates disguise their actions through tactics such as tucking bills inside envelopes, cards, or small gifts and by refusing to touch, or even acknowledge the presence of, the money. When Veronika, a young single mother who had come to Moscow for work, lost her job, she waited until she had depleted her savings and had exhausted all possibilities for work before she unexpectedly contacted a foreign friend via e-mail. In her letter, Veronika chattily asked about her friend's affairs and then described her own circumstances in vague terms, but never asked directly for money. The friend shared the letter with me and several other people who were close to Veronika. Because Veronika's actions were out of character, especially because she rarely mentioned the specific details of her finances, we decided that her letter was in fact a plea for help. Another friend arranged with a colleague in Moscow to give Veronika a New Year's card and "present" of a hundred dollars. Veronika later thanked each of us for the card but never mentioned the money. In a similar instance, I was present when another friend received a letter from a foreign friend. The young woman opened the envelope and commented on the letter but did not acknowledge the cash tucked inside, even as it fluttered to the floor. Her daughter picked up the money and attempted to call our attention to the bill, but her mother told her to leave it alone.

Conversations about loans, payments, or other more commercial, and hence impersonal, transactions are typically deferred until after acquaintances have socialized over a cup of tea. These practices extended to my fieldwork: when I interviewed Muscovites in their homes, my hosts refused to let the "business" part of my visit begin until after we had enjoyed a sufficient period of socializing. Even when I conducted interviews in settings where I was the host, I found that the amount of information I received during conversations improved after my informants and I had chatted informally over a snack.

In the CCM soup kitchens, Muscovites are hesitant to ask foreign friends and acquaintances directly for assistance. When they do make such requests, they veil them in disinterest. Recipients and volunteers carefully monitor the timing of each foreign volunteer's return home. In the weeks preceding a person's departure, several enterprising women subtly suggest that perhaps the visitor might not have enough space in her baggage for all of the souvenirs she has bought as indispensable memories of Russia. These women then generously offer to "hold" those clothes, books, linens, towels, and appliances the visitor will not be able to take home. One woman makes her plans known further in advance by commenting on the quality or color of a visitor's clothes and then casually asking, "Don't you think that I would look good in that as well?"

Outright requests for money and other material goods generally occur within restricted contexts, such as interactions with foreigners and strangers. Requests made to strangers are frequently couched within a familiar stereotype that all foreigners are wealthy and that Westerners in particular have a responsibility to support the local economy. Street vendors who recognize a customer's foreign accent may advertise their wares by weaving together tales of personal hardship about life in Russia and requests for financial assistance. An incident that took place while I was shopping with an American colleague is representative. While my friend and I were inspecting the fresh fruit at a sidewalk stand, the saleswoman commented that we must be Americans. When we confirmed her guess, she began a lengthy narrative about how she had come to Moscow from Belarus to earn extra money to support her children at school and then asked if we might "help" her in addition to our purchases. When my friend offered her a ten-ruble note (all she had left in her pocket), the woman angrily refused it as an insulting pittance. Comparable attitudes were expressed by CCM recipients who argued that it was the duty of wealthier countries such as the United States to support Russia's less fortunate people.

Transactional Knowledge

Knowledge is another crucial resource that percolates most effectively through informal connections. One of the legacies of a socialist state that enforced secrecy and privileged spying on one's neighbors was that the successful diffusion of news depended to a great extent on face-to-face, personal interactions.[3] During Soviet times newspapers and television news programs offered state-sanctioned polemical reports about events selected by officials, and personal letters were purged of potentially inflammatory details by censors. Today, despite the potential for the more autonomous role for the media that was suggested by President Mikhail Gorbachev's proposal of glasnost and the commitment of Russia's journalists to an unfettered press, Russian authorities continue to monitor the content of news programs on state television and radio. At the same time, privately owned media have also been strongly influenced by both state officials and individuals rumored to be associated with organized crime movements. More recently, President Putin directed state forces to seize NTV, one of the country's independent television networks. The journalists, who not coincidentally have been critical of the Russian government, and other employees were removed, and pro-Putin staff were installed in their place. To avoid accusations that the move heralded a clampdown on freedom of speech and a return to a more authoritarian state, Kremlin officials claimed that it was precipitated by the network's nonpayment of taxes. Nevertheless, several months after most of NTV's former staff had fled to TV6, the last remaining fully independent television network in Russia, state authorities also seized that channel and installed new staff there. Even more significant is that not just information but also personal safety is at stake: Russia has been one of the most dangerous places for journalists, because reporters and others who have exposed criminal activities have been murdered at an alarming rate.

Citizens learned to circumvent these official information channels by relying on the "private talk" (Ries 1997:21) that existed among personal contacts to pass on details about politics, economics, and the arts, as well as more intimate knowledge about friends and family. Tiny kitchen apartments and strolls through parks or forests became relatively safe havens for friends to engage in serious discussions about otherwise dangerous topics.[4] Queues, signs of socialist inefficiency, acquired secondary importance as sites of collective knowledge, where people could alert their neighbors to goods that had become available, discuss current events, or simply chat. When both domestic and foreign literature and music were heavily censored by authorities, groups of friends carefully protected and circulated books and tapes that had made it past the censors. On a visit to the home of one CCM recipient, the woman's daughter brought out her collection of Soviet-era *samizdat* (self-published) materials. Earlier in the Soviet period, citizens carefully copied forbidden books by hand. By the time this woman was in university in the mid-1970s, copy machines had appeared, although in very limited supply. The woman and several friends managed to gain access to a copier at the university, and they took turns "making Xeroxes" *(my delaem kseroks)*—a few pages at a time—which they eventually collated and then passed out to one another.

Today Muscovites continue to rely on their social networks to pass on illicit information. In particular, I was interested to note how often conversations with high school and university students segued into comparisons of Russian and American styles of education. Of great interest to Russian students (and their parents) were the strategies that American students employ to cheat on homework and examinations. Informants talked about cheating casually and often included their cheating tactics as one aspect of their overall academic accomplishments.

In Russia, education is a deeply social activity. Students typically matriculate through school, and later university, with a specific group of classmates; often students share desks with the same partner for several years. At the same time that this closeness reinforces communal practices of learning, it also creates groups of close friends. Most respondents identify their most intimate friends as former schoolmates, and even retired pensioners continue to maintain communication with former classmates. Liuba, the twenty-five-year-old wife of a CCM member, recalled that she and her classmates coordinated their activities so that they were always together: in school, they took the same classes and sat for exams together; outside school, they spent their weekends and holidays together. More important, however, they helped each other pass through school. Each student had a personal method of cheating: one of Liuba's friends folded up tiny "books" *(knizhki)* with answers, while another woman used the pockets of her dress to hide pencils with math equations written on them. Before an examination, several friends would meet to consult on answers and to prepare their cheating materials together. Parents also contributed to these exercises in collective education. Liuba described how her mother wrote out answers for her, while her father passed on cheating materials that he had saved from his own days at university. As Liuba explained, students and parents felt a collective sense of responsibility to help each other through school; the important thing was to pass, not necessarily to do well. Liuba said that her friends never felt a sense of competition among themselves.

The daughter of another friend confided that when she had sat for her final examinations to graduate from high school, the student ahead of her allowed her to read his answers so that she could pass her mathematics examination. With that help, the young woman graduated with a silver medal (salutatorian). Both she and her parents proudly acknowledged the assistance that she had received as testament to her intellectual resourcefulness. Several CCM recipients brought their grandchildren to the soup kitchen and asked other recipients and volunteers for help, particularly with English-language assignments. One woman went so far as to ask volunteers directly to do her granddaughter's English homework, citing the girl's frail nerves. Meanwhile, a university student complained bitterly when his American-trained Muscovite university instructor penalized him for plagiarism in a research paper. The student maintained that his act of "borrowing" was acceptable, because it was such a pervasive strategy and because knowledge belonged in the public domain. This last point is frequently given as a reason against honoring copyrights. In a conversation with my landlady and her son about the prevalence of pirated videotapes and compact disks available in Russia, my landlady commented that she thought copyrights are foolish because art and information belong to everyone.

The information that passes through personal connections is not always illicit, however, but can be public knowledge that is otherwise not successfully transmitted through Russia's bureaucratic structures. State and local regulations change with dizzying speeds, defying the abilities of both officials and residents to keep up with them. In some cases, government offices are themselves disguised in the deep recesses of apartment complexes and other buildings. Often informal channels are the only means for Muscovites to navigate the physical and symbolic labyrinths of everyday life. Andrei's wife commented that most Muscovites do not know where their local housing authority office (ZhEK, the acronym for *zhilishchno-ekspluatatsionnaia kontora*) is located, much less that inside the office is where various regulations and other community information are posted. Not only is this information passed through friends, but even the address of the office itself is circulated this way. In the CCM soup kitchens, several pensioner-activists keep current on recent changes in local welfare regulations through their contacts among the social workers. They then notify other recipients about new benefit requirements or aid possibilities by posting notices at the soup kitchen ticket desk or by visiting people at their tables while they are eating. Likewise, notification of the yearly reenrollment for the CCM soup kitchens is circulated only by word-of-mouth. Small community-based notices and newspapers offer yet another avenue for circulating information.

Information is thus not a private resource that individuals keep to themselves, but a socializing force that brings people together. In a sense, possessing information obliges one to share it with others. Moreover, not only does the circulation of information through personal channels protect it from official structures such as the state, but within a setting in which the state has actively created and revised "facts" to suit its own purposes, the element of personal contact also validates the accuracy of the news and the trustworthiness of the bearer. At the same time, these very acts of transmitting information affirm the viability of social ties. By selectively divulging and withholding information from others, agents delineate the parameters of trust and intimacy.

"Between Acquaintances": Irina and the Bus Ticket

Several times during my fieldwork, I visited Irina, the mother of a friend from Moscow and the woman whose exchange cycle of meat, eggs, and tomatoes I witnessed. Irina lived in a small town that had grown up around a group of research institutes, approximately 120 kilometers south of Moscow; but she occasionally traveled to the city for medical conferences and to visit her children and other friends. She preferred that I visit her, however, and on a number of occasions she invited me to use her spare bedroom when I needed a break from my research in the city. As I could buy only a one-way bus ticket from Moscow, Irina bought my return ticket at the bus station in her town. During my return trip to Russia in summer 1999, I again went to visit Irina. When I exited the bus at the first stop in the town, Irina greeted me warmly with a hug and led me to her apartment. She asked me about my ride, and I told her that it had been crazy with so many people on the hot bus. Irina nodded and commented that most of the passengers commuted to jobs in Moscow during the week and then returned home on the weekends. The others were most likely traveling to their dachas in one of the many summer communities along the highway connecting her town with the city. She congratulated me for finding—and keeping—an empty seat on the crowded bus and then confessed that she had been unable to buy my return ticket for the following afternoon, Sunday. By the preceding Wednesday, she said, the bus station had already sold out tickets for every return bus over the weekend. Irina quickly reassured me, however, that she would find some way for me to get back to Moscow.

Later that afternoon when the temperature had cooled off, we went for a walk through the town. After strolling through the woods near the research institutes, we made our way to the bus terminal. Irina explained that she knew someone who worked in the bus dispatcher's office and that she had hopes that this friend might be able to procure a ticket for me. On the way, we met Irina's neighbor, Elizaveta. During the week, Elizaveta works in Moscow as a doctor but commutes home on the weekends. Irina chatted with Elizaveta about her apartment in Moscow and then explained that she was trying to help another neighbor find an inexpensive apartment for her son, who was in graduate school in Moscow. The two women discussed various possibilities and strategies for finding an apartment. Elizaveta suggested a Moscow newspaper, *Iz Ruk v Ruki* (From Hands to Hands), a weekly publication that specialized in classified advertisements for apartment rentals, sale items, and work opportunities. (A second newspaper with a similar focus is named *Iz Pervykh Ruk* [At First Hand].) Despite Elizaveta's suggestion, however, Irina emphasized that she and her friend wanted to look for a place *cherez znakomykh,* or "through acquaintances." Elizaveta promised that she would help look, and the two women said good-bye.

When we arrived at the bus station, we found that the dispatcher's office had already closed for the day. Undeterred, Irina vowed to continue her search for a ticket. Later that evening while visiting friends, Irina described our difficulties in finding a bus ticket. Our host, Grigorii, mentioned that he had another friend who would most likely be driving on Sunday to the market in the next town, from which Moscow-bound buses were more frequent and less crowded, and said that he would ask his friend if he could help. The next morning at breakfast, however, Irina delightedly told me that she had successfully found a ticket for that afternoon. She had finally reached the friend who worked in the bus dispatcher's office, and the friend had located an extra ticket and set it aside for us to pick up right before departure. Irina confided that she had never asked this friend for help before, but this time was different: this time it was necessary. "*Ne imei sto rublei, a imei sto druzei*," she finished (Don't have a hundred rubles; have instead a hundred friends). She then wryly remarked that perhaps today in Russia it is more accurate to say, "Do not have a hundred dollars." When I later retold the story to Irina's son, Ivan, he nodded and replied, "It is not what you are, but whom you know."

Irina's efforts to procure a bus ticket reveal the extent to which material resources are often less important than social connections. Both Irina and I had money to spend, but the money was useless as long as tickets were unavailable. Moreover, Irina's acquaintance in the dispatcher's office neither gave her the ticket as a gift nor added an extra fee for her "services" in locating the ticket. The acquaintance simply had the means to look for an extra ticket—or possibly to create one, since the tickets were generic receipts with the date and seat number written by hand. No other fees were added, and Irina paid the bus company the official cost of the ticket. Nevertheless, even though economic capital moved through the official transaction between Irina as purchaser and her acquaintance as a representative of the bus company, the personal transaction that existed between Irina and her acquaintance was actualized by their social connections. Although Irina and the other woman had known each other informally for many years, the full potential of their relationship was not realized until the moment of the transaction. Through the reciprocal process of asking and helping, the two women cemented what had previously been an uncomplicated relationship into a solid connection based on mutual assistance and trust.

Trust and Real Friends

In Russian practice and discourse, *friendship* is a key idiom for articulating the parameters and directions of exchanges (Ledeneva 1998; Pesmen 2000), a point that appeared routinely in Muscovites' accounts about their exchange experiences. Informants reported that when they asked for assistance, they wanted to proceed "cherez znakomykh." As with information, goods and services that can be vouched for by a friend or acquaintance are perceived to be more reliable than those received from strangers. In addition, relying on one's contacts can facilitate negotiations. Saying that one has been sent from a mutual friend provides consumers with a strategic advantage over strangers, both in terms of gaining access and of being treated fairly. Moreover, by helping someone as a friend, one both initiates and invests in a social relationship that may be of use again in the future. This preference for working through friends and acquaintances implies both trust and an obligation to help, as well as the sense that both the asker and the helper belong to a common social group. One woman who asked me to watch for inexpensive clothing confided that she would ask only her closest friends for help of this kind. This emphasis on personal contacts extends to Russian communities outside Russia as well. An émigré in Boston who wanted to buy a used car called me to ask if I knew of anyone who might be selling an old car. The man told me that although he had looked at the classified ads, he preferred to go "cherez znakomykh."

A dictionary of Russian proverbs explains the one that Irina used— "Do not have a hundred rubles, have instead a hundred friends"—in these terms: "real friends always help, come to the rescue" *(nastoiashchie druz'ia vsegda pomogut, vyruchat)* (Zhukov 1998:211). Recipients of favors and other forms of assistance acknowledge those who have offered help—especially unsolicited assistance—with statements such as, "Thank you. You are a real friend" *(nastoiashchii drug)*, as occurred when a friend's daughter voluntarily brought an older relative a drink on a hot day. This emphasis on trustworthiness points to the importance of reliability within exchange relations: one can always count on a "true friend" to come through in times of need. Moreover, it is to "true" and "trusted" friends that one can direct explicit requests for assistance (see also Pesmen 2000).

At the same time, much more is at stake when exchanges are predicated on social relationships. Partners must deal with the consequences of exchanges that go awry on both economic and personal levels. The following story illustrates the ways in which social ties mobilize and disintegrate over issues of trust and assistance.

When I began planning my return to Moscow in summer 1999, I contacted Aleksandra Petrovna for help with my arrangements. With her extensive contacts in local welfare circles, Aleksandra Petrovna knew many of the residents in her neighborhood and prided herself on being able to match people with complementary needs. One of her specialties was finding housing for CCM staff and volunteers. Many Muscovites earn extra income by leasing their apartments or spare rooms, and among soup kitchen recipients there is fierce competition to offer housing to student volunteers. Although most students live in dormitories near their universities, six of the eight paid coordinators, as well as several young cafeteria employees, live in apartments or spare rooms rented out by pensioners who attend the soup kitchens. In the overall housing market in Moscow, rentals to Westerners are particularly advantageous, because most North American and European visitors work for multinational companies or embassies that provide substantial housing allowances. There is also a pervasive sentiment in Moscow that all foreigners—Americans in particular—are affluent and can afford higher prices. During 1997–1998, the average foreigner's rate for a two-room apartment in the suburbs was five hundred dollars; rental rates in the center of Moscow were as high as a thousand to fifteen hundred dollars (even higher for added amenities). By contrast, the rates that Russians and non-Western foreigners paid for similar accommodations in the suburbs were as low as a hundred to two hundred rubles (approximately seventeen to thirty-five dollars in summer 1998).

During my long-term fieldwork, Aleksandra Petrovna, among other acquaintances, had taken offense at the high rent I was paying and had insisted that she would locate more affordable and appropriate lodging for me when I returned to Moscow in 1999. After interviewing several friends and acquaintances, Aleksandra Petrovna recommended a pensioner who had a spare room to rent. An American colleague living in Moscow then contacted my future landlady, Marina Alekseevna, to discuss the specifics of my stay and to negotiate an appropriate amount of rent. Because rental rates for foreigners had dropped following the August 1998 financial crisis, my future landlady agreed that a hundred dollars per month for a bedroom and use of shower and kitchen were acceptable.

After I had settled in following my ride from the airport, I gave my landlady money for the first month's rent in crisp American dollars. Marina Alekseevna examined the bills curiously and then shyly explained that she had never seen American money before. She then explained that she was an invalid and thanked me for helping her with her financial difficulties. As a further expression of her gratitude, she took me to the kitchen and showed me a bottle of cognac and a box of chocolates that she had been saving for a time when she, Aleksandra Petrovna, and I could get together and celebrate our friendship. I was surprised, then, by what happened several days later. When I arrived home after a long day of interviews, Marina Alekseevna tearfully called me into her room to discuss a matter of some importance. Nervously, my landlady confessed that she had talked with her son and other relatives about our arrangement. They had scolded her for agreeing to such a small amount of rent and had advised her to demand $250 to $300 per month, because she lived in a prestigious section of town and, more important, because I was an American and should pay accordingly for the privilege. As she cried about the unpleasant predicament she was in with her angry relatives, she hinted that Aleksandra Petrovna had tried to cheat her; and she vowed never to trust the other woman again.

Thinking that perhaps my rent was indeed below market rates, I initially agreed to a fifty-dollar increase. After consulting with the coordinators at the soup kitchen, however, I came to understand that a hundred dollars was in fact a highly competitive rate for rooms in that area of town. As I subsequently learned through my contacts at the soup kitchen, Marina Alekseevna's previous boarder, a trader from outside Moscow, had paid only five hundred rubles (approximately twenty-one dollars) per month. Through the channels of the soup kitchen, Aleksandra Petrovna quickly learned of my landlady's demand. After scolding me for not telling her about the rent dispute, Aleksandra Petrovna announced that she was ashamed that her friend had treated me unfairly and declared that because she could no longer trust Marina Alekseevna to behave fairly, she would break off relations with her immediately. In addition, Aleksandra Petrovna effectively rescinded a previous act of friendly assistance that she had extended to my landlady through me. Several days earlier Aleksandra Petrovna had given me a bag of rice that she had received in the supplemental food package from her church. At the time, she had said that it was for me because we were "girlfriends" *(podruzhki)* and that I was to share it with Marina Alekseevna because she was also a friend. After the rent incident, however, Aleksandra Petrovna told me that I should keep the rice for myself and not share it with my landlady.

As further testament to the productivity of social networks, within hours after I had first told a friend about my landlady's demand for more money, other volunteers, recipients, and cafeteria employees had contacted me with potential offers for a different apartment. After several unsuccessful meetings with potential landlords, however, I ultimately convinced Marina Alekseevna to accept the price upon which we had initially agreed. Nevertheless, my landlady and Aleksandra Petrovna remained estranged. Even though I did not rescind the offer to share the rice with her, Marina Alekseevna refused to use any of it. During the next two months, whenever Aleksandra Petrovna called for me on the telephone, Marina Alekseevna engaged in exaggerated displays of formal civility before quickly passing the phone to me. A year later when I returned to Moscow for a short visit, Aleksandra Petrovna suggested that I contact Marina Alekseevna simply to be polite, although she admitted that they were still not on speaking terms.

Blat, "Pull," and Thank You

The literature on informal networks during the Soviet period has typically classified these unofficial exchange practices as aspects of *blat*. To obtain a good "po blatu" meant to obtain it "by pull," or through influential connections. In her ethnographic study of this "economy of favors," Ledeneva writes that blat "is a distinctive form of non-monetary exchange, a kind of barter based on personal relationship. It worked where money did not" (1996/97:45; see also Ledeneva 1998). Blat has often been likened to Chinese practices of *guanxi* (see Ledeneva 1996/97; Yang 1989), as processes by which actors attempt to gain access to people with influence in particular situations. As my findings suggest, when Muscovites acknowledged the practice of blat, it was also to qualify it as a viable activity primarily during times of scarcity. One man recalled, "You would call [the store] and say, 'I am from Anton Maksimovich. Please set aside a piece of cheese for me.' You would know one person for a hat, another for a coat, and another for something else."

Yet blat entailed more than simply accessing influence and scarce goods. In my conversations with Muscovites and other Russians about the specific nature of blat, respondents repeatedly noted that blat was a means to procure goods or services to which one was not otherwise entitled. As several individuals clarified, such goods and services could also be much more expensive than what one could ordinarily afford. Consequently, items obtained po blatu evoked distaste, because they suggested that one had an unfair advantage over one's peers and so were an affront to official and popular ideologies favoring social equality. For instance, Masha, the friend of several CCM members, was a young woman from Belarus whose father had been a high-ranking official in the Communist Party. When it came time for her to go to university, Masha chose to move to Moscow rather than attend a school in her hometown so as to avoid any suggestion that either her enrollment or her achievements were tied to her father's stature and influence.

Kostya and his wife, whose story about blat was detailed in chapter 2, offered the following example as elaboration: "Say that you are a professor at Harvard, and we ask you to help [our daughter]. You evaluate all the students, and you see that she is the worst student of them all. But you take her ahead of the others. She becomes your 'protégée.' That is po blatu."

In some cases, blat also entailed reciprocal prestations as means of thanks to recognize and reward assistance. A friend relayed the story of an acquaintance who had worked as a travel coordinator for a Moscow business. The travel job had initially been intended for a Communist Party member, but among the few party members already employed there, none was considered suitable for the position, so my friend's acquaintance was coerced into joining the party and accepting the job. Her coworkers believed that she wielded considerable influence, and they repeatedly made subtle requests for help. For instance, after she made travel arrangements for people in the office, they brought her gifts. Although these gifts were presented as thank-you gifts, the woman claimed that she felt uncomfortable receiving them because they implied that the givers might expect her to help them in the future. Jennifer Patico (2001a) has described how teachers, students, and parents in St. Petersburg exchange small gifts to express their gratitude at services rendered. Members of the medical profession also receive thank-you gifts for services rendered.[5] My friend Vera, from the soup kitchen, remembered that when she had been hospitalized for a serious illness many years before, her husband had charmed the nursing staff—and ensured better care for his wife—through his whimsical gifts to them. Other soup kitchen recipients detailed similar practices and advised that it was important to keep something useful on hand in case one unexpectedly needed medical attention.

These acts of thanks carried over to the day-to-day affairs of CCM soup kitchens, and many recipients presented gifts, such as sweets or pieces of needlework, to coordinators, volunteers, and cafeteria workers who had extended favors, such as a slightly larger serving of food, extended meal time, or extra meal tickets. In most cases, all of these individuals had long-standing relationships with each other, and gifts were offered either after a specific act or as a more generic thank-you timed to coincide with a day of public recognition, such as Christmas, Easter, or

International Women's Day. Recipients who were not as close to CCM staff and volunteers, however, occasionally offered small gifts as pretexts for initiating requests for help. Coordinators generally claimed they felt uncomfortable accepting items that they interpreted as subtle bribes and often redistributed them to other volunteers and then refused—or pretended to misunderstand—the requests implied by such gifts. In a more illuminating example, Svetlana Grigorievna, the manager of one cafeteria, organized an elaborate birthday celebration for Dr. Steve. During the height of the CCM serving period, the woman pulled Dr. Steve, several volunteers and cafeteria workers, and me away from our duties to attend a private gathering in her office. After making sure that we were all seated comfortably, Svetlana Grigorievna performed her role as hostess with a carefully orchestrated show of pouring tea and distributing pastries and chocolates. Dismissing Dr. Steve's repeated insistences that he needed to return to the soup kitchen, she initiated several rounds of toasts to the soup kitchen director's continued health and success. Finally, Svetlana Grigorievna and her workers presented Dr. Steve with several presents, including a bag of ripe apples and an expensive set of china dishes. In exasperation, Dr. Steve hurriedly fussed over the gifts and then rushed out of the room to get back to his duties. Later, he privately expressed his frustration with both the gifts and the public performance that had accompanied them, and then commented that they were all part of Svetlana Grigorievna's continuing efforts to curry favor with him and the CCM.

As Ledeneva (1998) has shown, few Russians willingly admit to their participation in blat networks, preferring instead to refer to them euphemistically as acts of friendship. Yet I found that Muscovites further qualified these types of friendship according to their forms and purposes. As one woman explained, "There were definitely different types of connections. When you had good relations it was simply 'friend to friend' [drug s drugom]. We helped each other. Po znakomstvu [by acquaintances], we said. It was just what you did. It was different from blat." The comments of respondents thus suggest that it is perhaps more productive to consider blat as one specific type of exchange geared at evening out inequalities of access, and not as a generalizing concept that accurately captures those everyday interactions between friends that are built on trust and social interdependency. More tellingly, several weeks after the economic crisis of August 1998, Irina casually remarked, "Blat has reappeared" (Blat poiavilsia), thereby reinforcing the notion that blat was a strategy associated more closely with shortages than with more ordinary acts of personal friendships.

Social Support

Muscovites approach these routine, non-blat transactions as forms of help *(pomoshch')* or support *(podderzhka)* that one extends to others. In an interview, the director of the United Way agency in Russia commented that the purpose of her organization was to help people help themselves and each other. She reflected that this was a culturally important goal, because there have always been times when Russians have helped each other. To illustrate the agency's commitment to providing social resources that would help clients achieve these goals, the woman directed my attention to the agency's logo—a hand supporting a person under a rainbow. Another woman cited the Russian children's story *Repka* (Turnip) as evidence for the value that Russians place on collective assistance. In the story, a man wants to pull a turnip from the ground, but it is so big that he calls on his wife for help. She takes hold of him, and they pull together but to no avail. A grandchild comes to assist, but even then they are not successful. Gradually, more parties—a dog, cat, mouse— come to help pull, until at last they succeed collectively in pulling the turnip from the ground. The woman finished her retelling of this story by reflecting that this was a commentary on Russian life: "They help each other" *(Oni pomogaiut drug drugu)*, she concluded.

This emphasis on cooperative assistance resonated with the comments of my landlady, Anya, during my first trip to Moscow in 1995. In one of our many conversations about Russia, Anya described the hardships of daily life with the comment that Russians have had to support each other "on our shoulders" *(na plechakh)*. Several days later, I walked into my landlady's kitchen and found her sweating over a hot stove, canning pickled cucumbers. According to Anya, her sister loved pickles but had little free time after working long hours, taking care of her husband and teen-aged son, and babysitting her grandchild. Because Anya was a pensioner with ostensibly more free time at home, her sister had asked her to make the pickles for her. "In Russia, we need to help each other" *(V Rossii nam nado pomogat' drug drugu)*, Anya explained.

A few weeks later we visited Anya's best friend, Tanya, at her summer cottage. The two women spent their days picking raspberries in the forest and their evenings turning the berries into preserves. Most nights they stayed up until the early morning hours, working and chatting. Invariably their arguments over politics turned into comparisons of how they managed to survive on their respective pensions. Tanya, a retired geologist in her late fifties, said that when her mother had fallen ill about five years earlier, she took a leave of absence from work to care for her. Although Tanya had intended to return to work, her mother's illness lasted far longer than anyone had expected. After her mother died, Tanya was too old to return to work and began drawing her pension. Because of the lost years of work, her pension was smaller than she had anticipated; there was barely enough to live on, she reflected. Her younger brother (a professor) helps her out every month, especially with the rent; occasionally he brings her groceries or fixes things in her apartment so that she does not have to pay a repairman. In turn, Tanya contributes what she can to help her brother's daughter's family. Tanya saves her money and passes on small amounts to her niece, as well as produce from her garden. By way of explanation, she remarked, "We all help each other; we are collective" (*my kollektivnye*).

These forms of help are not always solicited, and when they occur spontaneously they indicate one's membership within a social group. When I was preparing to leave Moscow at the end of my fieldwork in 1998, I casually mentioned to Irina that I was looking for a ride to the airport. Irina then began calling friends and acquaintances in Moscow. Within a few days she called me back long-distance and told me that she had found several people willing to help me. "We help our friends," she assured me. I did not think much more of Irina's statement until I returned to Moscow in May 1999. I was delighted to be so warmly greeted by friends and acquaintances whom I had not seen in seven months. Phone conversations and meetings were filled with reminiscences and gossip about what I had missed. Nonetheless, I was astonished when I realized that practically every conversation had turned to questions of what my friends could do for me. Repeatedly, close friends, and even people I considered more distant acquaintances, asked, "What can I do to help you?" or "Do you need any help?" When I later commented to another friend that so many people had offered their assistance, she nodded and commented that that is how one knows that one has friends: people want to help.

With friendship and acquaintanceship comes a personal sense of obligation to provide assistance. Aleksei Mikhailovich is the director for social welfare in a region of Moscow serviced by the CCM soup kitchens. When outlining the various services provided by his office and its affiliated charities, he commented specifically on the connection between charity and the assistance provided to his constituents: "We administer charitable actions, so that we help them." He further alluded to a sense of ethical and personal duty (*dolg*) to care for the well-being of the people who lived in his region, a commitment that was evident to his constituents. When he was removed from his position in the wake of departmental political struggles, pensioners at the CCM soup kitchens worried that his replacement would not be as responsive to their needs and concerns as Aleksei Mikhailovich had been. Similarly, Svetlana Grigorievna, the manager of one of the cafeterias serving the CCM soup kitchen programs and the director of her own food aid charity, named her organization Our Duty (Nash Dolg) out of what she said was a duty and responsibility to help other people. She explained that she chose this name because it reflected "the duty of every person to help those who are doing poorly. . . . We have the means, first of all, to feed people, because the government does not have any money, the labor unions do not have any money, and therefore the people of goodwill of our country . . . can now possibly help those who have found themselves in a hopeless situation."

The *Oxford Russian-English Dictionary* lists two meanings for the word *dolg:* "duty" and "debt" (Wheeler 1984:168). This dual meaning indicates the dialectical and reciprocal nature of assistance practices. When Aleksei Mikhailovich characterized the ways in which he and other affiliated aid workers supported their clients, he commented, "We try to interact *[vzai-modeistvovat']* with them." Another friend suggested that I use the word *vzaimovyruchat'* (mutual rescue or mutual assistance) to describe how people aid each other in social welfare programs. This suggestion is revealing in that it emphasizes the interactive component of support in Russia. In Russian the prefix *vzaimo-* means "mutual" or "reciprocal," and the phrases *"vziat' vzaimy"* (to take reciprocally) and *"dat' vzaimy"* (to give reciprocally) mean, respectively, "to borrow" and "to lend." Assistance is therefore closely implicated with ideas about the mutual constitution and interdependence of social relations and responsibilities.

At the same time, the importance of friendship as a specific resource that can be mobilized to guarantee personal security is frequently misunderstood, or "misrecognized" (Bourdieu 1977), by non-Russians, who focus on alternative economies as antagonistic, rather than complementary, to official economic channels. When acts of social diversion such as these have occurred among public figures—for instance, when former Russian president Boris Yeltsin and his close friends and relatives (collectively known as the family) and the networks around pro-West reformer Anatoly Chubais (known as the Chubais clan) have allegedly redistributed official funds and favors to each other—foreign analysts and politicians have suggested that these practices are forms of corruption that subvert the official economy (see also Wedel 1998a). The term *mafia* has also been used to describe these practices. By contrast, although public opinion in Moscow generally disapproves of these actions, Muscovites rarely profess to be surprised.

Going with the Flow

Key to Muscovites' exchange transactions is a strong moral code that regulates understandings about the appropriate directions in which aid flows, as well as the proper uses to which this assistance is put. At an immediate level, exchanges are perceived as cooperative and reciprocal endeavors, whereby goods flow back and forth, in multiple directions, among people who need and deserve assistance. Reciprocity does not occur according to temporal constraints, because needs rarely correspond to regular schedules or predictions. Instead, the system of informal exchange depends to a great extent on unpaid debts, because it is the potential for future exchanges that sustains these relationships. Participants invest in their networks both by making requests and by fulfilling them. Moreover, these expectations about proper exchange behavior not only regulate the actions of individuals but also maintain the boundaries of the social group in which these individuals interact.

Within the context of limited kin networks, even as relationships among parents, siblings, children, and grandchildren are especially valued, priority is given to the youngest members of the family. Parents worry that they cannot provide sufficiently for their children but assert that they will do whatever they can by going without meals or other necessities in order to save money for their children. CCM recipients save what they can from their tiny pensions to pass on to their children and grandchildren and rely solely on soup kitchen meals that are intended to supplement, not replace, their meager incomes. Holiday treats from CCM supporters are taken home for grandchildren to enjoy or for grandchildren to give to teachers as gifts. Other recipients bring young relatives to the soup kitchen and share their food with them. Children and grandchildren are not expected to reciprocate, but parents and grandparents praise offspring who selflessly give support in return. One couple praised their son and his wife for sharing their wages when they instead should have been saving their money for their new baby.

Nevertheless, Muscovites agree that there are limits to what children and grandchildren deserve as well as expectations about what they owe their elders. Both welfare officials and CCM recipients bitterly comment that too many elderly Russians have been abandoned by selfish children. Vera's encounter with her nephew and grandniece illustrates this tension well. Because Vera and her husband were unable to have children, they helped her sister's family when circumstances allowed. In recent years, Vera has hosted her sister's son Dmitrii for several months at a time when he comes to Moscow to work. In return, he contributes groceries but sends most of his earnings home to support his mother and teenaged daughter. Occasionally Vera's sister and grandniece travel to Moscow for holidays. One such family visit turned into a bitter dispute, however, and Vera found herself scolding Dmitrii and his daughter. First, Vera had discovered that Dmitrii was giving all his money to his daughter so that she could buy clothes, while his mother could not afford to buy even necessities. Then, the girl announced that she was not satisfied with what she had received; she demanded that both her grandmother and Vera should pass their belongings to her now instead of waiting for her to inherit them when they died. Vera responded that that was inappropriate, rebuked Dmitrii for not sharing with his mother, and then scolded her sister about allowing her son and granddaughter to leave her completely alone.

Misuse of networks and resources, inappropriate demands, and acts of neglect violate the trust and sense of "good faith" that are inherent in these support relations. As in the case of Aleksandra Petrovna and my landlady, they can also provoke bitter disagreements between friends and relatives or even cause partners to sever ties. Soup kitchen recipients who misuse their meal tickets or eligibility risk provoking the ire of other participants, who are willing to impose social sanctions by scolding or even reporting offenders to the director. This does not mean, however, that recipients refrain from attempts to subvert the system. One particularly striking instance of serious misuse included the case of Igor Ivanovich. Despite the careful efforts of CCM staff to ensure that recipients were not registered in any other program and particularly that they were not registered for multiple CCM soup kitchens simultaneously, Igor Ivanovich managed to enroll himself in two different CCM soup kitchens. For several years he evaded notice as he moved back and forth between the two locations. It was not until the two groups merged temporarily during renovations to one of the cafeterias that CCM staff discovered his dual membership. Igor Ivanovich was fortunate in that he was only scolded and forced to forfeit one of his cards. A slightly different set of circumstances brought other results. Viktor was a retired electrician who lived near one of the CCM soup kitchens and knew many of the recipients

through the pensioners' networks in the region. Although he was not officially registered as a CCM recipient, he volunteered faithfully several
days a week. For his service, he received free meals, just as the other volunteers did. Over time, however, Viktor's enthusiasm and expectations
for what he should receive in return for his efforts intensified to the extent that other volunteers and recipients felt uncomfortable around him.
With the overall harmony of the soup kitchen in mind, CCM staff were
forced to ask him to take a temporary "break" from his volunteering.

Muscovites denounce people who abuse the moral codes of "help" and
are quick to point out that these violations are extreme cases and should
not be interpreted as evidence that Russians are greedy or selfish by nature. I encountered such a reaction when I asked a friend to help me de-
cipher the handwriting in a note that I had received from a disgruntled
CCM soup kitchen recipient. The recipient had written, "Greed [zhad-
nost']—it is one of the characteristics of Russian people." The woman
then wrote that too many pensioners were taking advantage of charity so
that they could pass their pensions on to their children and grandchildren. When my friend read this note, she shook her head in amazement
and commented that the writer must be a person who wished others ill.

Individuals who ignore the moral standards that determine and regulate good exchanges violate the ethics of fairness and egalitarianism that
are implied by equitable allocations of scarce resources. Although such
actions may reflect creative acts of making do with available opportunities, they nonetheless set the perpetrators outside the social collectivity
and hence outside the very networks through which help flows. Immoral
agents are thus asocial agents. At the same time, these moral standards are
not absolute but flexible and ambiguous, a feature that offers individuals
possibilities for manipulating them in their tactics of making do. Personal
deviations can be reframed not as acts of selfish behavior but rather as acts
of resistance to other social groups—or, more commonly, to the anonymous bureaucratic structures of the state, the workplace, or an aid agency.
The tensions and contradictions that emerge from the ideals of fairness
and equity will be addressed more fully in this chapter in the discussion
of the "feud" in the soup kitchen.

The Contradictions of Charity

At the heart of the CCM soup kitchen program is another form of
exchange that complicates both academic and personal understandings

of the distinctions between commodities and gifts. As the previous discussion illustrates, the forms of "help" and "support" that constitute everyday transactions in Moscow blur boundaries between gift and commodity, because they are simultaneously intimate and instrumental. Moreover, the successful deployment of these interactions is not necessarily simultaneous or even immediate, as one would expect with a commodity-based transaction in which partners come together only at the moment of exchange and only for the purpose of engaging in a mutually utilitarian relationship. Rather, the mutual assistance system found among Muscovites depends solely on partners' trust that their actions will be reciprocated in the future. In anthropological terms, the simultaneously intimate and delayed nature of Muscovites' acts of assistance suggests that they belong to the repertoire of gift giving (Mauss 1990). Yet a comparison of these practices with the form of exchange that characterizes the way aid is dispensed at the institutional level of the CCM program—most notably in the relations between foreign aid workers and Muscovite recipients—reveals a vast chasm between the way members of the two sides view their relationships and the forms of assistance that they make available to each other.

In theory, philanthropic gifting, such as that of CCM and other aid programs, more closely approximates the ideal of the "perfect gift" (Noonan 1984:695), in which givers do not expect recipients to reciprocate. Reciprocity would, in fact, breach the anonymity and selflessness associated with charity by creating ties of sociality. Yet James Carrier (1990) has argued that the ideology of the perfect gift disguises tensions between the freedom of the gift and the obligation of the recipient. Although gifting interactions must appear voluntary and disinterested, this altruism actually masks a sense of obligation to receive and return (see, for example, Bourdieu 1977; Mauss 1990). Gifting partners are bound into a relationship where both refusals to accept gifts (Tapper and Tapper 1986) and refusals to return gifts (Yan 1996) indicate rejections of social ties. As Mary Douglas has noted, "A gift that does nothing to enhance solidarity is a contradiction" (1990:vii). Without reciprocation by recipients, moral imbalances are likely to emerge in charitable encounters (Cheal 1988). Hence for balanced social relations to exist, givers and receivers must engage in mutual, but not necessarily immediate or simultaneous, exchanges.

The rhetoric and practices of CCM and other foreign aid workers and donors highlight these tensions between giving and reciprocating. The larger foreign charity community in Moscow is composed of many vol-

unteers and donors who have uncritically adopted the rhetoric of international development agendas for the former Soviet Union and Eastern
Europe. Casting themselves in roles of benevolent givers providing services to destitute recipients who are unable to care or provide for themselves, these volunteers, who include many CCM volunteers (particularly
those from North America), see themselves as representatives of a Western form of modernity and hence claim a heightened responsibility to
care for the underprivileged during Russia's economic and political transition. A related perspective is that held by religious missionaries who
want to compensate for the aftereffects of Communist atheism by
spreading Christianity. Because both of these models of assistance entail
a unidirectional flow of aid and power, they do not allow possibilities for
Russians to reciprocate for the charity they receive. Indeed, as I discovered in conversations with CCM volunteers and other expatriates from
North America and Europe, many foreigners believe that Russians
should not attempt to reciprocate.

This vision of a paternalistic altruism quickly collides with the reality
of aid distribution in Russia. The very nature of the CCM soup kitchens
creates a space where exchange relations simultaneously exist among recipients and between recipients and donors/volunteers. On the one hand,
because recipients approach the soup kitchens as a node within their personal exchange networks, meals become opportunities to meet partners
and to affirm and continue existing circulations of goods and information. On the other hand, recipients also see the distribution of charitable
aid as national and international responsibilities. Some recipients view
the assistance provided by donors and volunteers as an appropriate return on the work they provided to the Soviet state during their younger
days, even if it comes from a non-Russian source and so is not directly reciprocal. Meanwhile, other recipients classify foreign aid as a form of international political justice. As one woman commented, it is only appropriate and responsible that American wealth be redistributed to other
countries. In both views charitable aid closes the cycle of reciprocity.

More significant, most CCM recipients perceive the meals they receive
as the beginnings of relationships with donors and volunteers that will
continue beyond the parameters of an individual meal at a singular moment in time. To recognize and sustain these connections, recipients give
back to donors and volunteers with formal letters of appreciation, poetry
(such as the epigraph at the beginning of this chapter), small gifts, and
other services. One woman collects discarded newspapers and magazines
that she gives to volunteers, and another person picks up free English-

language newspapers to distribute. In each soup kitchen, recipients organize birthday parties for the CCM coordinators; they collect money for a collective gift (usually an item of clothing such as a shirt, tie, or scarf) and pass around a card for all recipients to sign.

These acts of reciprocity are acknowledged and accepted primarily by a small group of African staff members and volunteers. North American and European volunteers, by contrast, generally refuse the acts of reciprocity that are offered by recipients. Aleksandra Petrovna, through her connections with the Veterans' Council and the local government, occasionally procures tickets for local festivals. As a gesture of appreciation, she invites CCM volunteers and supporters to attend these events. In most cases, non-African invitees refuse her offers. As several people explained, they do not accept her offers of social engagement because this would change their social relations with her, and they might later find themselves in positions of social obligation.

In another instance, Ekaterina Sergeevna moved to Moscow to work as a cleaning woman in order to save money for the time when her sons would finally be discharged from the army. A lonely woman, she often wept at the soup kitchen and told volunteers that she was grateful for the opportunity to eat there and to be with other people. Toward the end of her stay in Moscow, she invited several volunteers to take a walking tour of the city with her in order to create, as she said, some happy memories of her time in Moscow. Curiously, each invitee turned down her invitation. When I later asked those volunteers why they had rejected her offer, they all first cited busy schedules but then admitted that they suspected that Ekaterina Sergeevna might ask them for extra help. Later, I witnessed other distancing tactics at a meeting for the soup kitchen fundraising committee, where I relayed a message from recipients who wanted to help the CCM community raise awareness about the soup kitchens. Karina Andreevna, a recipient and activist for the elderly, had invited the non-Russian committee members to visit willing recipients at home to see how Russians really live. She had argued that this personal information would give committee members an advantage when they appealed to potential donors. After conferring, the committee members declined the offer. They explained that they did not want to visit recipients at home, because the recipients might be embarrassed and would likely extend offers of hospitality, such as food or drink.

By refusing recipients' efforts to reciprocate, non-Russian volunteers and donors not only place themselves outside a social network but also establish a powerful hierarchy in which they cast themselves in positions of moral and economic superiority over their Russian beneficiaries. These distancing tactics are further noticeable in the linguistic practices of volunteers and recipients. In Russian, degrees of social intimacy are designated by two forms of the pronoun *you: vy* is the form used for the formal "you," such as with strangers, acquaintances, and people in positions of authority, in addition to its general use for the plural "you," while *ty* signifies personal intimacy such as that between family members and close friends.[6] Few non-African volunteers are on an informal basis with any of the recipients. This is partly because most non-African volunteers do not speak more than a word or two of Russian. Yet even among those who speak conversational Russian, such intimacy is rare.[7] Those few volunteers who use *ty* or other intimate forms of address with recipients, or who have accepted return gifts, acknowledge long-term relationships with those recipients.

In these practices of englobing (Ardener 1975), givers delineate boundaries between themselves and their recipients by creating circumstances in which material and symbolic acts of reciprocity are impossible. Despite recipients' attempts to subvert the structural hierarchy of the soup kitchen program through acts aimed at creating intimacy and obligations of reciprocity, non-Russian participants reinforce the differences between them. Volunteers and donors who prevent recipients from reciprocating in charity exchanges not only disregard deeply entrenched local ideals about the nature of equitable exchange but also violate the logic of gifting as a mutual relationship (Douglas 1990:vii).

The Feud in the Soup Kitchen

A final series of events in the soup kitchens indicates just how precarious and potentially volatile the connections among sociality and informal exchange can be. During my return fieldwork in 1999, the CCM community opened a fourth soup kitchen. The recipient pool for this new kitchen was drawn from the local Veterans' Council rolls of the neediest elderly in the region. The few exceptions were twenty invalids recommended by the owner of the cafeteria in which the new soup kitchen was based; three elderly, frail recipients who lived closer to the new soup kitchen than to the one they had been attending; and Aleksandra Petrovna, who helped CCM staff find a suitable facility, obtain supplementary funding, and negotiate with officials and vendors. Although the third CCM kitchen and the new, fourth kitchen served Muscovites from the same neighborhood, the third kitchen was located in another region of the city and accessible only by a forty-five-minute ride on two or three different forms of public transportation. In some instances neighbors from the same apartment building were assigned to different soup kitchens.

CCM staff did not publicize these transfers, nor did they offer them as options for other recipients at the third soup kitchen. The main reason for this secrecy was the difference between the meals at the third and fourth soup kitchens: the portion sizes provided at the fourth soup kitchen were to be slightly larger than those at the other soup kitchens. A private charity in the neighborhood provided the supplementary funding for this soup kitchen with the stipulation that eligibility be limited to veterans. Many of the recipients in the third soup kitchen were not veterans, and CCM staff members and Veterans' Council representatives expressed concern that the differences between the two kitchens, no matter how slight, would become known and a cause for tensions if neighborhood friends moved back and forth. As one CCM coordinator put it, "People talk to each other."

Oksana is a recipient at the third soup kitchen. A middle-aged mother of eight, she actively participates in the CCM soup kitchen and church events, although neither she nor her children speak English. On the day the fourth soup kitchen opened, Oksana arrived at the new kitchen after her meal at the third kitchen and announced that she was there to help as a volunteer. Although I had never seen her volunteer at her own soup kitchen, I watched her energetically serving trays of food and removing dirty dishes at the new kitchen. Two of her children assisted by washing tables. Later that afternoon, Aleksandra Petrovna called me at home to chat about how well the first day had gone. During the course of our conversation, she asked if I had seen Oksana at the soup kitchen. When I replied that I had and then added that Oksana had informed me of her intention to help, Aleksandra Petrovna responded, "She does not want to help; she just wants to get food." Aleksandra Petrovna commented that Oksana wanted to transfer to the new kitchen but that CCM staff would prevent that from happening. Later that week at the new soup kitchen, I overheard Aleksandra Petrovna and Svetlana Grigorievna, the owner/manager of the cafeteria, discussing Oksana. It became apparent that both women had known Oksana for a long time, because they complained about how presumptuous she had been in her effort to move to the new site and about the frequency with which she had attempted to benefit from other opportunities in the past. My impression that Oksana's actions were a prime topic of conversation here and elsewhere was reinforced at church the following Sunday, when my conversation with two coordinators from one of the other soup kitchens segued into a discussion about their views on Oksana's arrogance at attending the new soup kitchen.

Oksana's subterfuge was a source of particularly great irritation for Aleksandra Petrovna, who on a later occasion described the younger woman as a person who abused social services networks: "She and two children eat at the soup kitchen; her younger children eat at the Red Cross Soup Kitchen. She is always first in line for something. She is cunning [khitraia] in working the system." In addition to their food aid programs, CCM members also collected used clothes and then redistributed them to congregants with severe financial constraints—ideally African student members of the congregation. Aleksandra Petrovna reported that Oksana and her children regularly flocked to the head of the distribution line and took all the best clothes. Then, instead of wearing the clothes, Aleksandra Petrovna alleged, Oksana stored them in the apartment of an adult daughter until they could be resold for a profit. Throughout the summer, Oksana and her abuses of various social services networks became a regular topic in my conversations with Aleksandra Petrovna.

Because of the way information passed through the CCM community, it was not long before Oksana learned that my interest in the soup kitchen program was more than that of a casual volunteer. She began seeking me out after CCM worship services or at soup kitchen events in order to share her opinions on a number of issues. She often alluded vaguely to "various people" who were allegedly conspiring against her and her children and impeding her efforts to transfer to the new kitchen or to receive aid. Over time, as Oksana apparently either came to trust me or (more likely) saw me as a resource to be used, she became more precise in her accusations and eventually focused specifically on Aleksandra Petrovna. One Sunday morning during the fellowship hour that followed CCM services, not long after she had volunteered at the fourth soup kitchen, Oksana took me aside for a private conversation. After looking carefully around the room to make sure that we could not be overheard, Oksana whispered that Aleksandra Petrovna was a terrible person and was interested in helping only her own friends. "You know what her husband was—he worked for the KGB. You cannot trust Communists like Aleksandra Petrovna," she complained. Several weeks later, I made a presentation of my research to a Russian group that supported the CCM project. Oksana was among those in attendance, and after the talk she passed me a note. In response to my remarks on the ways in which re-

cipient eligibility was tied to bureaucratic structures, Oksana had scrib-
bled, "Bureaucracy: the living, self-accommodating Aleksandra Petrovna
is a striking example *[iarkii primer]* of that; she is a former Communist,
the chief bookkeeper of the organization."

Although there was a hint of truth to this information about Aleksandra Petrovna—Aleksandra Petrovna's husband had indeed been an official in the KGB—Oksana's statements were not entirely accurate. Aleksandra Petrovna and her husband had divorced a number of years earlier.
On the few occasions when Aleksandra Petrovna talked about her ex-
husband, she consistently emphasized that he was an unpleasant person
and that she had found his choice of employment incompatible with her
emphasis on social service and altruism. As further evidence, she pointed
out that their children, with whom she was very close and whom she saw
regularly, seldom communicated with him. For his part, her ex-husband
had made it clear years before that he preferred his sister's children to his
own. Not only did he spend time with these relatives, but he also contributed a significant portion of his much more generous pension to
them while giving nothing to his own children or grandchildren.

This estrangement was especially remarkable because, owing to the
tight housing situation in Moscow, Aleksandra Petrovna and her ex-
husband continued to live together in a two-room apartment. They
shared kitchen and bath facilities, as well as a telephone line, but had their
own rooms, complete with individual locks, beds, tables, chairs, dishes,
and other items. Moreover, despite her great antipathy for her ex-
husband, Aleksandra Petrovna noted that she still felt some responsibility for his welfare. On one occasion when he failed to come home for
more than twenty-four hours, Aleksandra Petrovna spent several hours—
and a sleepless night—on the phone with his worried relatives, trying to
find him. (He eventually turned up but offered neither an apology nor an
explanation.) Even though her ex-husband has increasingly made life un-
bearable for Aleksandra Petrovna (his erratic mood swings and violent
temper have required police intervention on several occasions), she has
not stopped socializing and entertaining. She merely works around her
ex-husband by arranging visits from friends, CCM staff, and fellow activists to coincide with her ex-husband's absences from the apartment.
On the few occasions when he was in his room during my visits, Aleksandra Petrovna asked me to whisper when we talked about the soup
kitchen and other social services programs so that he would not be able
to hear us. Aleksandra Petrovna has also refused to let her ex-husband's
unsavory past taint her volunteer work. She adamantly maintained that

neither she nor any of her relatives had ever joined the Communist Party and offered as proof the story of how her grandfather, a respected icon painter before the revolution, had lost his private property, including a comfortable summer cottage, to Communists.

Yet despite Aleksandra Petrovna's denial that she was ever involved with the Communist Party, Oksana persisted in her allegations that the other woman was a Communist. In so doing, Oksana did more than simply suggest that Aleksandra Petrovna was untrustworthy. By making reference to a complicated and highly sensitive aspect of the Soviet period, Oksana strategically classified the other woman as an "enemy" of the people—and one with access to special privileges—thereby casting doubt on Aleksandra Petrovna's status as a legitimate member of the CCM community and on her allegiance to this community.

In the weeks before I left Moscow at the end of July, Oksana's grievance developed into a full-scale offensive against Aleksandra Petrovna. At the third soup kitchen, Oksana circulated a letter for other recipients to sign. She showed it to me after church one Sunday, shortly before giving it to the CCM pastors. Oksana contended that recipients at the third soup kitchen had written the text together; one recipient had borrowed a typewriter from a relative to make it look official. The letter began as a grateful "letter of thanks" *(pis'mo blagodarnosti)*, a standard format for letters from welfare recipients to those individuals who had provided assistance. The recipients thanked the pastors and coordinators for their work and extended their best wishes for the continued health, happiness, and success of CCM staff members and soup kitchen volunteers. After these remarks, the letter's tone changed drastically: the signers expressed their intent to alert the pastors to the fact that Aleksandra Petrovna, as a former Communist, was mistreating other recipients, that she was rude to them, unscrupulous in her dealings, engaged in activities that undermined the soup kitchen, and out of meanness was denying help to pensioners, invalids, and other people in need. The petitioners closed the letter by blaming Aleksandra Petrovna for a rent dispute between her son and one of the coordinators to whom he had leased an apartment, then accused her of giving preference to people in her own building for the soup kitchen rosters. The tone of the letter was, by the end, inflammatory and hostile. While I was reading the letter, Elena, a Russian congregant with whom Aleksandra Petrovna had chatted personably on a number of past occasions, walked up and noticed the letter in my hand. In English she complained, "Those Communists, they have no shame . . . terrible people . . . of course I am not talking about the rank-and-file Communists." Continuing in Russian, Elena and Oksana denounced Aleksandra Petrovna and vowed that she had to be stopped.

A few days later, a recipient at the fourth soup kitchen, a woman who occasionally attended CCM services, asked me privately if I had heard about the letter against Aleksandra Petrovna at the third soup kitchen. When I acknowledged that I had, she whispered that she was circulating a similar letter through the new soup kitchen. To counter the negative effects of these letters and the potential social divisions that had emerged through their circulation, CCM staff arranged a meeting at the third soup kitchen between Oksana and Aleksandra Petrovna so that the two women could air their grievances openly. When Aleksandra Petrovna received the invitation, however, she interpreted it as an opportunity to visit her friends and so took special care to dress nicely and fix her hair. She was surprised when she arrived and discovered the true purpose of the meeting—especially so, when Oksana took the opportunity to vent her frustrations and accusations fully and publicly. "It was such an unexpected shock. Of course I cried. I have spent my whole life helping people from my heart," Aleksandra Petrovna sobbed later. After the encounter, Aleksandra Petrovna suffered a mild heart attack and was confined to bed. When she had recovered sufficiently, she refused to return to the soup kitchen and wrote a letter of resignation from her volunteer activities. The CCM ministers rejected her letter and eventually, after several months, encouraged her to return to the soup kitchen. To protect herself against future problems, Aleksandra Petrovna relied on her friends in the CCM soup kitchen community to keep her informed of Oksana's activities.[8]

It is possible to interpret this series of events as the give-and-take of a long-standing personal feud between two women from very different circumstances and with a history of mutual antipathy. Yet this perspective reveals little about why these exchanges and accusations of diversions prompted such passionate outbursts not only from Oksana and Aleksandra Petrovna but also from other members of the CCM community who aligned themselves with one side or the other. Ultimately, this was a battle, waged largely through rumors and allegations, over the control of social networks. Specifically, Aleksandra Petrovna and Oksana were debating and marking the parameters and rules for appropriate exchange practices and partners. Although both women belonged to the larger CCM-related social community, each accused the other of belonging to a smaller subgroup to which she was diverting goods. Even Oksana's accusations that Aleksandra Petrovna was a Communist represent a tactical ploy to set the other woman apart as an immoral outsider. Moreover, these dynamics reveal the extent to which social networks, while overlapping, are neither coterminous nor necessarily linked with the same interests and objectives.

By conscripting their own networks of friends and sympathizers, both as evidence for their membership within a distinct social group and as visible support for their respective positions, Oksana and Aleksandra Petrovna seriously damaged the stability and solidarity of the CCM community. Through their bickering and manipulations, the two women revealed that the peaceful image of a unified and coherent soup kitchen community in fact disguised factions that corresponded to unequal power relationships. Recipients who were called upon to take sides had to weigh the value of their relationships with Aleksandra Petrovna and Oksana as well as the potential access to resources that each woman possessed. Recipients were thus compelled to evaluate their relationships with others not just in terms of their social and sentimental value but also in terms of their effectiveness.

The Gift of Exchange

The skillful manipulation of the practical rules surrounding exchange practices is, on the one hand, caught up in concerns over the equitable redistribution of resources. A system of morality guides the appropriate uses to which goods are put and the acceptable behavior of transactors. On the other hand, the ability to navigate these rules correctly and successfully demonstrates one's social worth and knowledge. More precisely, it emphasizes both the potential of individual actors and the ability of others to evaluate this potential accurately. Through the right connections, anything is possible; but some connections are nonetheless more fruitful than others, and one must recognize the difference.

The pervasive use of informal networks in Russia challenges theoretical explanations of the connection between exchange and social relations. In particular, distinctions between gift exchanges and commodity exchanges are complicated by the personalized nature of utilitarian redistributions of goods like those in Russia. The conventional distinction between commodity interchanges and gift giving is that the former are characterized by the immediate exchange of items possessing equal value between transactors whose relationship exists only for the duration of the exchange (Sahlins 1972). Gift giving, by contrast, involves a sequence of giving, receiving, and reciprocating over an extended period of time. Transactors are bound together by the obligations and expectations that determine when gifts are returned and under what circumstances (Bourdieu 1977; Mauss 1990; Yan 1996). Moreover, exchanges are understood to exist prior to sociality; it is through acts of exchange that individuals initiate and sustain relationships with each other (Bourdieu 1977; Mauss 1990).

These distinctions between commodity and gift economies, between the impersonal and the personal, and between interest and affected disinterest do not adequately capture the complexities of Muscovites' informal networks, however. In particular, the idiom of friendship through which informal networks are expressed disguises the extent to which displays of giving represent pragmatic distributions of material goods, as well as calculated evaluations of the ability of the recipient to reciprocate at a later time. More important, the possibilities for exchange emerge only after social relations have been established. Thus social relations precede offers of assistance and requests for help. Acts of exchange verify and concretize existing social relations and the trust that exists between partners. When Irina commented that she had known the woman in the bus dispatcher's office for a long time before she asked for a favor, she demonstrated that their relationship preceded the actual exchange of assistance. At the same time, Muscovites recognize that relationships can be voided through violations of the moral standards framing exchange practices, as when my landlady's attempt to renegotiate my rent breached the spirit of good faith that had characterized her relationship with Aleksandra Petrovna and ultimately severed their friendship.

Within an everyday survival system focused on material provisioning, social relations are themselves forms of long-term economic capital that Muscovites invest and cash in as needed. The personal connections that people cultivate may lie dormant, as a form of investment, until a future moment when they are needed, a phenomenon that Carolyn Stevens has called "deposits in the favor bank" (1997:231). In the following chapter I turn to this theme of social capital by looking at another economic system, "organic exchange," in which summer gardens and forests shape Muscovites' social relations and ideologies of collective assistance.

CHAPTER 4

The Forest Feeds Us

Organic Exchange

When Russia held its first democratic elections in summer 1991, people in the West watched to see Russians voting freely for the first time. Only a very small percentage of Russians successfully arrived at the polls to cast their ballots, however. Westerners were shocked to discover that most Russians could not vote because they were working at their dachas, and demanded to know more about this terrible thing called dacha that could prevent voting in a democratic country.

Anecdote told by Pavel, aged thirty-seven

The feel of everyday life in Moscow changes dramatically during the summer months. The frantic pace that marks urban life slows down noticeably, and the institutional drabness that characterizes winter gives way to the bright greens of trees and grass. Outdoor cafés spring up along busy sidewalks, *shashlyk* (shish kebab) stands make their first appearance, and the heavy bean-based soups and pureed potatoes that are the staple of the CCM cafeterias are replaced by vegetable salads, berry jams, and cold soups. Recipients switch their heavy coats and neatly pressed clothes with faded and patched gardening clothes, and people of all ages make time in their busy shopping and working routines to find a nice place to sit and enjoy the sun and warm air.

The air of relaxation that permeates the CCM soup kitchens and Moscow more generally, however, belies the extent to which the uncertainty and improvisation that infuses Russians' social practices during the rest of the year is only heightened during the summer. In particular, the allure of warm weather disguises the risks that Muscovites take with their personal well-being. Even as Russian newspapers publish daily death reports that detail how many people have died from eating poisonous mushrooms, Muscovites flock to the forests, armed with baskets and knives, ready to scavenge as many mushrooms as they can find. Public warnings about cholera bacteria and high pollution levels in lakes and rivers around Moscow go unheeded by eager bathers and anglers alike. Attendance at the CCM soup kitchens and other aid programs plummets drastically as recipients willingly abandon their free meals and opportunities for socializing with each other, sometimes for months at a time.

For most of the year, CCM staff consider themselves fortunate when the daily attendance rate at the four soup kitchens averages twelve hundred to thirteen hundred people out of fifteen hundred. Periodic dips in attendance are attributed to bouts of severe weather or illness, and most recipients explain unexpected absences to volunteers upon their return and inquire if they can be given credit for the meals they have missed. Between May and September, however, attendance levels drop to one-half or even lower. When recipients do attend the soup kitchen, they are more likely to request food for several days in advance and less likely to haggle with coordinators over making up missed meals. Recipients also curtail the amount of time they spend socializing with each other. These changes affect the overall rhythms of the soup kitchens. Whereas Mondays and Fridays are normally the busiest days in the soup kitchens, because they are the days immediately following and preceding a two-day period when the soup kitchens are closed, during the summer months, Tuesdays, Thursdays, and early on Friday mornings are peak times as recipients quickly rush in to get meals that they take home with them. For several years CCM staff have considered reducing the number of operating days to three days a week in the summer because so few recipients attend on a regular basis.

These fluctuations in the pace of everyday life are evident throughout Moscow during the summer months. Weekends and midweek are quiet times in shops and on the streets. On Mondays and Fridays, however, stores, markets, roadways, and public transportation teem with people, their carts and suitcases, pets, and assorted buckets, bags, and fishing poles. Thirty-minute journeys from the city turn into one- to two-hour bumper-to-bumper traffic snarls as thousands—perhaps even millions—of Muscovites attempt to leave the confines of the city for summer cottages (dachas), forests, health spas, and vacation camps in the countryside. During the summer, companies and research institutes decrease their work load or close completely, because so many employees take time off to spend at their cottages.

There is something exceptional, and almost mystical in some cases, about the appreciation that Muscovites display for the Russian country-side and the risks and creative efforts they take to incorporate it into their lives. One CCM recipient confided that dachas have their own spiritual-ity: she explained that *dacha* comes from the Russian verb *dat'*, for *to give*, in the sense of "given from God" *(dannaia ot Boga)*. Themes of dachas, forests, the countryside, and natural produce regularly permeate conver-sations with friends and strangers alike. Discussions about fresh herbs and berries can prompt nostalgic reminiscences about past meals, social events, and the healing qualities of the earth. In public spaces, complete strangers ask each other for advice on finding the perfect berry bush or on selecting the proper fertilizer or packet of seeds. Urban residents who would never dream of living anywhere but Moscow describe their ex-citement about leaving the city for cleaner air in the country. Anna Niko-laevna, a retired professor, once devoted an hour to recounting her va-cations at a lake outside Moscow, where she and her friends swam, hiked, read, and picked fresh herbs that they ate without washing. On another occasion I arrived at a friend's apartment for a weekend visit, only to find that the grandfather, an eighty-year-old World War II veteran, had walked several kilometers (up and down several hills) to the family dacha to pick fresh garlic.

Muscovites often claim that the countryside offers a form of escape from the rigors of urban life. As a result of the previous ten years of "transition," many Muscovites have found their personal time curtailed by the regimented schedules required to hold several jobs and adhere to North American–style workdays. The temporal constraints that charac-terize everyday life in Moscow are fewer in the country. As Aleksei Antonovich, a CCM member, remarked, "Time runs differently in the country." Two friends, Evgenii and Olga, remove their watches as soon as they arrive at their cottage and transfer the clock hanging on the wall to a less conspicuous location. Spontaneous visits with neighbors can happen at all hours of the day or night. One woman explained that she merely checked to see if lights were on inside someone's cottage before dropping in at midnight or later. Children play freely within the com-munities, periodically descending upon one another's cottages and gar-dens for snacks. Yet even as Muscovites celebrate the personal freedom and relaxation they associate with their summertime rural activities, most people hastened to impress upon me that gardens and forests were not simply vacation destinations but also crucial components of their repertoire of survival activities.

Nancy Ries (1997) has argued that private gardens belong to a "natural economy" that Russians use to support themselves during times of shortages and poverty. Nevertheless, as the comments and actions of Muscovite respondents reveal, there is more to dachas and the countryside than simply their role within Muscovites' schemes to ease the urgency of material needs. Although Muscovites acknowledge the exertion that is involved in dacha life, often captured in accounts of extraordinary gardening, the potential rewards of the countryside far exceed the possible losses that might be incurred by missing work or as a result of inclement weather or invasions of rodents, bugs, and other pests. Rural spaces provide opportunities for agents to satisfy a combination of social, spiritual, and symbolic needs that cannot be met in, and may even be caused by, life in the city. Because the importance of the rural extends far beyond immediate material needs and is in fact tightly entwined with Russians' sense of self within a larger nexus of social relations, I prefer to consider these practices as features of an economy of "organic exchange." Moreover, this perspective better reflects local perceptions that this economic sphere, when juxtaposed to a capitalist market economy, is more faithful to a collective sense of Russianness.

In this chapter I examine the phenomena of dachas and the Russian countryside, and I explore how this organic economy, derived from the earth, fits into Muscovites' everyday survival practices. I ask what it is about dachas, gardens, and forests that Muscovites find so compelling. Why do people devote so much attention to their gardens and cottages and seize every available opportunity to leave the city, even when this means forfeiting valuable forms of public assistance such as CCM meals in order to engage in hard, physical labor? In addition, why do Muscovites value so highly the natural produce that they take from their summer gardens and other rural spaces, even when these preferences carry potential risks such as picking poisonous mushrooms or produce from contaminated soil? And finally, if Muscovites' everyday survival tactics contribute to their hurried, frenetic lives in the city—where the common refrain among acquaintances seems to be *"bystro bystro"* (quickly, quickly)—how do they incorporate the rural life into their schedules? I suggest that answers to these questions lie in an understanding of the Russian countryside as a place where material and social resources converge. By escaping to both the physical and the imagined environs of the countryside, a simultaneously mystical and actual place where food and possibility abound, Russians create spaces in which they can manage daily life more simply, completely, and directly.

Rural Ideals

Simon Schama (1995:15) points out that national identities owe much of their legitimacy and endurance to the landscapes in which they are embedded. Similarly, in his study of Viennese gardens, Robert Rotenberg has suggested that "landscape is a powerful language for asserting ideologically based models of community life" (1999:139). These observations are especially apt for Russia, because rural spaces and urban centers have been important cultural counterpoints throughout Russian history.

In particular, the countryside has occupied a privileged position in the Russian cultural imagination as a symbol for social identities and experiences. Before the formation of the Soviet Union, ordinary nonnoble Russians were generally tied to the land, both figuratively and literally. As peasants, most people made their livelihood from working the soil. Before serfdom was abolished in the 1860s, serfs were bound to the land and thus bought and sold with parcels of property, just as agricultural implements and animals were. Rural peasant life was captured in art and literature in romantic terms, with images of peasant life featuring happy, simple farmers laboring beneath beautiful skies and on productive land.[1] With industrialization and the growing expectations for modernization that characterized the late nineteenth and early twentieth centuries throughout Europe and Russia, many peasants left their agricultural roots and moved to the cities. During the Soviet period, the regime linked urbanization with the nation's larger modernization project (Kotkin 1995). Yet at the same time that cities were growing in importance as centers of industrial production and consumption, Russians recognized that urban spaces were limited in other respects. In his study of Magnitogorsk, Stephen Kotkin (1995) has vividly described how planned cities that were envisioned by Soviet leaders as the means to socialist prosperity were nonetheless unable to meet the very real demands of residents. To satisfy the food-production needs of the state, the Soviet state engaged in massive agricultural-based projects through a system of collective farms (kolkhoz) and state farms (sovkhoz). As a result, rural spaces acquired prominence as agricultural sources for the entire nation. More recently, with the privatization efforts of the 1990s, these farms have been reconfigured into privately owned corporate farms. Nevertheless, despite the political significance of large farms during both the Soviet and post-Soviet periods, the most important source of supplemental food assistance has consistently come from private garden plots.[2]

Dacha Life

The centerpiece of the organic economy in Russia is the dacha (pl., *dachi* in Russian), the cottage around which private garden plots are organized.[3] Perhaps the most widely recognized symbol of Russian private life and leisure, dachas typically conjure up in both Russian literature and foreign media accounts images of comfortable summer residences where political and intellectual elites retreat in order to relax and entertain guests. In reality, however, luxurious cottages, sometimes complete with swimming pools, expensive electronics, communications devices, and even extensive surveillance systems, belong to the realm of Russia's rich and powerful and are not representative of the small dwellings that most Russians make their homes in the summer months.[4]

Most dachas are technically known as *sadovye uchastki,* "garden plots," or as *ogorodi,* "kitchen gardens," and are far more spartan and utilitarian than the homes of the elite. When I asked people about their dachas, most corrected me and said that they are not members of the elite and thus own work cottages, not vacation homes. Tanya confided that her cottage is not really a dacha—"It is actually a garden plot community to help people live," she said, although she admitted that she, her friends, and relatives prefer to use the word *dacha.* Others further deemphasized their cottages by referring to them as sheds *(sarai)* in response to my research questions. Yet when people either talked among themselves or initiated the subject with me, they almost exclusively used the term *dacha.* In conversations about their plans to visit the countryside, most people simply said, "I am going to the dacha" *(Ia na dachu).* Moreover, even though Russians' primary activities at their cottages are geared around food provisioning, most people combine their work activities with relaxation activities such as swimming, visiting, sleeping, and reading.

Previously, most people received their garden plots through their jobs. Parcels of land were issued to work units that in turn distributed small patches to workers, so that generally all the residents in a particular dacha community were related to each other through the workplace. Those who were not fortunate enough to receive an assignment or could not afford to buy one visited relatives and friends who owned dachas. Others rented entire cottages and gardens or, sometimes, just a room and small subsection of a dacha's yard. These renters were known locally as *dachniki.* Today, with the changes brought about by Russia's economic reforms, including privatization and more lucrative salaries for some workers, Muscovites are more likely to inherit or buy their cottages. Tanya inherited her dacha from her parents, who had received it some forty years earlier through her father's job as a geology professor. Although many of Tanya's neighbors in the dacha community were originally linked to the geology network, the occupational composition of the area is changing as outsiders buy cottages in the community and then erect new structures. In the outskirts of Moscow, developers are carving up former farmlands and forests for new dacha communities. Tanya's brother bought land in one of these new areas outside Moscow, as did many other friends and acquaintances.

Dacha owners generally erect the structures themselves over a period of several months to several years, depending on the availability of supplies, personal finances, local construction regulations, and free time. Formerly, buildings were usually wooden structures that were insulated with newspaper and rags stuffed between the walls and behind the wallpaper, because Soviet legislation forbade dacha owners to insulate their cottages. Restrictions that dictated size, sanitation and plumbing facilities, and heating ensured that dacha buildings remained rustic and unsuitable for year-round habitation. One woman recalled that her grandmother had once told her that the dimensions of houses in their community could not exceed four by six meters. Food preparation areas were generally confined to small alcoves in the cottages or to sheds that were located separately from the main building, while toilet facilities were provided by outhouses or visits to the woods.

Officials conducted yearly inspections, and owners paid large sums of money for permits and for taxes on the produce they grew. Tanya recalled that, every year, she and her relatives and friends hoped the inspectors would not notice alterations and clever circumventions of the laws. No one could understand the laws, she said, and in order to make the buildings habitable, everyone cheated and improvised. Tanya argued that the restrictions were the result of state leaders' fears that people would leave the cities and live in their dachas permanently. Another woman recalled that during Soviet times her father had worked in a construction company that made dacha materials. Through his job he received a garden plot, where he decided to erect a cottage. Because of the stringent nature of local building regulations, he could not install a toilet in the same building as the living quarters, nor could he construct a sturdy fence to separate his property from his neighbor's. These challenges did not prevent him from engaging in a cat-and-mouse game with the building inspector, however: he continually looked for inventive ways to circumvent the regulations, even as the inspector repeatedly pulled down the new structures.

In recent years, these restrictions and the zeal with which they are enforced have diminished, prompting many Muscovites to initiate intensive renovation projects on their cottages and gardens. A growing number of middle- and upper-class Muscovites are constructing year-round homes in newly created dacha communities. Telephone and electrical lines, satellite dishes, barbecue grills, and paved driveways characterize these areas, some of which have been transformed into gated communities. Other dacha owners are slowly adding insulation and indoor plumbing to their old cottages when they find the time and money. Building supply stores offering lumber, bricks, tubing, insulation, glass windows, expensive bath fixtures, hot water tanks, heaters, and fireplaces have sprung up along the highways leading out of Moscow. Posters advertising state-of-the-art farm implements, rodent traps, and bio-toilets cover the inside walls of Moscow subway cars and walkways. Department stores and specialty gardening shops offer imported flower and vegetable seeds and high-quality fertilizer. Despite this availability, the high cost of building materials still prevents many people like Tanya from making substantial changes to their dachas all at once.

Individual cottages typically consist of only two or three rooms (and sometimes only one): a small eating space, perhaps with a tiny hot plate; living room; sleeping alcove or bedroom. Many people, like Olga and Evgenii, collect rainwater in cisterns for bathing, hand washing, and watering their gardens. Others bathe in nearby streams. In some areas, dacha cottages are highly decorated with gaily painted outside walls and carved decorations around the doors and windows, whereas in other places, owners have eschewed adornment for simple whitewashed walls. Although garden areas are in most cases not very large, they are intensively farmed; visits to people's dachas require guided tours to see and sample the fresh produce. On one such visit, my friend Olga walked me around her neat beds of lettuce, parsley, dill, garlic, onions, potatoes, tomatoes, peppers, cucumbers, and zucchini, and then around her gooseberry and currant bushes. She finished by pointing out the young fruit trees that Evgenii had recently planted. Because the couple bought their land less than five years ago, their plot retains its open spaces. By contrast, older yards often have the feel of overgrown forests, with dense thickets of berry bushes and fruit trees crowding the pathways. Elaborate flower beds and herb gardens fill out available spaces. Dachas are organized into distinct communities with paths, roads, house numbers, and utility lines, and a typical dacha settlement might have up to eight hundred cottages.

Many communities are located near forested areas, and people spend much of their time gathering wild herbs, nettles, raspberries, wild strawberries, and mushrooms from the forests around their dachas. Buses, trains, and private taxis connect these dacha communities with nearby towns and cities.

Self-Reliance and the State

The organic system in which dachas are embedded occupies a realm that is distinct from that of the state and the formal economy. Neither is it fully controlled by the state, nor does it compete with the state. Instead it provides an alternative assemblage of assets, much like that of the informal economy, that Muscovites can exploit and piece together to supplement what they receive from the state. In a tangible sense, the organic economy offers Muscovites a means to be self-sufficient. Moreover, because local ideology holds that these resources come from nature, which does not belong to any single individual but is available to everyone, Muscovites' gardening and provisioning activities neither oppose nor subvert the state; they coexist as a parallel system.

One afternoon in July 1995, while I was visiting the dacha of the family of my landlady, Anya, she and her sister Yuliia sent Yuliia's husband, Sergei, and me on an errand to pick wild sorrel (*shchavel*) in the fields outside the dacha community. Eager to be out of the house while his wife was canning, Sergei chose an extended route through the nearby forests and fields to reach our destination. During our walk, he pointed out various edible plants, berries, and mushrooms and then led me to a field of beans that belonged to a private farm nearby. Saying that no one would miss a few beans, Sergei encouraged me to eat as many as I liked. Our impromptu snack break prompted Sergei to contemplate Russians' intimate relationship with the land. Reciting a Russian proverb, "The forest feeds us" *(Les kormit nas),* he proposed that Russians love their forests and gardens because the earth gives them food that is not only free but also healthy. In the past, when the state could not feed its citizens, he concluded, the forest could (figure 9).

This appraisal of the organic economy as a remedy to the woes of the official economy emerged in the comments of other Muscovites. On several different occasions, CCM recipients told me that natural grasses such as sorrel and stinging nettle *(krapiva)* had saved their respective families from starvation during World War II, when food supplies were in short supply. In a similar comment, Aleksei, whose aunt attends a non-CCM

FIGURE 9. Common land areas just outside this dacha community are prime spots for picking wild grasses.

soup kitchen in Moscow, stated that the special pleasure that Russians derive from their cottages and nature comes about precisely because nature has provided Russians with things that the state could not. Aleksei further remarked that he felt more intimately connected with nature than he did with bureaucratically determined structures. Gardens and cottages are personal and private, unlike buildings that are subject to official scrutiny and regulations.

The necessity of these alternative means to self-reliance points to a great irony in the Soviet system of production and supply. At the same time that state officials curtailed people's reliance on sources, such as dachas, that diverted attention from the state, Soviet citizens were nonetheless forced to mobilize resources from their gardens and forests as means to cope with state-conditioned consumer scarcities. Moreover, officials' attempts to reinforce a publicly oriented social order contrasted with individuals' efforts to engage in personal activities.

Katherine Verdery (1996) has argued that through state-oriented compulsory projects such as forced labor and directed agricultural activities, the socialist state in Romania coopted the bodily rhythms and tempos of its citizens as part of an elaborate system to sustain the state's production efforts. In the Russian version of this process of "etatization" (Verdery 1996:40), tensions between the public and the private, the state and the personal, appear clearly in the system of "voluntary" agricultural labor that characterized the Soviet period. As a technique to support the Soviet state, military personnel, workers, and students were conscripted to assist in agricultural production and other public welfare projects. In addition to Subbotniki (Saturday) service, in which students and employees spent their Saturdays engaged in so-called voluntary labor such as trash collection and tree pruning (see also Shlapentokh 1989:100–101), students spent their summer holidays engaged in collective agricultural labor. In times of need, state officials also released them from school to help with harvests. Likewise, in early fall 1998, soldiers were sent to farms to help with the harvest.

Olga and Evgenii, both professionals in their midforties, remember their service with a mixture of fondness and recollections of the physical exhaustion they endured. During their university days in the early 1970s, they and other students were assigned to various agricultural sites across the Soviet Union. Evgenii, a superb amateur photographer, pointed out pictures in his album as he recalled his experiences harvesting watermelons. He and his schoolmates traveled by bus or train to kolkhozes in the Russian countryside, where they worked all day, picking watermelons. At night they ate in the canteen and sang songs for entertainment. On weekends, students stationed at kolkhozes throughout the region traveled to a central place for dances and other social activities. It was at one of these events that Evgenii and Olga first met. Olga was part of a student group picking tomatoes on another farm. Through the student networks, they exchanged mail and packages during their courtship. Although Evgenii and Olga acknowledged that the work was difficult, they remembered their experiences more in terms of nostalgic reminiscences about the fun they shared with friends and schoolmates.

Verdery maintains that through these bureaucratic measures to appropriate personal time and energy, the socialist state consolidated its control and power over its citizens and their social relations (1996:41). I would suggest, however, that the experiences of agricultural workers such as Olga and Evgenii in fact restored the loss of control over time and the lack of agency that Verdery sees as missing in this system. Olga's and Evgenii's attentions to personal interests while officially employed in tasks for the state were not acts of resistance that challenged or subverted the power and authority of the state (cf. Scott 1985). Rather, they were individual strategies whose expression depended on the presence of the state's interests: by harnessing their own needs to those of the state, Olga and Evgenii were able to deploy their personal time and effort for two different purposes simultaneously. In this sense, their activities more closely approximate what de Certeau calls the practices of *la perruque*, in which "the worker's own work is disguised as work for the employer" (1984:25). Although the Soviet state established the parameters of people's activities, volunteers and laborers in fact seized these structures for their own use and converted them into opportunities that could be exploited for personal gain, so that official work and personal work were always performed concurrently.

This dual nature of work in the Soviet system is reflected in the benefits that Olga and Evgenii claim to have enjoyed from this forced service. Evgenii recalled that even though his agricultural service occurred during a time of severe food shortages in which urban residents were coping with empty store shelves, he and his friends had never eaten so well or with such abandon. After the good watermelons that he and his companions had picked were loaded onto trucks and taken away, the remaining melons were dumped into the backs of other trucks to be driven to nearby farms, where they would be fed to pigs and cattle. Evgenii and his friends took turns digging through the piles of rotten and smashed melons to dig out whole melons that had inadvertently ended up in the bad pile. There were so many good melons, Evgenii remembered, that he and his friends could pick and choose which ones they wanted to eat: "We would cut one open, take a bite, and if it was not tasty, throw it away and take another one." Olga, meanwhile, recalled the crates of tomatoes that she and her friends loaded into their belongings and balanced on their laps for many hours during the long train rides home from their service location. Despite official emphasis on public agriculture for collective food consumption, citizens such as Olga and Evgenii regularly reworked these activities to satisfy their own private uses. These acts were not forms of resistance to state structures but rather practices of personal survival that creatively patched together multiple sets of resources.

The countryside is a setting where time itself has become a critical commodity at the center of strategic manipulations. While state programs dictated the routines and schedules of everyday life and leisure, ordinary people found practical and symbolic ways to circumvent these regulations and to reassert their own forms of control over the most intimate aspects of their lives. Today time remains an important factor in home and workplace negotiations, and dachas and garden produce represent tangible sources and imaginative manipulations of temporal capital. Because self-provisioning efforts are so time-intensive, people must first have sufficient resources to spare the necessary time to go to the country, work their gardens, and process the produce. The following vignette illustrates the amount of time embodied in dacha life.

In 1995, my landlady, Anya, and I left Moscow to spend a week at her friend Tanya's dacha. We left the apartment at 6:30 A.M. in order to be at the train station for our 7:40 A.M. train. I later wrote in my field notes that we resembled packhorses because our backpacks were stuffed with towels, clothes, bread, eggs, meat, butter, cheese, tomatoes, and a chocolate cake. Before we had left the apartment, Anya had inspected my backpack and made me remove my extra clothes, field journal, and tape recorder so as to create extra space for the food products (I managed to retain some paper and my camera). Despite Anya's hopes, the *elektrichka* (electric suburban train) was completely packed. There was standing room only in the aisles and by the doors. After some negotiating, Anya found two seats together. The other passengers on the train also appeared to be going to the country: people carried baskets, bags, backpacks, and buckets; many were wearing work clothes and boots. Those who could not find seats—including old people, small children, and dogs—stood up, clinging to seats or doors, sometimes for several hours.

The train car was suffused with a relaxed, friendly atmosphere of genial camaraderie as strangers chatted with each other. Anya and the woman seated next to her compared notes on how well the raspberries were doing and where the best berry bushes were rumored to be located in the regions around Moscow. After a ninety-minute train ride, a twenty-minute walk, and finally a short car ride after a man kindly offered us one, we arrived at Tanya's dacha in time for a morning snack of tea and cake. By 10:45 A.M., Anya and I were in the forest, picking raspberries. The area was crowded with people, both those who were staying at their dachas and those who had come just for the day. As people met each other around the thickets, they stopped to chat and to compare buckets, picking spots, and picking strategies. Anya and I spent all day picking berries. Upon our return to the dacha in late afternoon, Tanya fixed us a quick dinner. Immediately after dinner we began processing the raspberries, first by weeding out the "bad" berries, and then mashing the good berries through a meat grinder, adding sugar, and pouring the mixture into large glass jars. We worked until midevening, when we went for a walk with Tanya, who wanted to pick mushrooms. Once back at the dacha, we continued processing raspberries and then mushrooms until after midnight. The days that followed were similar.

When we returned to Moscow at the end of the week, Anya and I were loaded with several enormous jars of raspberry preserves and bags of fresh cucumbers, tomatoes, mushrooms, and dill. The train was even more crowded than it had been on the previous Sunday, with people toting bags and bundles like ours. Back in Moscow, Anya continued her efforts, and spent twelve to fifteen hours a day turning the items we had brought back with us—as well as other fresh produce from the market—into pickles and other preserves. When she was not canning, Anya carried on long phone conversations with friends and relatives about where and how to find more jars and other supplies. Over the next several days, Anya worked late into the night, stopping only for a quick snack or to catch the news.

Similarly, over the weekend that I spent with Anya, Yuliia, and Sergei at their family dacha, most of our activities centered around food provisioning activities. While Yuliia picked fresh vegetables from her garden, Anya and I collected ripe red and black currants, gooseberries, and several other types of berries from the bushes alongside the cottage. Later we took turns mashing them through a grinder, mixing them with sugar, and spooning them into jars. Sergei rotated between making repairs to the cottage and kitchen and sealing the jars. Later, after we had returned home to Moscow, Anya showed me the jars of preserves she had already stacked up around the dresser in her bedroom. She confided that her summer goal was to line one wall of her bedroom with enough preserves to sustain her and her son through the winter. In a worst case scenario, she said, if she ran out of money to buy staples such as bread and sugar, she could sell the preserves to bring in extra cash. Similarly, my friend Olga proudly gave me a tour of her balcony and spare bedroom, showing me her jars of preserves and the burlap bags and used nylon stockings filled with potatoes, onions, and garlic that her family would use for the winter. When I visited my professor friend, Anna Nikolaevna, I found it difficult to walk around her apartment, because every bit of available floor space and counter top was piled with herbs that she was drying for the future. Many people invest in a second refrigerator or freezer for storing preserves and dried products.

For Muscovites like Anya, the long hours spent picking and processing foods represent a significant investment of both time and energy. People forfeit vacations, doctors' appointments, and even opportunities for paid work to engage in rural provisioning activities. Yet because this food is considered to be free—or at the very least incurs minor expenses for ingredients such as sugar, salt, and vinegar—the proceeds to be gained from these endeavors are worth the effort. By spending time during the summer to gather and prepare food for long-term storage, Muscovites can stock up on supplies that will help them protect their financial resources and sustain them through the long winter months or any other unexpected hardships. Thus, dacha activities are important precisely because of the material resources they provide.

Such practices also reveal the amount of time that people invest in their provisioning activities. People devote every available moment during summer and fall to store food they will use during winter months, when fruits and vegetables can be scarce and expensive, and these preserved fruits and vegetables provide tangible resources that can be mobilized as forms of security for the future. In a conversation I had with two pensioners, the two friends reflected on the importance of summer gardens. Oksana Valentinovna commented, "This year it is manageable to live on one's pension, but last year it was absolutely impossible." Her friend, Lidiia Konstantinovna, agreed and added, "There is hunger [golod] in the city! If people didn't have their little kitchen gardens [ogorodki] it would be impossible to survive. But pensioners and other people have their kitchen gardens, and they use that food to feed themselves. They can also sell the produce and flowers. Have you seen them? It is only the kitchen garden that saves them."

In a separate conversation about Russia's economic hardships and his recent pay reduction, Sasha, a CCM congregant, volunteered that he was not concerned about surviving through the winter. He said that as long as his family had their dacha, they would be fine. He continued that hunger had never been a real concern in Russia as long as Russians have had dachas and forests. To prove his point, he mentioned his wife's family in Ukraine: even though Valya's brothers and parents have not received their salaries in several years, they are not going hungry because they have a dacha and they know how to farm their garden. Any Russian or Ukrainian with access to a garden, or at least to the forest, will never be hungry; this is what foreigners do not understand about Russia, he finished. The next summer, however, several months of bad weather had taken its toll on his wife's family's garden, and Sasha remarked that his in-laws were fearful that they would not be able to salvage enough to get them through the winter.

Retired Muscovites in particular approach rural provisioning activities as time and effort well spent. Public transportation is relatively inexpensive, and pensioners generally ride for free. Enterprising individuals make day trips out of Moscow to forests or dacha communities, where they gather fresh produce. They then return to Moscow and can either keep the food for their personal use or sell it. Hopeful peddlers line city side-walks and the areas leading to marketplaces and hawk their wares: bundles of fresh flowers, herbs, and lettuce; mushrooms that are spread on pieces of plastic stretched on the ground; and berries piled in plastic buckets that the peddlers have tied around their necks. During the winter, elderly women walk through the city, holding up strings of dried mushrooms to potential buyers.

Ultimately, Muscovites can raise large sums of needed cash by selling their dachas. Galina Anatolievna, a pensioner, entertained the possibility of selling her dacha to pay the medical expenses incurred by her husband's cancer treatments. At the same time, she worried that she had forfeited her winter security by not working her dacha garden sufficiently during the summer of her husband's illness. She was distraught at the thought that she had "thrown away" (vybrosila) her dacha. Irina, meanwhile, contemplated selling the dacha she shared with her father in order to give her son a college education in America. Although neither Irina nor Galina Anatolievna particularly relished the thought of losing her dacha, each acknowledged the potential economic benefits that her cottage and garden would bring.

Muscovites who do not have direct access to the country use other strategies to enjoy the benefits of the natural economy. Many people grow herbs on their balconies or in their kitchens, and others swap services such as babysitting, needlework, or housecleaning for fresh produce. Another option is to share gardening and provisioning tasks with friends and relatives. Like many CCM recipients, Vera has severe arthritis that prevents her from venturing far beyond her neighborhood, and it has been several years since she has been able to travel to the countryside and gather her own produce. Instead, she has entered into a mutually productive partnership with relatives and friends who bring fresh fruits and vegetables for her to process into jams, pickles, cakes, or other products. After Vera keeps a small portion for herself, she redistributes the rest to the individuals who brought the raw materials.

In addition, the natural resources found in rural spaces can be cultivated within the city. In keeping with Soviet leaders' interest in providing recreation for workers, urban planners designed city spaces that include large tracts of scenic forests, fields, and rivers. Just minutes from the center of Moscow, people can visit "rest parks," where the sounds and smells of metro stations are left behind as dirt trails wind through thick forests and around marshes and rivers. During the day mothers and grandmothers wheel baby carriages through the parks; at lunchtime, workers sit on logs while eating their lunches and reading. In the evenings children, families, and older people stroll or sit in clusters and talk. Children romp in playground areas, while parents and grandparents sit and read nearby. On weekends, groups of friends gather in the brushy areas off the trails, where they roast meals over campfires, drink beer and wine, and sing. Older adults meet to play chess or to dance, and musicians perform in bandstands. One of the CCM soup kitchens is located next to such a park. This close proximity pleases recipients, who can eat their meals while looking out at the trees and then enjoy a postmeal recuperative stroll through the woods.

During spring and summer, CCM recipients and other Muscovites who cannot go to dachas or other rural spaces use these city parks as sources of food. For teenagers and young adults out with friends, wild berry bushes or abandoned fruit orchards are merely fun, temporary diversions. Anya's son Dima and two former schoolmates enjoyed visiting a neighborhood park that had once been a royal estate but was now a popular place for sunbathing and picnicking. During their strolls through the grounds, they would sneak into the abandoned cherry orchards and, with one eye open for roving policemen, climb the trees and eat their fill of warm, ripe fruit. Nearby, older adults filled buckets with cherries and other fruits. Anya frequently made pies and preserves from apples she had taken from the park and from other old orchards in the neighborhood. In the fall, the huckleberry bushes along the main walkway to the park proved irresistible for pensioners, who gathered the berries for homeopathic teas.

Like many CCM recipients, Larissa Antonovna always carries extra plastic bags in her satchel in case she finds mushrooms or herbs while on her travels through the city. Several acquaintances expressed concern over such practices, claiming that plants growing along heavily trafficked streets or near factories would have absorbed poisonous chemicals. Similarly, people who fished from city rivers were warned about the dangers of water pollution. Larissa Antonovna, however, laughed at such fears and claimed that she was careful to pick mushrooms and herbs in areas away from traffic. Whenever I saw Larissa Antonovna during the summer months, her satchel was brimming with an assortment of grasses and twigs that she had collected. In the soup kitchen, she occasionally used these items as trading currency with other recipients.

Social Resources

The organic economy offers more than material resources, however. It is also a system that is deeply embedded within and sustained by social networks and interpersonal exchanges. Friends and relatives come together in the country, both to work and to socialize. In many ways, leisure and labor, the social and the material, coexist at the dacha, as commodities and acts of assistance and exchange circulate through both extended informal social networks and ideologies of assistance and trust. At the dacha, the cooperative efforts of friends and relatives ensure the maximization of labor, harvests, and the distribution of resources. It is not uncommon for people to coordinate their vacations so that friends and relatives gather together to harvest, process, and transport the fresh produce. Tanya's brother plans his time off work in order to drive his car and help his sister transport her jars and bundles back to her apartment. Evgenii and Olga are like many Muscovites who consult almanacs to predict summer weather cycles so that they can schedule their vacations to maximize their time at the dacha. In many families, grandparents are entrusted with the task of living at the family dacha during the summer. While their adult children work in the city, older relatives water the gardens, pick ripe fruit and vegetables, begin the preserving processes, and serve as security against pillaging of the gardens. Grandparents also serve as babysitters, because many parents send their children off to the country for the summer and see them only on weekends. Among CCM staff it is common knowledge that these family obligations significantly contribute to the lower attendance rates at the soup kitchens in the summer.

Hence at the same time that dachas are important work spaces, they also facilitate social interactions between friends and relatives. Unlike in the city, where visits with friends must often be arranged in advance and accommodate such inconveniences as work schedules, transportation time, and communication difficulties, the flexibility and informality of "dacha time" encourage neighbors to drop in on each other spontaneously and walk directly through the front gate into friends' gardens or cottages. Work never ceases completely, as hosts turn excursions through their gardens into opportunities for spot weeding or nibbling. Spaces just big enough for several tea cups and a plate of cookies are cleared on tables piled high with potting soil and newspapers. Although meals are often slightly more organized affairs, with all adult members of the household sitting down together, places can always be made for the unexpected visitor. Barbecues can last well into the night as friends drop by to eat and visit. The heightened sociability at dachas means that in some sense, guests are always expected at the dacha, and people worry when they have not seen friends for several days.

Muscovites identify the countryside as the most desirable space for celebrating special events. One young couple who was married in midwinter organized the reception and dinner to take place at a vacation camp in a forest outside the city. Birthday parties, in particular, are special occasions that prompt people to invite relatives and friends to their cottages. For Tanya's sixtieth birthday, her brother and several friends made the four-hour round-trip journey to her dacha for her party. Aleksandra Petrovna always celebrates her birthday with two parties: one in her Moscow apartment for several close friends and CCM volunteers, and one for family members at her nephew's dacha several hours outside the city. The importance of the dacha as a special setting for social events was underscored by the coordination of the festivities at the dacha of Aleksandra Petrovna's nephew with her actual birthday, even though the date fell in the middle of the week, which required family members to take time off work, whereas the dinner at her apartment was arranged according to her schedule and the commitments of her guests.

Social Trust

Although dacha life occupies a "time out of time" away from the hustle and bustle of the city, it is still circumscribed by practical rules for appropriate behavior. In particular, the theme of trust that inflects Muscovites' exchange practices more generally shapes the interpersonal relations that characterize the circulation of natural produce. Dacha produce is somehow in its purest, healthiest, and least dangerous form when it is gathered personally or by a friend or neighbor and taken directly from the earth. From a practical standpoint, because items such as mushrooms grow in both poisonous and nonpoisonous varieties, one must be certain that one's hostess or exchange partner possesses the appropriate knowledge and skill to distinguish and prepare them properly.

In addition, from a nutritional perspective, Muscovites maintain that dacha produce is healthy and pure because it is packed with natural vitamins and minerals and lacks the additives and preservatives found in commercially processed foods. At the CCM soup kitchens, cafeteria workers claim that summertime meals are supplemented by fresh vegetable salads, cold vegetable soups, and fruit juices in order to enhance the overall health of recipients. Friends assured me that there was no need to wash, or even to question, dacha produce picked by relatives or friends. Olga expressed her certainty that Russian children's health improves when they can eat produce taken directly from the soil in the country. One friend acted insulted when I innocently asked if I should wash off the dirt clinging to the roots of the fresh dill she had picked from her garden. Similarly, while making preserves at Tanya's dacha, we separated the raspberries into piles of "bad" berries and piles of "good" berries. As Anya and another visiting friend instructed me, bad berries were those that had been chewed by worms (sometimes with the worms still present), draped in cobwebs, dropped in the mud, or splattered with bird droppings. We set these berries aside in a separate bowl, and I simply assumed that these berries were to be discarded. Anya then took the good berries straight from the sorting table to the meat grinder and began processing them without washing them. When I asked if I should wash the berries, she responded that water would hurt them. I was more surprised, however, to observe Anya processing the blemished berries in the same manner as the other berries—that is, without washing them and then adding sugar— and put them in a small bowl on the table. When I asked why she had processed these berries, she replied in amazement, "They are the bad berries, and so we must eat them first." (Noticing the expression on my face, she pointed out that the berry preserves I had eagerly eaten upon my arrival were made from bad berries as well.)

The emphasis that Muscovites place on safety and purity also has commercial implications. Moscow residents who do not have access to dachas, gardens, forests, or friends who can help them must resort to buying fresh produce from vendors from privatized commercial farms or from individuals who have brought in provisions from their own gardens (figure 10). Yet the commodification of these items violates the spirit of social exchange inherent in the organic economy, whereby dacha foods should be passed on to friends as gifts or bartered for services. Friends commented that they pitied both Muscovites and foreigners who had to buy natural produce in the cities. Although these individuals acknowledged that for the sellers these were necessary transactions, they suggested that dacha produce brought in from the countryside and sold in the city was inferior to produce brought directly in from the country for personal consumption and distribution to one's exchange partners. Through the processes of commodification and commercialization, organic products are removed from their symbolic and physical "state of nature" and become polluted (Douglas 1994).

In a related perspective, a common complaint among middle-class Muscovites and CCM recipients alike was that Russia's new economic elite are losing touch with an authentic Russianness because they are buying preserves instead of making them at home. Some people speculated that wealthy Muscovites who do not know how to grow their own food and prepare it have lost an essential survival skill. In a savvy ploy to counteract the "polluting" nature of market transactions, some mass-produced jars of preserves or pickles are packaged to resemble homemade

FIGURE 10. In the middle of summer, the Tver market produce section is filled with locally grown produce and food from other regions.

products, while others are linked with images of the countryside and grandmotherly figures. Nevertheless, Muscovites who privilege the social intimacy associated with dacha products find these tactics problematic. One woman claimed that the high prices attached to these products in elite grocery stores are an insult to her hard work and minimal income.

When Muscovites do resort to buying dacha and forest produce in city spaces, they are picky consumers and employ various tactics to ensure that they find the most reliable resources and vendors possible. Some people recommend asking potential sellers where the food comes from in order to make sure that it has indeed come from the countryside and not from along a road or from an urban place where there is much pollution. Fears about radioactivity are another important consideration. In recent years, Muscovites have become concerned that unscrupulous and desperate people from Ukraine and Belarus are trying to pass off produce that has come from the area affected by the Chernobyl disaster. In summer 2002, Moscow safety officials reported that during inspections of city markets, they had seized over six hundred kilograms of radioactive blueberries from Ukraine and Belarus. Television news programs featured dramatic coverage of city workers holding up portable Geiger counters next to piles of berries.[5] Uneasy consumers attempt to discern if vendors are Ukrainian or Belarussian by carefully checking their speech, facial expressions, and style of dress. Close friends advocated buying goods from elderly women, who are believed to be most truthful about where they have gotten their goods and can be trusted to have cleaned and prepared the foods properly. One CCM volunteer who had purchased fresh mushrooms at the local market asked her Russian neighbor how to prepare them properly. The neighbor first asked the foreigner the conditions under which she had made her purchase. When the woman replied that she had bought them from an elderly Russian woman, the neighbor announced that that was fine and that the mushrooms would be safe.

Another tactic falls neatly within larger and more obvious practices of discrimination against outsiders. When local newspapers warned about the dangers of eating Azeri watermelons, friends chided me for not asking about the origin of the fruit that I had bought and then hinted ominously that Azeri melons would cause great harm. That Azeris and other dark-skinned peoples from the Caucasus and Africa are regular targets of police harassment and public scorn is not coincidental but reveals how attitudes about race, ethnicity, and foreignness are refracted through multiple spheres, including food. Many produce vendors in Moscow, and particularly in my neighborhood, were Azeris; I watched on a number of occasions as Russian customers treated them less politely than they did lighter-skinned vendors. Once when I was buying pears from Raya, an Azeri woman whose family ran several fruit stands in my neighborhood and with whom I had become friendly, a policeman approached her and bluntly told her that if she did not pick up the trash around her stall, he would tear down her stand. When she replied that the trash belonged to another vendor, the policeman simply asked for a payment instead. The two argued and Raya advised him to speak to her husband, the leader of their group. The policeman left and Raya grumbled that he was always harassing her for money while ignoring the Russian women who sold produce nearby.[6]

Given the flexible ideology that in Russia everything is possible, however, even liabilities such as race, age, and nationality can be overcome when produce is at stake and savvy business practices are employed. Many vendors stay with their stalls for the duration of the summer season, or during the entire year if they work at booths in established markets, and develop a steady clientele. Vendors encourage and reward repeat customers with such tactics as friendly conversation (for instance, "I am so happy that you came back to me"), extra pieces of fruit, or especially high-quality items that they have set aside. Efforts such as these go a long way toward fostering trust and dependability in a commercial transaction.

Natural dacha foods further cement social relations by embodying and conveying sentimental meanings between givers and recipients. In a local context where meals are highly charged performances of hospitality that mark the parameters of social intimacy between actors, exchanges of fresh foods signify even closer ties between people. Within the soup kitchens, friendship groups of women transform their meals into social occasions where they can prepare and exchange jars of pickles and preserves, both among themselves and with cafeteria workers and other volunteers. Dinner guests are treated to fresh jams or pickles and are sometimes asked to sample and evaluate a hostess's unusual or novel dishes, such as pickled melon rind or sugared lemons. Bags of fresh dill or onions may be pressed into the hands of departing guests with murmured statements such as, "Please take this. I have so much already." Although Sasha and Valya are young professionals and have more financial resources than many Muscovites, during the summer and early fall, most of their produce comes from their garden. During the summer, they frequently receive packages from Valya's parents in Ukraine. Apparently concerned that their daughter and her husband were not getting enough food from their garden and likely wistful that they could not see their daughter more often and help her more directly, Valya's parents mailed boxes of produce from their own garden. Typically their boxes contained several kinds of berries, fruits, and vegetables. When I asked Valya about customs restrictions concerning fresh produce coming through the mail from another country, she laughed and told me that of course there were no problems, because this was dacha food.

In the days before I left Moscow at the end of my fieldwork in 1998, several CCM recipients and other friends gave me parting gifts of fruit preserves as culinary "souvenirs" and "memories" to remind me of Russia when I was back home in the United States. (At the end of my parents' visit, Vera made a special trip to the soup kitchen to give my mother a jar of homemade black currant jam.) My efforts to decline these gifts on the grounds that I did not have room in my luggage proved futile, and I found myself with a hefty collection of newspaper-wrapped jars inside my purse and suitcases. As I was going through airport security at the Moscow airport, my hand luggage set off the X-ray machine. A suspicious and stern Russian customs official pulled me aside and demanded to know what was in the jars in my purse. As soon as I replied, "Homemade black currant preserves from a [Russian] grandmother," his scowl turned to a broad smile and he waved me through.[7]

Gifts for the Spirit

The anecdote presented in this chapter's epigraph gives a glimpse of the power that dachas exercise in the popular imagination as places that occupy a spatiotemporal moment far removed from the everyday affairs of Russian political and urban life. The precious antidote that rural social life provides for the real shortcomings of life in the city is evidenced in city dwellers' appreciation for dachas as opportunities to recuperate in "mind, body, and soul" (Ries 1997:133, 135). Fields, forests, and gardens offer contemplative moments for Muscovites to get away literally and figuratively from the crises and uncertainties of the city and the nation at large.

The organic life is somehow healthier and less wearing on the body and the soul. Moscow residents claim that they go to the countryside for relaxation and entertainment because they feel healthier in the countryside where the air is purer. While Irina's son Ivan was studying at university in Moscow, he went home every weekend to his family's apartment in a small town surrounded by forests and rivers. He breathes easier at home among the trees, he said. Now that he is working full-time in Moscow, he makes the four-hour round-trip journey several times a week to recover from the strains of work. On my visits to his mother, Irina and I have spent much of our time together walking slowly around the town, along the river, and through the forest. Likewise, Sasha, the young man whose wife receives packages from her parents in Ukraine, compensates for hard weeks at work by driving several hours to his dacha and sleeping. Whenever I have visited friends at their dachas, all have solicitously inquired if I was tired and then invited me to take a nap. Olga explained that one gets more tired and sleeps better in the countryside because the air is so fresh and pure. "There is so much oxygen," was a common sympathetic response to my yawns and comments about how well I had slept at people's dachas.

Muscovites regularly talk about outdoor spaces as places of healthful sustenance, and many people take every available opportunity to be outside. Throughout the year, including winter, rural spaces are full of people enjoying the fresh air. It is not uncommon to walk through seemingly deserted areas in forests and parks and stumble upon people reading books, enjoying picnics, taking naps, or even singing and dancing (figure 11). In the summer, friends share advice on proper bathing attire in order to get maximum benefit from the sun and air. My attempts to apply sunscreen were often met with both laughs and incredulity at my desire not to get deeply tanned. During the 1995 cholera outbreaks around Moscow, Anya's sister and brother-in-law urged me to go swimming with them in the brisk

FIGURE 11. On a summer evening, residents of the Fili region of Moscow gather in the local park to dance and socialize.

stream nearby because it would be good for my health. When I expressed my hesitation, they quickly assured me that their stream could not possibly be infected because it was in the countryside.

In an ironic twist on these ideas of spiritual purity and pollution, Larissa Antonovna discovered that the "healthfulness" of Russian dirt and natural foods is not always recognized by outsiders. An agnostic with a "philosophical" interest in religion, Larissa Antonovna enjoys visiting different churches around Moscow. Her favorite is the Hare Krishna temple, which she visits every Sunday evening to attend events that are open to the public. In the particular incident that Larissa Antonovna described to me, she had arrived at the temple one evening after having spent all day digging mushrooms and herbs in the forest. Her clothes and shoes, although neat, were nonetheless spotted in a few places with fresh dirt, and she had soil under her fingernails. A Hare Krishna member who knew her well from previous visits took her aside and politely informed her that she must leave because she was dirty and so violated the purity of the spiritual environment. Larissa Antonovna protested that the dirt was clean because it was from the forest, but the other man insisted that she leave. When Larissa Antonovna related this story later, she added that she still did not understand why the Hare Krishna members did not recognize that dirt from the forest is not polluting.[8]

Mushroom Picking

Finally, no account of Russia's natural economy would be complete without a description of mushroom picking, probably the most evocative example of Russians' appreciation for the countryside as a place where the economic, social, and spiritual merge. Mushrooms (*griby*) occupy such an integral place in Russian social life that the progression of time is marked according to the natural rhythms of the different mushroom seasons, and social worth is measured in terms of an individual's knowledge and skills in gathering and preparing mushrooms. Anya introduced her friend Tanya by explicitly praising Tanya's knowledge of mushrooms and her ability to cook them perfectly. On our first night at her dacha, Tanya welcomed us by first leading us through the woods on a mushroom-picking excursion and then frying the mushrooms she had picked. During the meal, Anya and another visiting friend talked of nothing else except the wonderful taste of the fresh mushrooms. With Olga, another self-proclaimed mushroom expert, most conversations ultimately lead to her favorite topic: mushrooms, where to find them, how to cook them, and how many jars of pickled mushrooms she has made. Visits to Olga's apartment and dacha, like visits to many Muscovites' homes, frequently entail consultations with picture books and cookbooks about mushrooms and comparative sampling sessions.

When my parents visited Russia at the end of summer during my fieldwork, we went to visit my friend Lena, a doctor, and her husband, Anton, a traffic cop, in their home city just outside Moscow. In order to give us a taste of real Russian life, Lena and Anton organized what they deemed to be a truly Russian mushroom-picking excursion. After whizzing around mud-filled potholes in a borrowed police car, the five of us went tromping through the woods, up and down hills, waving long butcher knives and looking for perfect mushrooms. The weather was cold and wet, and our shoes quickly became soaked. Lena and Anton debated about finding the right place: at different times, each announced that we were picking in an unsatisfactory place or that there were too many people nearby and then proposed to find a new spot. We eventually made our way to a small forested area that had not yet been heavily trampled by other visitors. As we were picking our way up a steep hill, Lena casually informed us that during the Great Patriotic War (i.e., World War II), that area had been the site of intense tank warfare. When my father asked if we should worry about unexploded shells (there had recently been several stories in the news about schoolchildren in and around Moscow finding unexploded World War II–era shells in wooded areas), Lena confidently waved off his concerns and explained that this was "safe" ground.[9]

In the end, we found only a few edible mushrooms. Lena and Anton both confessed that they were not mushroom experts and so picked only the mushrooms that they knew for certain were not poisonous. As we drove back to their apartment, where Lena would cook the mushrooms for our dinner, Anton revealed that those few hours were the first time off work he had had in several weeks. In fact, while we were eating, Anton received a call from the police station, and after he hurriedly finished his meal, he dressed and left again for an emergency shift. Nonetheless, despite the disagreements, uncomfortable weather, meager yield, and limited time, Lena and Anton pronounced the event a perfect excursion, because we had been in the woods, picking mushrooms and enjoying each other's company.[10]

Nature's Bounty

In its most visible incarnation, dacha life is suffused with ideals of naturalism, spirituality, and sociability. It is about rejuvenating the spirit and the pantry as much as it is about reconnecting with friends and the earth. It is also what motivates people and keeps them going throughout the year. In the summer, Muscovites work their gardens tirelessly in order to stock up on provisions, so that during the winter the natural economy continues to sustain them as part of their everyday survival strategies. At the same time, the memories of leisurely, warm, sunny days and rambling walks with friends in the country make life more bearable in the city.

At another level, dacha life is about escapism and the relationship between citizens and the state. In the countryside, Muscovites see themselves as fully self-sufficient. They are not subjected to the political wranglings and bureaucratic hurdles that structure daily life, nor are they clients and consumers of what is offered to them—or withheld—by the state or aid agencies. In the countryside, Muscovites are free to set their own schedules and to prioritize and satisfy their own needs. Moreover, they are actively engaged in the production of material provisions and social relations. Thus, Muscovites rely on the earth to compensate for what the state cannot provide, especially in times of political and economic uncertainty.

CHAPTER 5

Strategic Intimacy

Communities of Assistance

The well-fed person does not understand the hungry person.
(Sytyi golodnogo ne razumeet.)
Russian proverb told by Nina, a fifty-five-year-old CCM member

Personal strategies of inclusion and exclusion are part of everyday life in the CCM soup kitchens. The protocol of friendships and familial ties dictates who is offered admission to the program, who sits with whom, and who gets extra servings behind the scenes. In chapter 3 I described the feud that erupted between Aleksandra Petrovna and Oksana over the ways in which informal networks were mobilized to distribute scarce resources. Although this disagreement originated in the soup kitchen, it acquired additional complexity, because it filtered through the CCM congregation and pitted congregants, recipients, and volunteers against one another. The divisiveness of this conflict brought to light fissures and competing interests within the seemingly united community that gathered around a set of shared religious experiences and a common commitment to providing food aid.

At the heart of many disputes over religious affiliation, nationality, ethnicity, race, and age in Moscow are concerns about the connections that exist between social identities and the allocation of resources. Potential aid recipients voice their fears that outsiders are unfairly taking resources that belong to group members. In the case of the feud between Aleksandra Petrovna and Oksana, the issue of religious affiliation became especially acute. Oksana, who was officially a member of the CCM community, questioned the right of Aleksandra Petrovna, who belonged to another church but frequently attended CCM services and other events, to influence decisions about the distribution of food aid in the CCM soup kitchens. By no means are such concerns over the demarcation of insiders and outsiders unique to this congregation. Elsewhere in Moscow local churches have closed their doors to needy petitioners and demanded proof of affiliation from their own members. At the national level, popular conspiracy theories in Moscow hold Jews, refugees, and other minorities responsible for single-handedly ruining the Russian economy by channeling funds to foreign accounts and draining the state's resources through demands for material assistance. "Blacks," an expansive category that includes Africans, Roma, and Central Asians, are commonly represented as lazy, nonworking, irresponsible outsiders who are burdening Russia's welfare system with demands for public assistance. A political opinion that I encountered among pensioners and other people receiving small amounts of federal assistance was that the Russian government should grant independence to Chechnya so that Russians would no longer have to support the Chechens.

This chapter focuses on the problematics of ascriptive identity by investigating how Muscovites' memberships in social groups are constituted through a complex tangle of bureaucratic taxonomies and personal relationships. I question the extent to which Muscovites feel personally invested in these identities and explore the ways in which individuals balance imagined communities that coalesce around shared sentiments and experiences against more utilitarian relationships. CCM participants play with the reductive logic of identities as strategies for associating themselves within assistance programs and for excluding the access of others to these programs, so that membership within social groups offers a valuable social currency that can be exploited for material gain.

Positioning Identity

Although identity politics may be about disputes over the ownership of tradition, the past, culture, or territory, they are at heart negotiations over how to create order out of perceived similarities and differences. As E. E. Evans-Pritchard (1940), Fredrik Barth (1969), and Anya Royce (1982), among many others, have pointed out, the aims of identity processes are to erect and maintain stable boundaries between groups. Identities are then reified and bolstered by the allocation or appropriation of

a unique combination of cultural traits, practices, and beliefs to each social group (Bourdieu 1984; Douglas 1990; Douglas and Isherwood 1979;
Dumont 1970; Gellner 1983). This essentialist project of "culturalism,"
what Arjun Appadurai describes as "the conscious mobilization of cultural differences" (1996:15), characterizes much of the earlier cultural
studies work that has looked at Russian and Soviet identities. Paradigms
of "possession" (Beissinger 2001) and "innatism" (Herzfeld 1992) have
distinguished Russian and Soviet citizens along axes of high culture versus popular culture, aesthetic appreciation versus base materialism, rural
versus urban, and powerful versus powerless, among others (Lotman
1994; Stites 1992). In particular, the "elites" in Russia have long been portrayed as having exclusive ownership of culture and cultural knowledge
(Barker 1999a).

Michael Herzfeld warns, however, that stereotyped representations
depicting characters as "fixed, simple, and unambiguous" deflect attention from the very complexities, contradictions, and particularities that
in fact exist behind them (1992:73). Claims made on the symbolic reper-
toires associated with identity taxonomies are always partial, because actors do not necessarily mobilize all the resources that are available to
them at any one time. Instead, claims are based on strategic choices of
which symbols to invoke, in which combination, and at what moment
(Handler 1988). There are often significant discrepancies between ideology and practice when identities are at stake (Hayden 1996). The significance of theories of essentialism, then, is not whether essentialized traits
are in fact real or even accurate, particularly because their inventedness
becomes ever more apparent during moments of upheaval, but rather
that essentialized traits are the vehicles through which individuals position themselves within society. As I will describe in this chapter, Muscovites carefully reduce themselves and each other to idealized character
types in order to deal with bureaucratic structures and interpersonal relations alike. The realities of everyday life in Moscow are always experienced and understood through the shifting parameters of performed
identity.

The common thread that links the perspectives on identity proposed
by Herzfeld, Handler, Hayden, and Giddens, among others, is the suggestion that identity construction is an intentionally "reflexive project"
(Giddens 1991:32) to carve up the social world into spheres corresponding to Self and Other, Us and Them. An understanding of identities
as strategic and poetic claims for specific purposes and in front of specific audiences (Aretxaga 1997) focuses attention on the ways in which

agents evaluate the potentiality of similarities and differences, maneuver among them, and negotiate their content and meaning through everyday interactions and activities. Although classifications may be mapped discursively and practically on individuals, they do not replace these persons. Rather, identities, as tactics of making do, are ever-changing roles through which social actors apprehend the world around them.

More important, however, is that identity practices are always social processes. At the same time that acts of "strategic essentialism" assign "Others" to "culturally coded roles or identities" (Herzfeld 1997:26), they are also the media through which members of social groups recognize one another and acknowledge one another's familiarity. Stereotypes are not simply labels that are applied as heuristic devices to understand and manage others; they are also codes that agents appropriate to explain and define themselves and their place in the world. Thus essentialisms are themselves personal tactics that both establish and maintain distances between the Self and the Other, Us and Them, insider and outsider; as such, they solidify a unique social group around a "cultural intimacy" that is based on the "assurance of 'common sociality' " (Herzfeld 1997:3). The social solidarity that emerges through practices of stereotyping the Self and the Other is what I have termed strategic intimacy.

The Bureaucratization of Russian Identities

Although the Soviet project of social engineering was ostensibly a reaction to the class structures of the Imperial period, the successes of the Soviet state relied in large part on a similarly rigid vision of social ordering. Work-based divisions replaced aristocratic hierarchies, while gender and ethnic differences were emancipated by a generic citizenship. According to these distinctions, citizens were given roles to play and rules to follow in order to maintain the mechanical solidarity of the Soviet state. It was in this new system that the new Soviet citizen was to live and make productive contributions to society. Moreover, Soviet citizens depended on this system for their everyday survival, because the allocation of goods, services, jobs, education, vacations, health care, and all other forms of public welfare was tied to this bureaucratic taxonomy.[1] Individuals whose identities did not fit into the state's identity system were not only outside the official channels through which the means of everyday life were dispensed but also outside the social order that was normalized through the state's possession of its citizens through categories (Humphrey 1996/97).

Despite the carefully constructed routinization of this system, Soviet identity politics were based as much on perceived innate qualities as they were on social constructions. Citizens were assigned a set of identities according to their occupational and military experiences, family relationships, biology, and physiology. Each characteristic was then ranked within the hierarchy of privileges and benefits through which resources were allocated. For instance, former military personnel were given status as "veterans," but those who fought in World War II were given the greatest preference as veterans. Survivors of the Leningrad Blockade were placed even higher than veterans in the hierarchy. Motherhood offered a separate category (cf. Haney 1999), and the greatest motherhood status was given to women who had given birth to multiple children. Orphaned children received another classification and system of benefits. Physical, mental, and emotional disabilities were recognized by yet another set of classes for "invalids," while individuals who suffered disabilities due to wartime service or other catastrophic events were further marked by such designations as "veteran invalid" or "Chernobyl invalid." For the analogous system of Ukrainian benefits, Adriana Petryna (2002) has created the term *biological citizenship* for these designations that are based on physiology.

These practices have continued into the present post-Soviet period. As late as 1995 in Moscow, many shops, banks, post offices, ticket offices, or any other place queues might be expected to form, displayed posters announcing that veterans of the Great Patriotic War and veterans of labor, as well as members of several other privileged groups, were entitled to move directly to the front of queues and be served first. By 1997, I saw such signs only rarely, and primarily in small towns outside Moscow. Buses and subway cars, however, continue to have benches and standing areas that are designated specifically for elderly people, invalids, and mothers with small children. It is still a common practice for younger people, men in particular, to give up their seats voluntarily to elderly people, although it is also not unknown for an elderly person to demand a seat from a younger person.

Nationality poses a special problem within this classification scheme. Although people living in the Soviet Union were nominally Soviet citizens, all persons were further identified according to their *natsional'nost'*, which was calculated primarily by genealogy and "blood" *(krov')* and listed in their domestic passports. Ethnographers contributed to this enterprise of constructing identities by assisting state authorities with census questions and ordering the numerous possible identities in a finite list of nationalities (Hirsch 1997). On the one hand, these ascriptive nationalities were intended to galvanize minority groups and to celebrate the diversity within the Soviet population by recognizing the unique contributions and cultures of members of these groups and by ensuring that they were given equitable access to resources. On the other hand, the reification of perceived differences facilitated repressive practices such as quota systems in universities and workplaces, police harassment, and deportation (Simonsen 1999).

This insistence on innate characteristics features in both popular and academic discourses about social difference (e.g., Bromley 1974), for Muscovites talk about identities and the differences among identities in terms of blood-based, inherited traits. In one conversation, Anya, my former landlady, argued passionately that social conditioning was one of the great myths of socialism and that inner qualities were the real determinants. Jews are particularly vulnerable to these essentialisms, because most bear the official category *"evrei"* (Jew) in their passports, even if they have never practiced Judaism.[2] Although my friend Vera from the soup kitchen has lived in Moscow her entire life, her official nationality is listed as evrei. She reflected that her in-laws had never considered her to be a true Russian and that they had made it clear that her husband had married beneath himself because she was Jewish. This correlation of blood and identity is so strong that public officials have lost political and personal credibility and authority simply by having a family name that might be interpreted as being Jewish. In other instances, ordinary "Russian" citizens risk being stopped by the police or suffering physical harm for having skin, hair, or facial features that do not precisely match a stereotyped list of "Russian" phenotypes. Typically these typologies privilege those with fair-skinned complexions. Once while riding an intercity train, I witnessed a fight between two young men that began when one pointed to the other's face, commented on the latter's darker pigmentation, and called him *chërnyi* (black). Even as the second young man tried to protest that he was Russian and to show his passport as proof, the first young man pummeled him while repeatedly calling him black.[3]

Meanwhile, friends frequently bragged that they could identify Americans simply by looking at a person's eyes or mouth and insisted that bodily practices such as smiling and a steady, directed gaze (typically seen as markers of Americanness) are not culturally shaped bodily practices but rather reflections of internal qualities. Even personal tastes were seen as evidence of natural dispositions. When I asked people about their personal food practices, those who professed to prefer "Russian" foods commonly explained that there was something about the taste of Russian food that appealed to them.[4]

This classificatory system derived its authority not from any quantitatively provable "facts" but rather from the version of reality that it created and perpetrated over time.[5] Edward Said's remarks on the analogous process of reification in the ideology of Orientalism are appropriate for this case as well: "If we agree that all things in history, like history itself, are made by men, then we will appreciate how possible it is for many objects or places or times to be assigned roles and given meanings that acquire objective reality only *after* the assignments are made" (1978:54, emphasis in the original). This comment points to the arbitrary and artificial nature of categories, like those of the Russian identity system, that are crafted as natural and rational.

Nevertheless, in the Russian case these techniques of bureaucratic Othering have succeeded, because the individuals who are constituted through them are themselves complicit and active participants in the system. Moreover, they have often gone to great lengths to essentialize themselves by strategically manipulating both the interpellative labels and the accepted rules for negotiating bureaucratic structures. Individuals who wish to have their identity status and benefit levels amended in order to receive greater levels of assistance must apply and supply the appropriate supporting documents to verify work history and military service. Supporting evidence for claims to self-ascription can be further traced on the physical bodies of applicants. Within the CCM soup kitchens, recipients openly advertise their status as veterans or invalids by displaying their physical disabilities. Georgii Mikhailovich's wife tells soup kitchen volunteers about her husband's wartime heroism in reference to his partial blindness and deafness from artillery fire, while Galina Vassilievna shows off her stiff fingers as reminders of the severe cold she suffered during the Leningrad Blockade. Boris tells everyone about his heart attack several years ago as a prelude to a fuller elaboration of his military service. Meanwhile, Aleksandra Petrovna complains that her severe wartime injuries do not qualify her for additional status as a war invalid because she was not yet eighteen when she was injured. For many people, physical infirmities are as much a source of pride for the experience behind the disability, such as for war veterans, as they are a validation of the category of disability and benefit to which the bearer is entitled. CCM recipients who hope to increase the number of meals they receive try to use physical ailments, both permanent and temporary (such as a cold), as leverage in their negotiations with church staff. During the registration period for the fourth soup kitchen, would-be applicants lined up in front of the director and lifted articles of clothing for him to inspect their scars and wounds.

Self-Identification and the Burden of Proof for Social Participation

Among the various techniques through which the politics of identity are waged, written documentation has been one of the most powerful avenues for producing the version of reality in which those politics are themselves generated and legitimated (Hayden 1996; Humphrey 1996/97). The use of written documentation also represents a form of social administration in which, once identities and social groups have been assigned, the burden to prove the rightful ownership of a classification falls on each individual citizen, not the state. Consequently, the ordinary people whose lives are recorded in the pages of files or passports actively participate in their own surveillance and management by carrying their documents with them or by making the proper documentation available upon demand by authorities. To counter the potential consequences of being caught without the means to substantiate one's identity, Muscovites create elaborate strategies to get around the system.

Like other Russians, CCM recipients generally carry their domestic passports with them at all times. These documents, which were instituted during the Soviet period, verify the bearer's name, age, and citizenship, as well as nationality, benefit status, and housing registration. They are a potent form of social control, because one's identity and existence can be verified only through these documents, which must be presented upon demand to policemen and other officials, including welfare officials and aid workers. CCM staff expect recipients to present their passports during the yearly registration period or whenever questions arise over a person's eligibility status. A conversation between two CCM recipients over a change in the soup kitchen protocol attested to the importance—and long history—of passports in Russian social life. In spring 1998, the directors of two different cafeterias stopped offering spoons for the recipients to use because in the months leading up to the change, spoons had been disappearing at an alarming rate. (Cafeteria employees blamed recipients for taking them home, while recipients blamed cafeteria employees for stealing them and reselling them.) From that point on, recipients were expected to bring their own spoons from home if they wanted to eat in the cafeterias. Invariably every day several people would forget their spoons and would desperately beg volunteers to sneak a spoon for them from the dishwasher's room in back. The two recipients whose conversation I overheard were complaining about this new practice and comparing it to events during World War II, when one could gain admission to a soup kitchen only if one presented "a passport and spoon" *(pasport i lozhka)*.[6]

CCM soup kitchen regulations further resemble those used by Russian institutions and other aid programs in Moscow in their requirement that potential recipients present proof of residence in the region served by the program in order to be admitted. A *propiska*, or residence permit, is a stamp in an individual's passport that marks both that person's legal domicile in Russia and the right of that person to reside there. Although officially Russians may now move freely throughout the country, in Moscow and elsewhere they must still provide residence permits to obtain jobs, apartments, or other social services. Announcements about distributions of food or other commodities are frequently qualified with a notation specifying that the opportunities are exclusively for Moscow residents.

Yet simply possessing a legal propiska is not necessarily enough to guarantee one access to public assistance. For many programs, such as the CCM soup kitchens, the address listed in a person's propiska must correspond to a particular region of Moscow, usually the immediate neighborhood in which the program is located. On one occasion when I was dispensing meal tickets at one of the soup kitchens, an elderly woman approached me and asked which documents she needed to present in order to receive a meal. I presumed that she had been contacted by her social worker about an opening on the roster, and I informed her that she needed to show her propiska and certification from the social services agency to the coordinator in charge. The woman went to the coordinator and presented her documents, but her request was refused because she had a propiska for a different region.

Propiski became a central issue during the initial enrollment period when the fourth CCM soup kitchen first opened. The coordinators issued attendance permits only to those persons whose names were on the list created by the social services office and whose addresses, as recorded in their residence permits, corresponded to a narrowly defined geographic territory. Despite the efforts of the social workers and CCM staff to publicize and enforce these stringent parameters, the procedural process erupted into heated arguments, insults directed at the coordinators and volunteers, and creative attempts to manipulate the system. Ineligible applicants endeavored to convince the coordinators that they lived in the appropriate region by advising that the street boundaries used by the CCM were inaccurate or by arguing that the information recorded in their residence permits was incorrect. Others tried themselves to alter the data listed in their passports or claimed that they had left their documents at home but would bring them the next day after they had been issued an attendance pass. When Dr. Steve told one woman to present her passport, she refused. When he asked her to provide her telephone number instead, she jabbed her finger at the roster in his hands and brusquely said that the number was "what is written there." Dr. Steve denied her request and later confided that he suspected the cafeteria director had told the woman, most likely one of her workers, to try to get on the list in order to receive free meals. I will discuss this registration period more fully later in this chapter.

In contrast to the bureaucratic insistence on residence, however, propiska regulations are ambiguous (see also Morton 1980:237) and depend largely on local practices, especially the vigilance of the local police department. Previously, nonresidents were required to register their movements with the local police; unlawful outsiders could be fined, jailed, and sent away. The extent to which this is enforced varies tremendously, as do the official regulations concerning this issue. The issue is further clouded by the greater ease with which people can travel around Russia and the growing number of people who rent apartments from private owners. Many people do not know whether they are supposed to register themselves when they rent an apartment or to report visiting friends and guests. In summer 1999, Marina Alekseevna, the woman from whom I rented a room, asked me on my first day if I needed to pay a visit to the detective station on the first floor of her building. (I explained that my documents were already registered with the Foreign Ministry.) Another landlady requested that I use another address if I had to register my documents. In some neighborhoods, policemen routinely visit apartments and demand that the inhabitants present their documents for inspection. If people cannot provide proof of residence, the police can levy fines on the spot or drag people down to the local precinct for questioning. Enforcement also correlates with the extent to which bribery is condoned in a particular region. Friends who did not possess propiski for their apartments reported being harassed by policemen, who periodically dropped by to demand a bribe for not taking them down to the police station and starting legal proceedings against them.

The topic of the propiska arose in a number of conversations with friends both in Moscow and elsewhere in Russia. These individuals come from a variety of economic, social, and geographic backgrounds, but they have had similar experiences with the hassles of trying to get a propiska and of trying to get by without one. Sveta's story is representative of these experiences. Fifteen years ago, Sveta came to Moscow as a university student from her home in a region that had originally belonged to Ukraine before the creation of the Soviet Union. After the dissolution of the Soviet Union, the region was legally incorporated by Russia but symbolically "given back" to Ukraine. Although Sveta considers herself to be Russian and classifies herself as such, when she went to exchange her Soviet documents for Russian ones, she was told that she first needed to get Ukrainian papers. She does not have the money to pay for train tickets to Ukraine or even for the necessary exit visa to leave Russia. Moreover, in an ironic display of the contradictions inherent in many Russian legal procedures, Sveta can receive an exit visa only after she presents her legal Ukrainian papers to the Foreign Ministry. Even if Sveta were able to find both the financial resources and the know-how to circumvent this paradoxical system, go to Ukraine, and receive the proper documents, there is no guarantee that she would easily get back into Russia. Because she is currently not legally registered, she fears the regular visits from local policemen who extort money from her. Both her landlord and her employer have used her "illegal" status as leverage when negotiating rent and wages. In summer 1998, in order to cut expenses, Sveta's boss presented her and several similarly unregistered workers with the option of either working for reduced and delayed pay or quitting. Sveta took the first option and now worries about feeding herself and her beloved cat.

Because the bureaucratic channels are closed to Sveta, she has resorted to more extreme measures in order to get a propiska. Before her wages were cut, she was optimistic that she could save enough money to buy a small one-room apartment in the outskirts of Moscow. Legal ownership of an apartment entitles one to a residence permit. Now, she despairs that that goal is completely out of her reach, particularly because none of her friends are able to loan her the ten thousand dollars that she says she needs for such a purchase. Most recently she has investigated the possibility of arranging a fictional marriage *(fiktivnyi brak)* in order to get registered through her husband's apartment. Although friends have located several potentially willing men, none of the leads have panned out. Sveta reported that she did not feel comfortable with the physical advances made by one man, and the others demanded more money than she could afford for the arrangement.

Masha, a friend of several CCM volunteers, is in a similar predicament. After she graduated from university, she elected to remain in Moscow to work, although her parents live in Belarus. She has had to pay bribes to continue her status as a "student," which carries some weight as a category with privileges, notably reduced prices for transportation and admission to museums, and to be registered to live with relatives who are Moscow residents. Because she has her own apartment, however, she has experienced many problems with members of the local police who stop by periodically and ask for money in exchange for not reporting her.

Even though Sveta, Masha, and other Muscovites in similar circumstances face financial constraints that are even more extreme than those of some CCM recipients, they are ineligible for public assistance because they cannot prove they are legal residents. There are many people who are similarly shut out of programs and opportunities because the realities of their circumstances conflict with the official identity categories that are used to calculate need. People like Sveta are fortunate, however, in that they have a place to live, belong to work groups, and can count on friends and relatives who can offer assistance, either by sharing their personal reserves or by diverting the resources they receive through their networks.

Other Moscow residents, however, lack even these most basic forms of social security and are so marginalized that they are not officially counted, registered, or even acknowledged in most demographic figures. One such group is the homeless population in Moscow, the *bezdomnyi* (without a residence), or more pejoratively *bomzh*.[7] Although the CCM program and most other assistance organizations in Moscow serve only people with propiski, at least three charitable programs offer their services to homeless and other unregistered, destitute people in Moscow: the Center for Humanitarian Aid (CHA), the Salvation Army, and at least one Orthodox church.[8] In addition to homeless persons, recipients at these programs include people who have recently been released from prisons or hospitals and cannot find work or a place to live; individuals and families who have lost their homes or have come to Moscow and been stranded; and foreigners who find themselves alone in the city.

Potential recipients at these programs are not required to present any documents or registration materials certifying their need or establishing their identity. People identify themselves as members of the community simply by showing up and helping out. Moreover, in contrast to the distinctions between volunteers and recipients at the CCM soup kitchens, which are made visible through the structured rules and practices governing the roles and responsibilities of each group, the distinctions for those affiliated with the CHA are more ambiguous, for people move between roles as volunteers and recipients. Not only do CHA volunteers include many more Russians than are in the CCM program, but also many long-term CHA recipients offer assistance by handing out food and plates, monitoring the serving line, making sure that children get second helpings before adults, cleaning up, and policing the general area around the agency's office and serving area.

Despite the status of these people as outside the extensive networks and institutionalized structures of society, CHA recipients have formed their own community. Recipients learn of the program through word-of-mouth and other channels for homeless persons, such as a newspaper that homeless people sell to earn extra money. People help each other reach the soup kitchen, sit together to eat and talk, and share their food with one another. Thus, in contrast to food programs like that of the CCM, in which recipients' membership is shaped by their claims to officially defined identities, the solidarity and community that characterize the CHA population spontaneously develop around an absence of institutionalized identities.

The Routinization of Public Assistance

On paper and in practice, CCM regulations allow the selective distribution of meals and other forms of assistance by differentiating among participants according to institutional categories. When CCM staff established procedures for the soup kitchens, they replicated the social services model used by Russian welfare agencies, so that the allocation of resources was determined according to the identity classes and benefits established by federal authorities. Priority for enrollment in the CCM program is given first to pensioners who receive the smallest pensions, with an internal ranking of those who are eligible according to their status as veterans of the Great Patriotic War (World War II), veterans of labor, heroes of various classes, invalids of first and second class, and mothers with many children. The number of daily meals that are assigned to each recipient further depends on each person's specific financial circumstances.

Most recipients are entitled to only one meal per day, although a few are given two because their monthly retirement incomes place them at the lowest end of the pension scale. In a few cases, long-time recipients who also support needy but otherwise ineligible relatives at home are given additional meals to sustain the entire family. This predictable system for dispensing benefits gets complicated when supplemental foodstuffs are donated to the CCM program. In some cases, donors give exactly one item per each recipient. In others, donors give according to the numbers of meals that are served, which includes the extra meals that some clients receive. In cases where there are enough products for only one per person, recipients who are eligible for more than one meal demand that they receive the appropriate number of gifts. Hurt feelings and angry words have been known to result from these tensions.

Recipients' identities are further reduced to material representations through the use of passes (*propuski*) with a personal registration number. Access to most businesses, libraries, universities, dormitories, and other public and private buildings in Moscow is gained only through a *propusk* that identifies the bearer as a worker or authorized visitor. Like their counterparts at other food aid programs (except those that serve unregistered persons, like the CHA), Muscovites who eat at the CCM soup kitchens present their propuski in order to receive their meal tickets. At the check-in desk, coordinators mark off the registration numbers on a weekly attendance sheet and then give recipients the appropriate number of meal tickets, which recipients then exchange for their meals. CCM staff also use the weekly attendance lists as a form of social surveillance by keeping tabs on which recipients are eating regularly. This process ensures that attendance passes not only indicate the identities of recipients as members of the community, but also in a very tangible sense become the physical representations of their identities. It is rare for volunteers or church staff to know the names of the recipients. Even though soup kitchen coordinators have, on average, worked closely with recipients for several years and know intimate family details about many of them, most recipients are known to them only by their card numbers and not by name. Several coordinators can dispense tickets and check off most recipients' numbers without ever looking at attendance cards. More than once I asked a coordinator about a specific person, only to have the coordinator ask me to provide the person's card number or a description of the person and not the name. Through this system the identities of individual recipients are collectively compacted to numbers and pieces of paper.

Although these passes are no more than photocopied squares of colored paper printed with the CCM logo and the bearer's identification number, they are nonetheless treated as precious commodities by recipients, who go to great lengths to safeguard them. Most people have laminated their cards or fashioned some kind of plastic sleeve in which to keep them dry and uncreased. Some people insert them into the second flap in their official passport holders or hide them in "secret" pockets created inside wallets. One woman carefully tucks hers into a novel. The loss or theft of a propusk is cause for anxiety and fear among recipients. People who misplace their cards but do not remember their identification numbers risk forfeiting meals until CCM staff can verify their eligibility through the official membership list. Soup kitchen supervisors have sent recipients home to locate their cards or directed them to telephones to contact relatives who can go to their apartments and look for the missing cards. On one occasion a middle-aged woman who was not a recipient came to get food for several relatives who could not leave their apartments. The relatives had not given the woman their passes or their numbers, only their names. The coordinator would not accept the names as evidence and ordered the woman to get either the cards or the numbers. The woman spent at least one hour on the telephone, trying to reach the recipients. Even as time was running out, the coordinator refused to release food without the numbers. Finally the woman succeeded in getting the numbers and came back to the soup kitchen with only minutes to spare before the soup kitchen closed.

People who abuse the system risk more severe penalties than those experienced by people who merely try to circumvent it, such as being banished from the program for a period of time or losing their eligibility altogether. There have been occasions in the past when recipients claimed they have lost their cards but have in fact given their passes to friends not affiliated with the program, thereby trying to fool the CCM system. One man ripped his card in two, gave half to a friend, and then claimed that he had been accosted by a local hoodlum who had stolen half of his card. Soup kitchen supervisors try to deal with both honest losses and unscrupulous tactics fairly and are slow to remove recipients from the program without cause and due process. One supervisor generously remarked that he felt he had to be tolerant and understanding with recipients, because most were elderly and likely to be more absent-minded, forgetful, or even desperate than younger people.

The connection between attendance pass and identity is a tenuous one. Even as bureaucratic procedures and regulations reduce people to the material statistics represented by their attendance and residence permits, thereby delineating them as people outside a larger social group of secure

Muscovites, cards such as those carried by CCM recipients simultane-ously verify these individuals' status as members of a distinct group within the aid community. Moreover, as tangible and official documents that prove recipients' identities and their legitimate claims to these iden-tities, these cards become tangible resources that recipients manipulate in their efforts to position themselves even more advantageously within the assistance game.

Ours, Not Ours, and Tactical Communities

In his *Konstanty: Slovar' Russkoi Kul'tury* (Constants: Dictionary of Rus-sian Culture), Stepanov questions what it is that makes cultures and peo-ples distinct from each other. He writes that the Russian ideological con-cepts *"svoi"* (one's own) and *"chuzhoi"* (other's; also, foreign) are the very "oppositions where are created not only objective data, but also their sub-jective expression in consciousness" (1997:472; cf. Okely 1996). More commonly encountered in everyday discourse in Moscow, however, are the classifiers *nash* (ours) and *ne nash* (not ours), which may be applied to everything from claims about nationality and kinship to consumer goods, politics, advertisements by the federal tax authorities, and cloth-ing styles (Caldwell 2002; Humphrey 1995). In its practical realization, the nash / ne nash distinction is embedded within the logic of instru-mental sociality. Muscovites see it as a malleable discursive strategy for identifying and embracing those individuals who are not only similar to themselves but also, and perhaps more important, potentially useful. As was explained to me on several occasions, it is to "nash" individuals that one offers assistance or emotional sympathy. Likewise, "nash" individu-als or commodities are more trustworthy and reliable than those who are unfamiliar or are somehow seen as being foreign (Caldwell 2002). The flexibility of the "nash" distinction disengages it from specific communi-ties based on such features as nationality, race, religion, and gender, and endows it with a capability to be both expansive and constrictive.

Within the CCM community, the nash / ne nash distinction plays out regularly in the ways that recipients, volunteers, and aid workers under-stand and articulate their relationships with each other. Individuals who are not part of the CCM program but attempt to bluff their way through the system are informed by both staff and other recipients that they are *"ne nashi"* and thus ineligible to eat. When clients from another feeding program, which met several hours after the CCM program, mistakenly showed up during the CCM's serving time and insisted that they were in the right location at the right time (even as they presented passes that were clearly for a different system), Dr. Steve tried to sort out their confusions and direct them to their own program. When all of his explanations failed, he resorted to the simple statement, "Our time *[nashe vremia]* is now; your time *[vashe vremia]* is later." During the registration period at the fourth CCM soup kitchen, Svetlana Grigorievna and Aleksandra Petrovna told applicants whose names were not on the list that they should leave because they were "ne nashi." Later, in her speech at the festivities to celebrate the grand opening of the fourth soup kitchen, Svetlana Grigorievna advised the recipients to be grateful for the CCM's efforts to help "our people" *(nashi liudi)*.

The expansive and socially responsible aspect of nash may under certain conditions extend to strangers with whom one shares a similar background or experience, such as the interactions between Muscovite pensioners and Siberian miners that took place during the summer months of 1998. A group of miners from Siberia had traveled to Moscow and set up a tent village outside the Russian White House to protest the fact that they had not received their wages for many months and that their families were suffering from shortages of food and other supplies. For the duration of the miners' stay, Muscovite supporters of the Communist Party and elderly pensioners with very limited personal means took it upon themselves to bring the protestors hot meals and other food supplies as powerful empathetic gestures to a shared experience.

At first glance, these instances of social communities that are founded on both shared practices and a shared acknowledgment of those practices resemble Gellner's description of the bonds that unite conationals: "It is their recognition of each other as fellows of this kind which turns them into a nation" (1983:7). Gellner's emphasis, however, points to a nation-oriented social cohesion that is missing in the transnational nash interactions that take place within the CCM soup kitchens. Specifically, according to the logic of nash, concerns with race and nationality are supplanted by emphases on reciprocal assistance and trust. When the CCM program first opened, interactions between Russian recipients and African volunteers were strained. Dr. Steve and other volunteers recall that many recipients refused to accept food that was served by Africans. Similarly, some African volunteers refused to serve Russian recipients. After the CCM minister at the time informed recipients and volunteers that their only alternative was to leave the program, relations improved between the two groups. Over time, the economic and personal relationships that developed among participants have contributed to the formation of a distinct social group whose members engage in similar pursuits, look out for each other, and identify themselves as belonging to a shared community with shared interests. The city politician whose jurisdiction includes three of the CCM's soup kitchens has in the past offered legal assistance and sponsorship to CCM coordinators and long-time volunteers. When Muscovites who are not part of the CCM network have directed racial slurs and violent behaviors at African volunteers, recipients have stepped forward and defended the volunteers.

The power of nash as a pragmatic strategy for recognizing and maintaining social intimacy is that it offers a flexible medium for dealing with the messiness of interpersonal relations. Differences such as race, age, gender, class, ethnicity, and nationality that might otherwise operate as impermeable boundaries are deemphasized within the logic of a nash system that privileges sentimental familiarity, social connections, and economic trust. The strategic flexibility of the nash community is most evident when it expands to include outsiders who might otherwise not include themselves as members of the group. This was evident when a tragedy struck the soup kitchen community in fall 1998. Antonio, a coordinator who was popular among recipients for his warm, gentle personality, fell ill. Days later he was hospitalized with acute stomach cancer, and within the month he died. CCM recipients and congregants grieved that they had not had time to say good-bye. The ministers organized a joint memorial service for recipients and congregants that was held in the soup kitchen. From all accounts the event was extremely well attended. Several years later, recipients still talked fondly about Antonio and recalled the service. The memorial was even more significant because the embassy for Antonio's home country had refused to transport his body back home for burial, and he was buried instead in Moscow. The outpouring of support from the soup kitchen community demonstrated that although Antonio was far from home, he was not without a supportive community in his adopted country. Moreover, for the people who attended the service, it was an important reminder that they too belonged to a larger community through the soup kitchen.

Contingent Spirituality

Religious affiliation offers another set of resources that Muscovites can exploit for personal ends. Throughout Moscow, churches and synagogues have become volatile settings where Muscovites symbolically—and physically—wrangle over identity categories, the appropriate social behaviors assigned to those identities, and even the amount of aid that should be correlated to those identities. Such conflicts are apparent not only when Jewish cemeteries and synagogues are vandalized, but also when officials with the Russian Orthodox Church try to convince Russian authorities to regulate and restrict activities of foreign religious congregations in order to preserve an ordered and unpolluted version of Russianness. In one revealing set of events, leaders of an Orthodox church that was located next door to a charitable organization that provided food and medical assistance to homeless persons in Moscow locked the church's doors and requested that the charity keep its clients away from the church and congregants. Even within religious communities, preceived differences among worshipers can turn into physical violence (Goluboff 2001).

Many CCM worshipers acknowledge that they attend church services and participate in church activities not simply for spiritual reasons but also to feel that they belong to a community and have friends. Some members travel several hours from cities outside Moscow just to attend Sunday-morning church services. Several North American families periodically make the eight-hour airplane ride from Russia's east coast to Moscow's CCM services. For many CCM congregants, however, these social connections are not their sole inspiration for active participation. Membership in the CCM community also provides access to food, clothing, jobs, and legal and diplomatic assistance. High-ranking diplomats at several foreign consulates attend CCM services and have quietly assisted members of their respective countries with problems concerning visas, student rights, and police protection.

Despite CCM congregants' avowals of feeling a spiritually based fellowship and equality with one another, informal moments such as the social hour after Sunday services and the break after the biweekly students' fellowship meeting are spaces where members' strategic and partisan wrangling for assistance comes to the fore. These negotiations are most visible during distributions of clothing and supplementary food packages to members of the student group and several Russian congregants. In the specific case of the clothing distribution, prior instances of individuals either taking more than their share or taking items that they later resold (such as Oksana is rumored to have done) have prompted student leaders to organize an underground distribution chain with intermediate relays. A church staff person first hands out bags of clothing to several dependable individuals, who in turn distribute the items in their bags to the respective members of their "teams." Problems still arise, however, when particularly desirable articles of clothing are at stake. One woman confided that she sometimes asks church staff to keep an eye open for particular items and then set them aside for her.

Comparable issues arise when food packages are distributed after student group meetings. Only church members are eligible for this program, but because student membership has recently far exceeded the number of available packets, church staff have created an additional requirement for eligibility: recipients must also demonstrate a commitment to the soup kitchen program. Soup kitchen supervisors issue time sheets to volunteers who receive assistance. When decisions are made at the monthly supervisors' meeting to determine how food packages and transportation passes are allocated, staff members take into account how often volunteers serve and for how long. The package distribution after one student meeting turned contentious when several individuals complained that they had been denied food. Dr. Steve, the director, reminded them that if they were to show initiative and help at the soup kitchens they would be eligible for assistance as well.

Other churches in Moscow provide similar forms of assistance to their members. Members at one Korean-Russian Methodist church service include several elderly Russian members. At the tea and sandwich fellowship hour that followed the service I visited, I watched as several Russian members removed plastic bags and containers from their tote bags and filled them with sandwiches, tea, and fresh tofu and bean sprouts that other congregants had brought. Although Aleksandra Petrovna is a staunch supporter of the CCM congregation and regularly attends their services and programs, she belongs to a Korean Presbyterian church. She confided that she enjoyed her home church not just for the lovely music and feelings of spirituality that she experienced there but also for the food packages and other forms of material assistance that were available to her. Without church, she commented, she would not be able to survive. The weekly free meals at the Hare Krishna temple are generally crowded with pensioners and homeless persons who have brought containers to fill with food to take away with them. Similarly, when clergy at the newly rebuilt Cathedral of Christ the Savior offered fresh, blessed apples to mark an Orthodox holiday, hundreds of people (including several CCM recipients) stood in line for hours to receive apples, which they then piled into bags, boxes, and even shopping carts they had brought with them.

At an Orthodox church that sponsors a soup kitchen program immediately following that of the CCM at the Moscow Scientific Institute, weekly prayer meetings attract Muscovites who use the introductions and participatory prayer segments of the service to articulate their personal problems and ask for assistance. On the evening that I attended one of the prayer meetings with a delegation from the CCM congregation (as part of an exchange program between the two churches), one woman spoke and cried for almost ten minutes while she described her daughter's illness and begged church members and God to help her. Beggars routinely gather outside churches and synagogues and approach worshipers, visitors, and passersby for spare change. Some solicitations are further couched in pointed remarks that people who are entering a church should be willing to offer assistance. Outside one church in St. Petersburg, I observed two women jostling each other as they competed to be the first to approach each visitor who walked through the gates leading to the churchyard. Later that same day, I was followed into a synagogue by a young woman who informed me that she was an invalid with a small child and then commented that I seemed like a nice, understanding person who might be able to spare her some money. When one of the synagogue staff came out of his office, the young woman quickly scuttled away.

Although opportunities for assistance and fellowship offer compelling incentives for Muscovites to attend church services, they also create contentious issues over language and personal declarations of faith. Although the Korean-Russian Methodist Church offers simultaneous translation from Korean into Russian, the CCM congregation and most other foreign churches provide services in English or French only. Congregants who do not speak English or French must either find friends who are willing to translate for them or sit through services without understanding the proceedings. These linguistic challenges do not prevent non-English-speakers from participating actively in CCM services, however. Nobody in Oksana's family speaks English, but her children readily attend Sunday School; and Oksana joins the choir every week, holding her hymnal and humming the music. Other congregants find their participation in CCM services awkward for spiritual reasons. Several African students who are not Protestant attend services anyway in order to take advantage of the supplemental food packages that are offered to church members. Edward, a graduate student in engineering from Liberia, reflected that he felt frustrated because he was forced to divide his time between the Christian Church of Moscow in order to receive assistance and the Catholic Church, which was the faith in which he had been raised.

As this young man's comment reveals, not all worshipers attend church for purely spiritual reasons, thus problematizing the significance that foreign missionaries and Russian Orthodox leaders alike have placed on raising conversion rates in Russia and the tactics they have employed to attract Muscovites to their services. Eliot Borenstein (1999b) and Judith Kornblatt (1999) cite survey data indicating that regular church attendance in Russia is declining even as professions of faith are increasing. The elision of religion during the Soviet period has meant that church rituals and doctrines are unfamiliar and a source of curiosity to many Muscovites. Larissa Antonovna, the CCM recipient who introduced me to the Hare Krishna feeding program, voiced a sentiment that I frequently encountered from other people when she said that she visited different churches in order to understand them from a philosophical perspective. What she left unsaid, however, but was evident in the care that she took to arm herself in advance with empty containers, was that she also viewed these churches as opportunities for receiving free or low-cost food. Vera openly acknowledged that even though she is Jewish, she has started attending Bible study at an evangelical Christian church, because a young man in the congregation has generously brought her reading materials, helped her with her grocery shopping, and driven her to and from services. Aid workers report that several churches offer food and other forms of assistance with the condition that recipients attend church services and engage in prayer consultations with church leaders.

When forms of public assistance and material resources are at stake, spirituality and religious fellowship converge with economic concerns as Muscovites remake declarations of faith into strategies for making do. This goes for those who distribute aid as well. In his study of recent religious movements in Russia, Borenstein remarks that "the manner in which these organizations allocate their resources leaves them open to charges that they are purchasing respectability with foreign currency" (1999b:442). Religious organizations such as the Unification Church and the Japanese community Aum Shinri Kyo have donated educational, medical, and other supplies to local communities in Russia (Borenstein 1999b).

Similar efforts to link spirituality with self-interest have occurred within the CCM community as well. The most notable instance of this occurred when Svetlana Grigorievna, who manages the cafeteria that is contracted for the fourth CCM soup kitchen, marketed her services to CCM staff and local journalists by emphasizing her Christian beliefs and her commitment to helping others. On separate occasions shortly after the new soup kitchen opened, however, both Dr. Steve and Aleksandra

Petrovna criticized Svetlana Grigorievna for attempting to get her workers added to the enrollment list. Aleksandra Petrovna commented that the cafeteria manager was not a Christian. I suggested that perhaps she was a businesswoman. Aleksandra Petrovna tartly responded that that was an accurate assessment: Svetlana Grigorievna was a businesswoman and *not* a Christian. Dr. Steve, meanwhile, had earlier commented that Svetlana Grigorievna had disappointed him because, although she had claimed to have Christian beliefs at the heart of her actions, in reality she was scheming and trying to swindle him.

Registration in the CCM Soup Kitchen

The events that took place during the last several days of May 1999, when the CCM congregation opened its fourth soup kitchen, offer a glimpse into the ways that identity labels and claims to membership in a group get invoked, contested, and tweaked when forms of assistance are at stake. During the episodes that I describe below, potential recipients, welfare officials, cafeteria employees, and volunteers collectively engaged in overlapping classificatory techniques to define and organize the social parameters of the soup kitchen. Potential recipients positioned themselves according to established conventions that associated identity categories with forms of assistance. Through the cooperative invocation of classificatory strategies, recipients and volunteers distinguished eligible recipients from those who were ineligible and founded a solid community of "insiders," composed of recipients, volunteers, and workers, in (sometimes) hostile opposition to those who were from the "outside."

Although the official notice about the opening of the new soup kitchen had not been made public until late the night before (owing to last-minute negotiations between church staff and the cafeteria director), by thirty minutes before the scheduled opening a long line of elderly Muscovites had formed in the hallway and along the sidewalk outside the cafeteria. Inside, white-coated cafeteria workers bustled around, setting tables, while CCM staff and local officials from the Veterans' Council and social welfare office conferred over lists and directions for the proceedings. To facilitate the distribution of meals, CCM staff had decided that for the first day, food would be served to anyone who arrived. Recipients would then register and receive their attendance cards on their way out of the cafeteria. At noon, the two coordinators began handing out meal tickets, and recipients made their way to the tables, where they waited to be served by volunteers and cafeteria workers. After recipients had eaten their meals, they were to make their way to the registration tables.

The proceedings went smoothly until recipients reached the registration tables. Initially, recipients were to return to the table from which they received their meal tickets and present their documents to James, one of the two coordinators, who would verify their information on the soup kitchen roster. Alan, the second coordinator, would assign each recipient a membership number and an attendance pass. Two factors contributed to the chaos that quickly ensued, however: the two coordinators were African students who had not been in Russia long and spoke limited Russian; and the soup kitchen roster that had been created by the welfare office had been put together late the night before and was only roughly in alphabetical order and was largely incomplete. The resulting confusion that was generated at the registration table led to more than a hundred people pushing and shoving, breaking line, and arguing with the coordinators. Dr. Steve and I were quickly enlisted to monitor two additional stations. I was put in charge of the welfare office's master list, which included soup kitchen recipients and a waiting list. Individuals whose names were not listed on either the soup kitchen roster or my master list were to present themselves and their documents to Dr. Steve, who would write down their names and investigate their claims.

Despite the ordered system, as soon as Dr. Steve and I sat down we were each surrounded by people who were shoving their passports in our faces and shouting their last names and addresses at us. As I went through the list, people peered over the top of the papers in my hand, over my head, and under my arms from behind, looking on the list themselves. Most people were not on my list, so I directed them to Dr. Steve. I repeatedly asked people if they had even checked in at the first station; most had not, so I directed them back to the coordinators. The following exchange, which I had with one woman, was similar to those I had with many potential recipients. When I was unable to locate the woman's name on my master list, I sent her to Dr. Steve. A few minutes later she came back to me and said that she needed her attendance pass. I asked her if she had been successfully registered. She replied that she had and that I was supposed to give her a card. When I turned to Dr. Steve for confirmation, however, he informed me that I was not to assign her a card. I relayed this information to the woman, but she insisted that I give her a card. The three of us went back and forth in this manner for several minutes until Dr. Steve eventually informed her firmly that she would receive her card another day and that she needed to go home.

The following days proceeded in a similar fashion. The lines remained orderly for only a few minutes before potential recipients began breaking line and approaching Dr. Steve, James, Alan, and me from all sides. After the first day, caseworkers at the welfare office had alphabetized the list so that it was easier for us to find people's names. Nevertheless, we quickly discovered that very few of the people who came to us were officially entitled to be enrolled. Although each of us verified whether a person's name was on our list or not, most people who were turned away did not accept the first answer they were given and so went to another station to try again. Some people insisted on reading through the lists themselves to prove to us that we had been mistaken.

Potential recipients recognized that spaces in the CCM program were limited, and enterprising individuals employed several tactics in their efforts to plead their respective cases and convince CCM representatives to enroll them in the program. The first ploy that most applicants used was to suggest that they had special connections that entitled them to preferential treatment. Applicants based their claims in the logic of referrals and said that "someone" had called and told them to report to the cafeteria to be registered. The popular response to the coordinators' questions about the precise identity of the caller seemed to be a vague reference to "some woman" whose name could not be readily recalled.

Other applicants made their claims by directly manipulating the rules and structure of the Russian welfare system. Specifically, these individuals capitalized on their knowledge about the hierarchy of disability categories, housing requirements, and the types of aid that corresponded to those classes, as well as local understandings about how the power and authority that aid providers were presumed to possess correlated with age, experience, and nationality. After it became clear that eligibility was limited to recipients who lived in a specific set of apartment buildings, several petitioners invented for themselves fictitious apartment numbers at those addresses. When I asked one man how he had learned of the soup kitchen, he simply replied, "I live here." When CCM staff confronted persons who had given addresses that did not match those recorded in their passports, most claimed that their documents were incorrect. A more explicit invocation of the welfare system occurred when potential recipients went beyond simply offering their names and addresses and asserted that they had status as a veteran or invalid and then detailed their various infirmities, described the battles in which they had participated, and even showed their scars.

Issues of race and nationality were also subtle factors in these negotiations over how to work the system and who would be enrolled in the program. At some point during the second day, I realized that the line in front of my station was always substantially longer than the lines in front of Alan, James, and Dr. Steve. As best I could, given the rather disorderly circumstances, I began paying attention to the interactions between recipients and each of us. I noticed that even when I directed applicants to one of the other three tables, most people simply wandered to the back of my line. When people reached the head of my queue again, I asked if they had gone to the table to which I had directed them. Some replied that they did not know they were supposed to do that, and others lied that they had and had been referred back to my line. I also sensed that among those who had been given an answer they did not like from Dr. Steve, Alan, or James, many returned to my line and presented their case again. Although Dr. Steve had been publicly introduced as the director of the program by CCM ministers, the cafeteria manager, and the regional welfare director, applicants who were told to address their claims to the director maintained that they did not know who that person was. I once overheard one woman explaining to another person that Dr. Steve, the director, was the *"negr"* (Negro). On another occasion, I overheard a conversation between two women who were looking curiously at one of the coordinators and standing less than three feet away from him. Evidently trying to decide who the young man was, the first woman finally asked her friend, "Is it a black [person]?" *(Eto chërnyi?)*

It is important to note that the terms *Negro* and *black* do not provoke the same widespread discomfort among Russians that they do among North Americans. In Russia, these terms appear routinely in both personal usage and official discourses (including dictionaries) to indicate people of color; as my informants have suggested, there are other words that are undeniably pejorative. However, a growing movement among intellectuals, members of the younger generation, and other Russians to replace these terms with others such as *African* or *African American* calls into question the alleged neutrality of the terms that my informants have used. Moreover, even if Russian members of the CCM community, and Moscow at large, claim that these words are not objectionable, their behaviors toward CCM volunteers continue to reflect residual attitudes about blacks and whites.

Even as I suspected that appeals and requests were frequently directed explicitly at me because I am white, it was clearer still that applicants assumed my authority and knowledge were limited by my nationality (and likely by my age as well). Frequently when I was going through the lists of names, hopeful petitioners would comment that my language skills were not sufficient to handle Russian names or addresses and then insist on looking through the lists themselves—even though these individuals evidently felt comfortable enough with my language skills to engage me in extended conversations about their eligibility status and petitions. One man whose name was not on my list returned after the soup kitchen had quieted down and asked me to look again, but this time to do it "attentively" *(vnimatel'no)*. As soon as either Svetlana Grigorievna, the cafeteria director, or Aleksandra Petrovna sat down at one of the tables, applicants immediately moved away from me and approached them instead. In one such instance, when Svetlana Grigorievna sat down next to me and we were approached by several people who had repeatedly badgered me with their requests, I started to explain to her in frustration that I had already gone through the lists several times and was quite certain that their names were not there. She put her hand on my arm to stop me and quietly said, "I understand." Svetlana Grigorievna then made a show of going through every page of the list and showing each person that his or her name was not on the list. Only after hearing Svetlana Grigorievna's assurances that their names were not on the list did those persons leave.

Later in the first week, my hunch that many of these applicants were in fact ineligible but were invoking familiar negotiating strategies in their efforts to "work" and "beat" the CCM system was confirmed by several incidents that took place after Grigorii Filipovich, the genial, seventy-five-year-old volunteer director of the local Veterans' Council, joined Svetlana Grigorievna and Aleksandra Petrovna in helping the CCM coordinators register recipients. The three Muscovites had lived in the neighborhood around the cafeteria and had been active in neighborhood activities for many years. Among the three of them, they recognized most petitioners either by name or by face. More important, they knew personal details about petitioners: for instance, whether they lived in the neighborhood, received a qualifying pension, or had the appropriate status. In many cases, while James and Alan were scanning their lists, looking for petitioners' names and addresses, one of the three Muscovites refused the applicant directly. A comment that Aleksandra Petrovna directed to a petitioner was representative of these encounters: "You do not live in this area; you are ne nashi."

At one level, these negotiations over who had the right to belong to the CCM soup kitchen community, how these claims were articulated, authenticated, and even rejected, and the ways in which frameworks of insiderness and outsiderness may shift, attest to the complex and tenuous nature of aid distribution. At another level, these machinations illustrate the contingent and calculated nature of social identities and social group-ings. The efforts of recipients, volunteers, welfare workers, cafeteria em-ployees, and hopeful applicants to define and redefine their relationships with each other through strategic positionings reveal not only how so-ciality itself is a resource to be objectified, exchanged, and invested but also how interpersonal relations that are conducted through stereotyped roles and expectations are always distanced to some degree from the ac-tors themselves. Access to aid is in many ways akin to a chess match, where both the givers and the hopeful receivers must first evaluate their positions and the resources at their disposal and then skillfully outma-neuver the other party.

Performing the Self

In this chapter I have suggested that identities are not absolute repre-sentations with finite cultural contents, but rather are symbolic reper-toires to which social actors lay strategic claim according to their partic-ular needs and interests in a given situation. As such, identities are always a partial amalgam of different traits and practices. It is this flexibility that allows for differences and contradictions to coexist. The collective per-formance of these identities produces a distinctive social group whose members share similar traits and practices. The "we" of the "nash" col-lectivity is not as cohesive or homogeneous as it is either purported or performed. Rather, it is an ideal that agents invoke to mask the ways that they shift among positional differences in their everyday lives.

Within the context of resource allocation, these negotiations and ap-propriations acquire special significance as opportunities for Muscovites to maximize their potential to procure scarce goods. As Margaret Beissinger has described for Romani musicians in Romania, "The poli-tics of ethnonyms, like that of language, is played out at the intersection of power, social status, and economic security" (2001:45). Practices of identification go beyond locating oneself within a community based on sentiment or attribute and are instead valuable tactics for positioning oneself within a productive community, a group through which one can attain both social and economic security. Moreover, the act of laying claim to a character type does not entail "ownership" but rather demon-strates Muscovites' facilities at being performers who make deliberate choices about the images that they present to each other and the circum-stances under which that occurs. Presentations of the "Self" take place not precisely within everyday life as much as they do on the stage in front of it (Herzfeld 1985). For CCM participants, then, essentializing discourses and practices do not represent a loss of either subjectivity or agency. Nor can the efforts of participants to reclassify themselves be read as forms of resistance against the power of the state or other institutions. In fact the rules and structures of the Russian identity schema are empowering precisely because they offer resources that Muscovites can use and play with for their personal and collective benefit.

CHAPTER 6

The Mythology of Hunger

It may be nice to live alone, but it is impossible to live alone.

Elena Antonovna, age seventy-five

A conclusion often heard in international circles is that Russia's chronic food shortages, unstable economy, and the number of soup kitchens and food aid programs currently operating throughout the country can be seen as compelling evidence that hunger is a pervasive problem in Russia and other former Soviet states (see also Giroux 2001). Similar to the representations of "starving Armenians" described by Barsegian (2000) and the recurring stereotypes of "hungry Africans," images of "hungry Russians" and stories about desperate Russians who have resorted to thievery, "subsistence" gardening, or general hopelessness circulate throughout international policy and media discourses. In many ways Russian food concerns have been degraded to a Third World status as foreign advisers launch interventionist efforts and churchgoers in North America link offerings for famine relief in Africa with contributions to hunger relief programs such as CCM and other soup kitchens throughout the former Soviet Union. Such representations of everyday life in Russia as perpetual material crisis have become powerful commodified essentialisms that inform public development, economic, and foreign policies.

Local Russian discourse, however, provides a different picture. Although soup kitchens and food package programs are, for the most part, acknowledged as important community resources, there is a pervasive notion that no hunger exists in Russia. During one of my visits to a CCM soup kitchen, I met a middle-aged man who was not a participant in the program but rather a paying customer in the café at the other end of the room. The man asked me what had brought me to the cafeteria, and I explained that I was researching the soup kitchen program. In response, the man became irate and informed me that I was mistaken. There was no hunger in that place, he argued. When I pointed out the soup kitchen activities that were taking place around him (at that moment two different soup kitchens were operating within the cafeteria, one for CCM recipients and one for Red Cross recipients), the man maintained that neither the programs nor the need for them existed in Moscow.[1] Although this was an extreme example, people from a broad range of socioeconomic backgrounds had similar reactions during interviews and general conversations about my research. Many Muscovites responded to my questions with statements such as "We have no hunger here" *(U nas net goloda)*, or "There is no hunger in Russia" *(V Rossii net goloda)*. Intriguingly, such statements often came from food aid recipients themselves.

In everyday usage, the word *golod* has a number of different meanings, including "hunger," "starvation," and "famine." In some contexts it carries special associations with the famine periods of the 1930s and with the starvation that accompanied deprivations during World War II, particularly the Leningrad Blockade. Scholars have further complicated any singular meaning by describing various types of scarcities with the evocative word *famine*, for instance, "goods famine" (Osokina 2001:51). As a methodological strategy to avoid prompting informants to use the word *golod*, I did not initially introduce this word in my interviews and conversations. Nevertheless, both informants and reporters in the popular media used this word and its derivative forms.

Despite these disavowals of widespread hunger, informants acknowledged that indeed individuals throughout Russia were in danger of going hungry. Raisa Ivanovna, the director of Russian Red Cross activities in the same region as the CCM soup kitchens, responded to my question about hunger *(golod)* with the following statement: "People are really going hungry *[golodaiut]*. Of course you understand clearly that, in the first case, we have a sharp stratification into poor and rich, and we still have a stratum like your [i.e., American] middle class—people like us, who have generally been living off their wages and are active in business. Well, they receive some kind of salary. In any case, in this period the population *[narod]* still has not realized that there really is hunger. That is, not everyone has realized, because we are still living on our old supplies *[zapas]*. We are accustomed to that in Russia." A CCM recipient who was an advocate for her fellow pensioners stated that she received telephone calls from people in her neighborhood who told her, "I fed my child for the last time last night. Today I cannot feed him," and "I had to kick out [*vybrosit'*] my children because I cannot even feed myself." One of the more usual terms of self-description used by beggars throughout the city was *golodnyi,* or "hungry." One elderly man who walked up and down a main Moscow street looking for donations wore a sign around his neck that read simply GOLODNYI.[2]

This contradiction about the presence of hungry people in the absence of hunger poses an intriguing vehicle for exploring why Muscovites participate in food aid programs such as the CCM soup kitchens. Are Muscovite aid recipients in fact truly hungry? Or does the concept of "hunger" have different connotations in Russia, so that there is a slippage between the understandings of Russians and those of foreign aid workers, donors, and interested observers? Moreover, do disavowals of hunger reflect a collective embarrassment, a moment of "cultural intimacy" (Herzfeld 1997), about a social reality that is familiar to all but nevertheless needs to be hidden from public, and especially international, view? In this chapter I explore how Muscovites understand the notion of "hunger" and, in particular, its connection with fears about social isolation. I suggest that in contrast to a more typical North American perception that soup kitchen recipients are people who depend on institutional support systems because they are otherwise marginalized from society at large (Ammons, n.d.; Glasser 1988), CCM participants point to the soup kitchen as tangible proof that they in fact belong to a defined and powerful social community. At the same time that recipients' visits to the soup kitchen are opportunities to get free food, they are also public displays that one belongs to a community and is tied into a social support network. Thus, the word *hunger* is better understood as a marker of the extent and durability of one's social wealth as expressed through networks, whereas *aloneness* is the idiom through which concerns with material poverty are articulated and understood.

The Social Life of Hunger

In the social sciences, accounts of food poverty encompass a range of interrelated issues such as scarcity, hunger, malnutrition, starvation, and famine, from a variety of perspectives. Most case studies rely on analytical frameworks that emphasize either the biomedical and physiological effects of food deprivation on victims (see the examples cited in Scheper-Hughes

1992:548 n. 8) or the material conditions that lead to hunger (Kates 1995; Riskin 1991; Sachs 1991). Although Jean Drèze and Amartya Sen have recognized that "famine is, by its very nature, a social phenomenon" (1989:46), they nonetheless continue to situate their analyses within a causal paradigm. In some cases, the very existence of hunger is produced in the interface of special interests and material circumstances (Lappé and Collins 1997). As Janet Poppendieck (1998) has persuasively argued, whether or not hunger even exists in the United States is a consequence of American political interests and negotiations at particular moments in the country's economic trajectory. In addition, the phenomenon of food deprivation is generally seen as a Third World concern. Graham Riches (1997) notes in his introduction to *First World Hunger,* a volume that addresses the politics of welfare reform and hunger in First World nations, the reality of hunger and poverty in First World countries is overlooked in international aid discourses that privilege the suffering of people in distant lands. Similarly, Janet Fitchen (1997) has argued that television depictions of abject conditions in Africa have been particularly useful in diverting the public's attention from the broader experiences of food poverty.

Anthropologists and sociologists in particular have offered valuable correctives to perspectives that privilege accounts of food poverty told from theoretical and geographic distances. Johan Pottier has convincingly argued for the necessity of including the perspectives of those directly involved in and affected by food shortages. By asking, "How does expert opinion compare with the perceptions and strategies of vulnerable groups and individuals?" (1999:10), he calls attention to what Scheper-Hughes has called the "lived experience of hunger" (1992:135). This attention to the multiple ways in which food poverty implicates material circumstances with the realms of the personal, experiential, symbolic, and psychological offers a much more complex picture of the ways in which social agents experience and make sense of food deprivation (Allahyari 2000; Aretxaga 1997; Brownell 1995; de Waal 1989; Hastrup 1993; Prindle 1979; Scheper-Hughes 1992; and Shack 1997). In addition, studies of hunger from the perspectives of insiders reveal the diversity of circumstances that constitute food poverty, ranging from severe and chronic food shortages (Scheper-Hughes 1992; Turnbull 1972) to acts of self-deprivation (Aretxaga 1997; Bordo 1997; Bynum 1997). In many cases, food poverty does not represent circumstances of complete deprivation.[3] As Alexander de Waal has suggested, "Hunger is in part an idiom. In part it is an experience" (1989:13).[4]

At the same time that food deprivation is an individualizing experience, it mediates the personal and the social. Where these connections have been addressed most successfully are ethnographies of the communities that form around food shortages—most notably, Rebecca Allahyari's 2000 ethnography of two church-based feeding programs in California, Irene Glasser's 1988 ethnography of a soup kitchen in Connecticut, and Barbara Myerhoff's 1978 ethnography of a Jewish senior citizens' center in California. By treating feeding programs as communities and by focusing on the social dynamics within these groups, Allahyari, Glasser, and Myerhoff have poignantly demonstrated that hunger and poverty are intrinsically social. In particular, for the elderly members with whom Myerhoff worked, center activities were preventative strategies for being ignored or forgotten by one's relatives and the rest of the world. Attendance at events affirmed participants' visibility within the community.

In many ways, this social component is representative of Russians' experiences with food shortages and food aid projects as well. Not coincidentally, soup kitchens, food packages, and pensioners' activities are known in local circles as social welfare programs, not as economic development activities. Intriguingly this perspective is noticeably absent in both popular and academic discourses about Russian and Soviet social history, despite the long-recurring themes of hunger and poverty—allegedly since the eleventh century (Fisher 1927:474). In the last two centuries specifically, the frequency with which food shortages have been reported and the issues with which they have been correlated have created a powerful sense that Russian history cannot be told or understood except through the lens of deprivation.[5] This emphasis has been particularly notable for the twentieth century, as the history of practically every decade has been told with attention to problems in food production and distribution.

In spite of the regularity with which food scarcities appear in the historiography of Russia, there is not a single, unifying narrative about scarcity and the way it has been experienced by Russians. At times it has been theorized as a political consequence; at others, as an economic crisis. The revolutionary events of the early 1900s, and the 1917 Russian Revolution in particular, have been associated with food shortages (notably bread) (Davydoff 1971; Kitanina 1985; Lih 1990; McAuley 1991). One especially common version of the events leading up to the 1917 Revolution contends that it was hungry women who mobilized in the very bread lines in which they were waiting and formed the first public protests against the monarchy (Bobroff-Hajal 1994; Leites 1922). Immediately following the revolutionary period, the 1920s and early 1930s were characterized by severe agricultural losses and widespread famines. In Moscow, a Famine Exhibition was constructed in a hall at the zoological gardens to show visitors the various stages of famine, aid programs such as children's cafeterias and mobile kitchens, and displays of substitute food items (*Russian Information and Review* 1921:78). It was during the Great Famine of 1921–1922 that the American Relief Administration, an aid program launched by Herbert Hoover who was then U.S. secretary of commerce, sent packages of food, medicine, and clothing to the Soviet Union (Fisher 1927; Weissman 1974).[6] Foreshadowing the circumstances surrounding foreign food aid to Russia during the 1990s, these earlier food programs strained relations between the Soviet Union and the United States, as Hoover's allegedly altruistic motivations were called into question by Soviet authorities (Weissman 1974:17).

Although natural environmental conditions undeniably factored into the food shortages that characterized the first several decades of the twentieth century, other circumstances have been given just as much attention in accounts devoted to the causes of hunger. For instance, one interpretation points to Communist Party policies regarding forced collectivization (Conquest 1986; Dolot 1985), while another perspective suggests that shortages of consumer goods resulted from shortcomings in production systems (Kingsbury and Fairchild 1935). The famine conditions of the 1920s and 1930s were followed by severe deprivations during and after World War II. Citizens of Leningrad suffered particularly severely during the Leningrad Blockade, when the city was under siege by German forces for nine hundred days. Casualty figures for Leningrad alone have been conservatively estimated at one million persons who starved to death (Moskoff 1990:226).[7] To acknowledge their suffering, the Soviet state awarded survivors of the Leningrad Blockade a separate benefit status that effectively allowed them to claim first priority for assistance and service, a preference that continues to be observed in Russia today.

The theme of scarcity continued into the postwar period. In the 1960s, even as food and other consumer goods were more readily available to consumers, Soviet leader Nikita Khrushchev (1964) observed that it was the market that remained unable to provide customers with the goods they wanted. Later, during the Brezhnev period of the 1970s and 1980s, grain losses and low economic growth again contributed to periodic shortages (Kroncher 1979; Pipes 1984). Finally, both the restructuring of perestroika during the late 1980s and the transition to market capitalism in the 1990s have also been associated with a decline in the national economy and shortages of both consumer goods and money (Burawoy, Krotov, and Lytkina 2000; Ericson 1995).

In the post-Soviet period, dire images of food shortages have continued to preoccupy the attentions of outside observers of Russia, particularly in commentaries on the underlying political and economic circumstances of the "growing pains" associated with Russia's transition to democracy and market capitalism. In many respects, a sense of crisis and social disruption characterizes the discourses of non-Russian analysts. In the early 1990s, a reporter for *Business Week* predicted that a widespread industrial depression and massive unemployment in Russia would lead to hunger and riots and perhaps even to another coup (Brady 1992). Five years later, an American newspaper article reported: "With their wages months overdue, millions of Russians [were] learning new survival skills . . . giving blood for money and making pancakes out of potato peelings" (McNabb 1997:A2). Meanwhile, a Moscow-based foreign journalist reported in the *Independent* that even before Russia's financial complications of August 1998, "miners, doctors and other workers have been surviving for months without any wages at all, . . . people regularly faint from hunger in trolley buses, [and] neighbours are reduced to stealing cabbages from each other's gardens to feed their children" (Womack 1998). A more specific genre of transition accounts has focused on the situations of elderly Russians who allegedly cannot afford to buy food. A previous minister with the CCM congregation wrote in a fund-raising brochure that was distributed to churches throughout North America that elderly soup kitchen recipients were in danger of starving because of the government's precarious financial situation. The minister described the relationship between one recipient and the government in this way: "She is hopeless, the government is broke, and the days of Communism don't look so bad through the hunger pangs of memory" (Ammons, n.d.).

The 1998 "Crisis"

Toward the end of my primary research period in late 1998, a series of events brought attitudes about food poverty into sharp relief by highlighting the disjuncture between outsiders' views of Russia and the views of Russians themselves. These events were the August financial crisis *(krizis),* when the official devaluation of the ruble from an artificially set exchange rate prompted severe depreciations of the currency and rapid inflation. In the first several weeks of these events, the scope of the crisis was imagined just as much as, if not more than, it was experienced in practical terms, particularly in the eyes of outsiders. Accurate pictures of what was really happening with the Russian economy were obscured by rumors that circulated throughout the international media about the impending withdrawal of foreign companies from the Russian market and further delays in the payment of wages and pensions. Typically the effects of these moves were envisioned in terms of decreasing food supplies and an increasing probability of widespread hunger. On an Internet list-serve devoted to Russian studies, a group of North American scholars focused their comments on predictions for the likelihood that bad harvests would further contribute to hunger conditions.[8] Additional stories in Russia's English-language community reported that private gardens were increasingly being pilfered and that villagers in regions outside Moscow were organizing vigilante groups to seek out and punish suspected food thieves (McMahon 1999). Meanwhile, friends and colleagues back in the United States related the bleak images of food lines and empty store shelves that were being depicted on American television and in American newspapers. A journalist writing for *USA Today* cited an International Youth Foundation bulletin that claimed family budgets were being strained to the extent that "14 million of Russia's 38 million children [were] literally starving" (Babakian 1999).

Even more gripping than the themes of economic calamity that were linked with the "crisis" were the connections drawn between food shortages and the ultimate fate of Russia's stability and continuity as a nation-state. Not only did outside observers question Russia's economic solvency (Clinton 1998; McGuire 1998:1), but even the extent to which Russia could remain a "modern" nation came under debate (Cohen 1998). Embedded within these perspectives were themes of blame and responsibility that offered strong views about the morality of Russia and Russians. In many cases, these outside perspectives retained an emphasis on material factors by alluding to Russians' supposedly reckless and immoral economic practices. One analyst suggested that Russia would never successfully reform itself owing to the "abnormality" of the local economy, particularly the pervasive practice of barter to distribute domestic goods (Steele 1998). Another writer speculated that postcrisis hunger was "less because of shortages of food or fuel than because of bad government"; the writer further predicted that foreign interventionist food aid would hurt Russia by "encouraging corruption" (*Economist*

1998). Lawrence Summers, then U.S. secretary of the treasury, vowed that American aid would be contingent upon Russian officials' acknowledgment of local problems and their guarantees to conform to U.S. examples (cited in Coleman 1998). Finally, American policy makers delayed promised food aid to Russia because of disagreements with Russian officials over the proper ways to distribute the aid to needy people (Slavin 1998).

Although discourses of food poverty provide important referents to Russian current events, perspectives that privilege this aspect overlook the complexities and inconsistencies that make up the everyday lives of Russians. At the very least, these narratives ignore the perspectives of Muscovites themselves, a common shortcoming in policy analyses and directives about the former Soviet Union. This omission of local actors and their voices elides the very ordinary realities that ordinary people experience every day. As a case in point, a particularly intriguing counterpoint to the speculations of outsiders about the impact of the 1998 crisis emerged from the reactions of Muscovites, who both criticized the pessimism of non-Russian observers and denied the likelihood of either food scarcities or widespread hunger.

In their conversations with me, Muscovites expressed a widely held sentiment that the events of fall 1998 were not particularly unique and that they had weathered similar events in the past and were confident that they would be able to live through (*perezhivat'*) these as well. Muscovites articulated a number of reasons to support their optimism. Several respondents mentioned the continued presence of inexpensive produce and other local products in the markets, and others noted the widespread availability of summer gardens, pointing out that another one or two months remained in the growing season. Many people had yet to exhaust their stores of supplies from the previous year. CCM soup kitchen recipients calculated which food products could still be gathered from the forest before the first frost; others described the elaborate shopping practices and informal networks they had developed and employed to cope with shortages during the Soviet period, which they could once again employ as emergency strategies. The possibility that Muscovites were somewhat reluctant or embarrassed to discuss their present material circumstances, as was suggested by several American analysts, was not supported by the willingness—indeed, almost enthusiasm—with which informants articulated their financial and material resources in great detail. Numerous conversations and interviews quickly progressed to comparisons of prices, wages, and pensions at different historical moments.[9]

Certainly, the first weeks of the "crisis" were confusing and chaotic as Muscovites tried to assess the rapidly changing world around them and to mobilize a set of coping strategies. Store shelves emptied quickly when shoppers stocked up on nonperishable items such as sugar, flour, rice, oil, grains, and tinned foods. Some bread shops imposed limits on the number of loaves that could be purchased at one time. In the CCM soup kitchens, demand for loaves of bread instead of complete meals exceeded supply; cafeteria directors restricted the amount of bread that recipients could take and forced them to take soup or potatoes instead.

Yet in spite of the heightened vigilance with which Muscovites approached their daily strategies of making do, people resolutely maintained that the need for such extreme measures would be temporary. Indeed, within several weeks stores had replenished their stocks. In the case of the small grocery store next to my apartment, supplies were available within a few days. Although there were significantly fewer imported or domestically produced transnational brands than before, Russian companies had capitalized on the moment and increased production, thereby prompting a resurgence in the availability and marketability of local goods. Consequently, contrary to the predictions of outside observers, a complete dearth of goods never materialized.

More significant than the material circumstances of the crisis, however, was the attention that Muscovites placed on social ties. Friends commented that just as in earlier periods, they could rely on relatives, acquaintances, and colleagues for help in weathering these events. Collective shopping practices reappeared, and people continued to circulate produce from their gardens and their emergency supplies.

The Insiders' Perspective: Social Scarcity

Often when I described my research to Russians, I was met with puzzling responses. Several university students laughed at my interest in studying food assistance, and one, a CCM congregant, asked seriously, "Would anyone find that interesting?" At a dinner party, three Muscovites who had been friends for more than twenty years, discussed the prevalence of local soup kitchens and agreed that such aid programs were misleading because there was not a widespread need for them. More intriguing, however, were the views expressed by recipients at CCM soup kitchens who argued that they did not know anyone who was hungry—including themselves. Even as respondents confirmed that the majority of the Russian population was constrained by severe financial limitations, they nonetheless adhered to a collective sentiment that material resources did not adequately indicate need or the potential for hunger. Several days before the International Red Cross launched its winter fundraising appeal, a Russian official with the organization stated that he could not confirm that Russians were in fact literally dying of hunger, although he could say with certainty that many people required supplementary food. Hunger, the official suggested, was "really more a social problem" that had to do with "the question of dignity." Similarly, Aleksei Mikhailovich, the regional welfare director who worked with the CCM programs, reflected that his most important task was to find assistance programs such as those of the CCM soup kitchens that would make each of his constituents "feel like a person" *(chuvstvoval sebia chelovekom)*.[10]

When Muscovites both inside and outside the CCM soup kitchen community discussed hunger and those who might be at risk for various forms of food poverty, they systematically mentioned people who occupied marginal and tenuous positions in society: specifically, housebound pensioners and invalids, homeless and mentally ill persons, and visitors to Moscow. Respondents explained that often people in these social groups were alone and therefore lacked the necessary social connections through which they could gain access to goods and services. In their reports to the World Council of Churches, representatives from several Russian Orthodox churches that sponsored soup kitchens around Moscow each noted that their programs served "poor and lonely pensioners," "the least protected social groups includ[ing] lonely old people, orphans, and the disabled," and "lonely sick people."[11]

Social isolation is one of the official prerequisites for assistance through CCM and other food aid programs. Social workers and volunteer activists at several regional welfare offices in Moscow meet monthly to consider letters of application from local residents who are in need of food assistance, which they then use to compile lists of eligible recipients for CCM and other soup kitchens. In their applications, petitioners describe their material circumstances, for example, the type of apartment in which they live (communal or privately owned; number of rooms; type of sanitary facilities; its overall state of repair), their pensions, and any additional sources of income. They also enumerate any extenuating circumstances, such as outstanding debts or the support they provide to other family members. Finally, applicants list living relatives and explain the amount and kind of assistance they receive from each person (i.e., money, living space, food, and so on). In many cases, committee members dismiss applications because petitioners' income levels exceed the imposed limits of approximately seven hundred to nine hundred rubles per month. In many other cases, applications are rejected because petitioners have strong family resources at their disposal. In still other cases, as further proof of the amount of information that is available through informal channels, especially in small communities such as those found in neighborhood welfare associations, committee members are aware of personal details that applicants have not disclosed, for instance, live-in relatives or the extra income that those relatives receive from informal employment. Committee members then turn down these applications on the grounds that family members should provide supplemental assistance. By quantifying kin relations, welfare workers reinforce the notion that although material resources are important, they are not as important as social resources. As both welfare workers and aid recipients have attested, food poverty is a social, not an economic, condition; and it is those individuals without social connections who are at greatest risk of lacking *access* to food and thereby go hungry.

Although family connections are privileged, it is worth noting that extended kinship networks are relatively scarce among Muscovites. On the one hand, persistent economic constraints have contributed to small family sizes, and single-child families are common. On the other hand, one of the consequences of the Soviet emphasis on population integration was that students, workers, and soldiers were often assigned to universities and postings far away from their family homes. During moments of upheaval, such as in the post–World War II period and poor harvest years, displaced persons and hopeful laborers left their parents and siblings behind and made their way to other regions to find work. Most recently, following the breakup of the Soviet Union, the appeal of high-paying work in Moscow and other Russian cities has enticed many Russians to move. Thousands of others have capitalized on loosening immigration restrictions in other countries to leave Russia altogether. CCM participants are like their peers in other aid programs in that they have either outlived their relatives or have been left behind by children and grandchildren who have moved abroad. Consequently, Muscovites often cite a dearth of immediate relatives living nearby as a serious constraint on the resources available for their everyday sustenance.

Raisa Ivanovna, the director of Russian Red Cross activities in the southern region of Moscow, supervises aid projects ranging from feeding programs and clothing distributions to youth activities and drug rehabilitation services. During our interview, which took place in fits and starts as she took care of other agency business and helped people who had come to her office for assistance, Raisa Ivanovna commented on the connections between the social and the economic in terms of the eligibility requirements for her program: "We generally take people who are alone. That is the primary criterion, because if there is an invalid or pensioner with relatives, of course it is easier for them to survive. When one is completely alone, that is difficult." Similarly, aid workers with another local, privately funded program strategically marketed their services to elderly Russians who lacked extensive social resources. In a program brochure, organizers invited people who were "over age 65, alone, and in need of social support and defense." The pamphlet continued with a description of the services the agency provided to accommodate "the fundamental living problems of single people."[12]

Marina is representative of CCM recipients in that she has outlived her spouse, children, and friends and has neither the material nor the social means to support herself. Two other CCM recipients who volunteer as *aktivistki* (activists) for their fellow pensioners note that many CCM recipients and hopeful applicants do not have relatives or friends to help them and so depend on the soup kitchens for both food and companionship. By contrast, a woman not directly associated with any food aid programs reported that several years ago her mother and an elderly neighbor each received an invitation to attend a soup kitchen located in their neighborhood. Her mother declined the invitation because she lived with her daughter's family and received assistance from them. The neighbor, however, received an adequate pension but lived alone and without family nearby. He chose to attend the soup kitchen because he had no one else to help him. When the woman told this story to me, she added that she supported her neighbor's decision, because he needed the social interaction that would be available at the soup kitchen. In an evocative example of the importance that Muscovites place on social connections, CCM recipients express their concern that foreign volunteers at the soup kitchens might suffer because they lack the social capital necessary to find goods and services and—perhaps more important—to navigate effectively the bureaucratic challenges of daily life in Russia.

CCM soup kitchen recipients endorse this image of food poverty as a socially constituted circumstance. In opposition to the images of hunger and poverty that are portrayed in CCM fund-raising documents as well as in most foreign accounts of Russia more generally, recipients suggest that these depictions, and the label "hunger" in particular, do not accurately represent their circumstances, even during the 1998 economic crisis. Sasha, a long-term CCM recipient and self-proclaimed activist for the elderly, refused to identify herself as hungry, even as she described her severe shortage of material resources. She receives a five-hundred-ruble monthly pension, with which she pays for food, medicine, and utilities. She also supports her daughter's family, because her daughter, an electrical engineer, has not received her salary in six months. Despite her scant economic resources, Sasha knows people in local businesses and government offices and procures supplemental goods and services through these connections. She explained that the label "hungry" more appropriately describes the circumstances of other neighborhood residents who lack these social relations. Recipients concede that hungry people might in fact exist in Russia but maintain that they are most certainly outside the soup kitchen community. In fact, this distancing maneuver reveals the "catch" that is inherent in the notion of "hunger": as Muscovites explained, if "hungry" people are those who are beyond the reach of social connections, then there is no means by which to locate and count them. Once those individuals have entered a social relationship, they are no longer hungry.

Effectively, not only are hungry people marginalized, but they are also invisible to the rest of society. This sense of the hungry as invisible vividly emerges in the efforts by members of the larger university community at the Moscow Scientific Institute to disguise and ignore the activities of the CCM soup kitchen. When classes are in session at the university, there are obvious distinctions between the CCM community and the university community, in terms of both the food that is served and the personal interactions that take place. In many ways, cafeteria workers actively distance the soup kitchen operations from those for members of the university. The meals that are prepared for soup kitchen recipients are simpler and often less aesthetically pleasing (for example, bowls of watery soup, plain macaroni, and white bread for recipients versus elaborate salads, caviar-filled boiled eggs, and brown bread for university customers), and serving staff discourage regular customers from requesting recipients' food for their meals. Although recipients, volunteers, and paying customers share the same physical space, soup kitchen recipients are forbidden to sit at tables beyond the halfway point in the room; this area is reserved for students and faculty. The cafeteria manager strictly enforces the division by yelling at offenders and making them move to different tables. Volunteers, however, are permitted to move freely throughout the space, although most elect to remain in the same area as the recipients. Recipients must also hang their coats on racks in the hallway outside the

FIGURE 12. In winter, the CCM soup kitchen at the Moscow Scientific Institute is a study in contrasts between recipients and volunteers.

cafeteria, unlike members of the institute community and volunteers, who hang theirs on coat racks located inside, near the tables.

Faculty and students cooperate in these efforts to hide the soup kitchen from public view. Customers silently push their way past recipients and volunteers and find seats away from tables occupied by CCM recipients. Several students who are active members of the CCM congregation occasionally walk past the cafeteria with friends or stand in the hallways talking with volunteers but never visit the soup kitchen during serving times or offer to help. In one striking incident, Mikhail Vassilievich, a jovial CCM recipient who enjoyed an easy and jocular rapport with CCM volunteers (young women, in particular), accidentally bumped into a young female student. He immediately apologized profusely and asked her if she was injured. The young woman, however, ignored him completely. Looking anywhere but at him, she gathered her belongings and walked past. These distancing techniques are not as evident at the other soup kitchens, where paying customers share space with program recipients. In some cases, paying customers share tables and conversations with CCM recipients.

The invisibility of the soup kitchen to other cafeteria customers sets recipients apart from the larger community at the Moscow Scientific Institute and relegates them to the nether regions of Moscow society, unreachable by public awareness or assistance. Nevertheless, for recipients and volunteers themselves, as well as for cafeteria employees such as the dishwashers, who remain otherwise unseen in the cafeteria's commercial transactions, the activities of the soup kitchen occupy a tangible physical space and delineate a visible and vibrant community (figure 12). Even if this group is visible only to its own members, their shared experiences affirm and validate both their membership within this group and their access to very real resources.[13]

The Sociality of the Soup Kitchen

Although food distribution is a critical component of the CCM's services, the actions of participants endow the program with a far more significant value. Specifically, the soup kitchens have acquired local appeal as lively community-oriented centers where the material and the social converge (figure 13). Recipients, volunteers, and cafeteria employees alike use the CCM soup kitchens as spaces where they can enjoy the company of friends and neighbors, as well as pass around information and commodities. Few recipients eat alone: most either arrive with companions or join friends at their tables, and it is customary for people to save places for each other. Although some people stay only as long as it takes for them to eat their meals or to repackage their food in take-away containers, others sit with friends for an hour or more, chatting about their health, the weather, local news, and recent events. One group of men regularly meets to eat and argue with each other about politics. Letters and pictures from relatives and friends—and even from former volunteers—are brought to the soup kitchen for other recipients and volunteers to read.[14]

Many recipients have favorite volunteers with whom they feel especially close. They seek out these volunteers to chat for a few minutes or even to invite them to the table for longer conversations. At times the line to the ticket table gets snarled when recipients gather in clusters to talk with each other and with the CCM staff person distributing tickets (who often has to shoo people along to keep the line moving). Musically inclined members of the community often entertain others by playing the

FIGURE 13. During the summer, the mood at the fourth CCM soup kitchen is relaxed as recipients enjoy the meal and conversation.

piano, singing, or dancing. In her younger days, one recipient traveled extensively throughout Europe as a member of one of the Soviet Union's most prestigious choral groups. When she has time, she organizes volunteers and other recipients around the piano, gives impromptu singing lessons, and then entertains the others in the dining area. Another man likes songs from Soviet musicals from the 1940s and 1950s; while he plays the piano, an elderly woman who is employed by the cafeteria as a dishwasher comes out from her work space at the sinks in the back to dance with willing partners.

Participants also spread news and gossip through the soup kitchen community. Several active members of the local Veterans' Council post notices for upcoming films, concerts, and lectures. Before the local elections in 1998, a group of friends distributed information about the various candidates and their respective platforms on social welfare and assistance to pensioners. Other people enlist their fellow recipients in such collective letter-writing campaigns as thanking local officials, expressing their opinions to local politicians, or showing their support for CCM staff and volunteers. Volunteers are asked to proofread letters, especially those addressed to foreigners, and occasionally to add their signatures or to mail them. Recipients have also approached volunteers and CCM staff for assistance with other problems. One woman requested help in dealing with the local police detective after her boarder stole money from her. At the same time, volunteers, especially African assistants who have worked with the program for an extended period of time, occasionally make requests of trusted recipients. One man needed medical attention and asked a recipient to help him locate a doctor who would not discriminate against him. Another man called on his contacts in the soup kitchen to help sort out his document problems. Others have passed on their intentions to locate housing or jobs through CCM recipients.

CCM recipients also rely on the soup kitchens as personal message centers for passing on information about each other as well as for communicating with each other. Participants even leave written and verbal messages and small packages for each other with the soup kitchen coordinators. Recipients inform CCM staff and volunteers when other recipients have fallen ill, are delayed, or have traveled out of town. Likewise, meals are opportunities for CCM staff and volunteers to keep track of recipients' health and well-being. When recipients first present their identification cards to receive their meal tickets, coordinators often take a moment to observe them and to ask personal questions about their health or home lives. When recipients have not attended for a period of time or have been in the hospital, CCM coordinators and volunteers inquire about them through their fellow recipients. On other occasions, coordinators have phoned recipients at home to ask about them. Although recipients can take meals for two days at a time, one coordinator restricts this privilege for individuals about whom he has special concerns. He explained that by forcing these recipients to come every day to collect their food, he ensured that there was at least one person who interacted with them on a daily basis and would notice if they had problems or had stopped leaving their homes.

The CCM community is also a space where members can mark the rituals of social life such as holidays, in addition to daily interpersonal relations. Although the soup kitchens are closed on Russian national holidays, these events are recognized in advance with small gifts of chocolate or staples such as rice, sugar, and cereal grains that are presented to recipients. Occasionally recipients mark such events with small items such as pieces of candy or flowers, which they give to each other or to favorite volunteers. Vera brings in a homemade cake on the yearly anniversary of her husband's death. Because it was fellow recipients and volunteers who had visited her during her husband's illness and after his death, Vera continues to observe his death anniversary within the same community. When Olivia, a graduate student volunteer from Sudan, defended her master's thesis, the first people she told were the recipients and volunteers in the soup kitchen. Recipients stopped by the ticket table to offer their congratulations and hear the details, and Svetlana Grigorievna, the cafeteria manager, donated several bottles of champagne and some pastries for Olivia and several recipients and volunteers to share. CCM staff solicit Western corporations in Russia for special donations of candy and toiletries, which they formally present to recipients on major holidays such as New Year's Day and International Women's Day, which are traditionally marked with exchanges of presents in Russia. In return, recipients keep track of the holidays of the volunteers. For the most part, recipients generalize volunteers into categories of "Christian" and "American," and so give all volunteers (regardless of their nationalities or religious affiliation) holiday greetings on occasions such as Christmas, Easter, Thanksgiving, and American Independence Day.

CCM staff and recipients proudly acknowledge that the soup kitchens provide a setting where recipients can socialize with each other and feel that they are members of a community. This importance is underscored by the frequency with which some recipients come to the soup kitchens simply to socialize and not to eat. Like a number of recipients, Aleksandra Petrovna takes her food home in glass jars and eats it later. Instead of leaving the soup kitchen after she has received her meal, however, Aleksandra Petrovna remains and helps the volunteers and visits with other recipients and cafeteria workers. Gennadi Sergeevich arrives early in the morning and works the room, talking with friends, mediating disputes between recipients and volunteers, and reading. Not until a few minutes before the soup kitchen closes does he collect his food and put it into containers to take home with him. Other people who periodically have sufficient food at home (particularly during the summer months or after relatives have visited) bring their own food to the soup kitchen so that they can still sit and eat with friends.

CCM congregants and supporters have expressed their frustrations with the limits they must impose on recipients' social opportunities and describe their hopes at being able to provide additional social opportunities for recipients in the future. When the CCM program first began ten years ago, the cafeteria in which the program met was closed to the public after the soup kitchen's serving hours ended. Recipients and volunteers frequently remained in the dining area after their meals to play cards, sing, and listen to lectures. Congregants have investigated possibilities to restore this type of social life to the soup kitchens but acknowledge that their budget cannot cover the costs of increasing hours in the cafeterias for soup kitchen recipients. The church does rent these spaces for occasional congregational activities, however. A biweekly students' youth group meets at the Moscow Scientific Institute cafeteria, and CCM staff have held soup kitchen volunteer appreciation ceremonies there as well. Although recipients are not discouraged from attending these events, the occasions are not generally publicized widely outside the CCM worship community, thereby creating subtle distinctions among recipients, volunteers, and supporters. Nevertheless, those recipients who are intimately connected to the CCM information pipeline (like Aleksandra Petrovna and Oksana) attend these events regularly. Several soup kitchen programs in Moscow are able to offer extended social services to recipients, but these programs are primarily sponsored by organizations with privately owned space, such as senior citizens' centers connected with regional welfare offices and a Jewish community center.

Moreover, because of the costs associated with renting space and services for the soup kitchens, as well as the need to maintain good relations with cafeteria administrators, CCM staff and cafeteria employees must carefully monitor the length of time that recipients spend in the cafeterias. The four soup kitchens operate for only one to two hours each day, and the managers of the four cafeterias request that recipients leave promptly to create space for paying customers. These same restrictions do not apply to volunteers; many African volunteers elect to remain after the serving hours to eat, chat, read, or do their class assignments. The majority of non-African volunteers, however, leave promptly when the serving period ends, if not before. To enforce the time restrictions placed on recipients, cafeteria employees have used a range of tactics to encourage recipients to leave. Such efforts have included "accidentally" running out of food and scavenging cold and unappealing leftovers from the refrigerators, putting away the food and dishes ten minutes before the official closing time, removing recipients' trays of food even as recipients are attempting to finish their meals, and going so far as to scold and shout at people to hurry up and leave. On one occasion the director in one cafeteria hollered "quickly, quickly" (bystro bystro) at a young man with severe physical disabilities that prevent him from feeding himself easily. The man (a researcher at a local economics institute) gamely tried to speed up his efforts, with the unfortunate result that he spilled much of his soup on his clothes before volunteers told him that he was in no danger of being evicted. The janitor at another soup kitchen removes trays from volunteers' hands and shoos the helpers out the door, thus preventing them from serving. On days when she is more benevolent, this janitor walks around to the volunteers, points at her watch, and simply commands, "Sit!" Volunteers and cafeteria employees jointly monitor the doors of the dining area before and after the serving times to ensure that recipients have left.

Recipients generally find ways to circumvent these time limits, however. One CCM supervisor reports that although the soup kitchen he directs opens at 9:30 A.M., it is not uncommon for recipients to congregate in the corridors by 7 A.M. On pleasant days, people continue their post-meal discussions outside, on the benches and railings in front of the cafeterias or on their journeys home by public transportation. In cold weather, recipients congregate in bathrooms and hallways, particularly those in parts of the buildings more remote than where the soup kitchens are housed. One man passed himself off as a researcher at the Moscow Scientific Institute and participated in lectures and meetings with faculty members until someone recognized him as a member of the soup kitchen community. The creative ways that recipients attempt to circumvent the severe restrictions on sociality that are enforced by cafeteria staff and volunteers reinforce the important role that the soup kitchens play as social arenas. The soup kitchen is very much a social necessity, because within its spaces both recipients and volunteers display and deploy their relationships with each other for multiple purposes.

Social Security

That food aid programs are locally affiliated with "social welfare" or "social defense" *(sotsial'naia zashchita)* departments is an important clue not only to the many ways in which material and social needs are entangled with each other every day in Moscow but also to the extent that this confluence is both recognized and institutionalized in social practice and discourse. The director of one regional welfare office explicitly recognized the material and social resources that are provided in the soup kitchens when he praised the CCM program for providing "charitable aid and social support to our members. . . . It is very significant support." A brochure for another domestic aid program advertised that the most important form of assistance it provided was "moral support for the single

FIGURE 14. This sign in a grocery store window informs
World War II veterans that the shop offers special benefits.

person." Similarly, the director for a Jewish soup kitchen in Moscow reflected in a newspaper interview that her staff actively attempted to make
recipients feel welcome: "We try to put them at ease by making them feel
that this is their home and that we are all in this together" (Ruby 1999).
One grocery store publicized that it offered special benefits to veterans
of the Great Patriotic War with a sign that read SOCIAL SUPPORT *(sotsial'-
naia podderzhka)* (figure 14).

This sense of community and mutual assistance emerges in the ways
that Muscovites learn about assistance programs and enlist them as part
of their everyday survival strategies. Many Muscovites explicitly draw
upon their social connections to help them apply to and enroll in assistance programs. Although CCM staff use residency requirements to determine eligibility (as I described previously, in chapter 5), these standards
are enforced most strictly in the fourth soup kitchen owing to restrictions
imposed by the local Veterans' Council. Coordinators at the other three
soup kitchens enjoy greater discretionary powers and occasionally make
exceptions for applicants who live outside the prescribed boundaries for
their groups.

In most cases, individuals who do not meet the necessary requirements but are nonetheless granted membership are not strangers; rather,
they are linked through their social networks to other CCM participants,
who act as advocates for them by describing their circumstances to coordinators and vouching for their merit and dependability. For example,
Larissa Antonovna lives in a region not covered by the CCM programs
but has been able to circumvent the rules because of a personal connection with one of the volunteers. Larissa Antonovna's apartment is located
near the university attended by most of the African student volunteers.
Several years ago she was befriended by a young African woman who
told the soup kitchen coordinator about her situation as a widow who
lives alone. It was through this contact that Larissa Antonovna received
her place in the soup kitchen. Likewise, another woman moved to
Moscow for several months to find seasonal work. The relative with
whom she was living was a regular CCM recipient and a welfare activist
who negotiated with CCM staff to create a temporary space for her. In a
more tragic instance, a CCM recipient who had attended for many years
died after being hit by a car as she left the soup kitchen. Instead of going
through their waiting list of potential recipients, CCM supervisors
agreed to give the woman's spot to her sister as a means to recognize their
family relationship.

Beneath the formality and regulation that characterizes the CCM's eligibility procedures, the soup kitchen program is in reality a flexible community that recognizes the importance of social networks by readily wel-
coming and accommodating participants' friends and relatives.
Recipients and volunteers do not have to leave guests at home when they
attend the soup kitchen. When Vera's sister visits from a town outside
Moscow, she attends the soup kitchen with Vera, receives her own meal,
and participates in Vera's conversation groups. Vera confessed that her
sister has a "crush" on the coordinator at that cafeteria and often asks her
to pass on messages or small gifts to him. As mentioned previously, several people bring their young grandchildren. Volunteers pay special attention to the children, playing with them and giving them small treats.
Other recipients who usually eat in the soup kitchen take portions of their
meals home and share them with visitors. At her birthday party, Aleksandra Petrovna served sweet rolls that she had saved from her meals at
the soup kitchen. Meanwhile, volunteers bring their visiting friends and
family to the cafeterias as well and introduce them to other helpers and
recipients.

The Morality of Social Security

The importance of social relations as the criteria by which people evaluate food poverty underscores the significance of group membership in everyday Russian life. People who are within the soup kitchen system do not see themselves as hungry precisely because they belong to a network. Instead, they perceive the people who live outside the soup kitchen network as those who are in danger of going hungry. Nevertheless, membership in a social network is not enough to protect people from threats of material scarcity, either real or imagined. A corollary to the importance of trust in social relations is the demonstration of morally appropriate behavior in the use of social relations. People are entitled to belong to a social community only if they can demonstrate that they are responsible members of that group. This sense of morality applies to all levels of social organization, from immediate exchange partners to society and the nation at large. Individuals who somehow deviate from the norms of social interaction are represented as forces that violate the social order and consequently are not worthy of public assistance.

A common reaction among people who did not have firsthand knowledge of food aid programs in Moscow was that all recipients must be bomzhi or alcoholics. A university student who disagreed about the value of my research asserted that I was wasting my time, because food aid recipients are drunks who have caused their own problems by squandering their apartments and savings on alcohol. In an intriguing contrast, his mother, a physician who has seen many hardship cases in her examining room, enthusiastically supported food aid and other public assistance projects and frequently expressed interest in my findings. In a similar vein, a professional woman in her forties contended that there is no real hunger in Russia and suggested instead that the only people who are hungry in Moscow are those who are too lazy to work. Citing the availability of such menial jobs as selling cigarettes by the metro stations, she complained that lazy people find it easy to stand on the street, hold out their hands, and beg, "Give me money." People such as these are embarrassments to Russians who support themselves, she concluded. On a separate occasion, the woman returned to this theme and further expanded her category of "lazy people" to include African students and refugees who depend on state subsidies.

The director of a soup kitchen for homeless persons acknowledged that his biggest obstacle to finding donors and volunteers and getting permission from local authorities for his program is to correct Muscovites' perceptions that his clients are lazy, dirty, and generally unworthy of public assistance. In summer 1998, Moscow hosted the World Youth Games. As part of citywide beautification efforts that included extensive landscaping and renovation of building façades, city authorities closed down this soup kitchen, as well as the activities of Doctors Without Borders, an international medical program that offers free health care to homeless persons in Russia. Homeless people and other "undesirable" persons were picked up by the local police and transported well beyond the city limits with the expectation that they would not immediately have the resources to return to Moscow. Officials justified these actions by citing concerns that homeless people might contaminate visitors with diseases, particularly because most aid programs serving the homeless are located near railway stations. Aid workers, however, reported that a reliable source had learned that President Yeltsin's sister had observed the feeding program and, embarrassed at the picture it presented to the outside world, had petitioned her brother to close the center in order to present a more appealing image of Russia to foreign visitors.

Comparable sentiments about the connection between responsible behavior and social assistance emerged in the comments of Russian members of the CCM church. One congregant, a Muscovite who works in a foreign company and portrays herself as a philanthropic-minded person, confided that she gave money only to invalids who begged. She claimed that other people could find ways to support themselves if they were truly in need of food. This theme of self-sufficiency and personal responsibility eventually played a pivotal role in an incident within the CCM congregation.

To foster fellowship and cultural awareness among members and to raise money for the soup kitchen program, CCM representatives organized an international potluck supper. Congregants were assigned to committees according to their countries of origin, and each committee was charged with providing foods that were representative of their homelands. Aware of the income disparities between African and non-African members, small subsidies were given to people with limited finances. Money was also given to several Russian members with extenuating circumstances; for instance, one man had just lost his job in the wake of the August financial crisis. The members of the Russian committee compiled a menu of the dishes they wanted to serve and then decided that Oksana would be given funds in return for preparing most of the food for the Russian table. Because Oksana was a single, nonworking mother of eight children, all of whom would be attending the dinner and eating (and all of whom benefited from various forms of CCM assistance), everyone agreed that she should be responsible for purchasing and providing the food. After committee members presented their plan to her, Oksana accepted the proposal and took the money. Privately, several individuals questioned Oksana's dependability; in the days leading up to the dinner, committee members periodically checked with Oksana to ensure that she had successfully bought the necessary goods and was ready to begin cooking.[15]

On the night of the dinner, CCM members decorated their respective tables and set out their food. The Russian members spread tablecloths over their table and artistically positioned decorations and plates of cookies. Oksana, however, was nowhere to be seen, although her children were running around the room and trying to snatch pieces of food from the tables before the meal had officially started. The Russian congregants gathered around their table and excitedly asked each other about Oksana's whereabouts and then speculated unkindly about why she was late. It was not lost on them that Oksana's children were the first in line after Pastor Rick's blessing signaled the official beginning of the dinner. In what seemed to be the consensus, one woman denounced Oksana and argued that she could not be trusted because she did not work and was promiscuous; for evidence, she cited the fact that Oksana's eight children each had a different father. When Oksana did arrive, several hours later, but carrying the promised food, she frantically explained to the others that her oven had broken and that she had had to use a neighbor's kitchen. In response to Oksana's explanation, the women who had previously criticized her so harshly suddenly changed their stories and adjusted the parameters of the "inside" group to include her. Sympathizing with Oksana, they offered supportive statements such as "What can you expect of a Russian oven?" Then they praised her for being responsible and resourceful and for meeting her obligations.

The necessity of social responsibility appears in other venues as well, including the strike that Siberian miners launched outside the Russian White House during the summer months of 1998 to protest their delayed wages. Although some sympathizers (mostly pensioners) brought food to the miners, many other Muscovites objected, claiming that the miners were doing nothing to help themselves and therefore could not complain that they were hungry. One popular view was that the miners could support themselves by finding other work, even if it meant leaving the mining region, but that they had instead preferred to take handouts from sympathizers.

During the Soviet era, concerns with personal and social decency *(prilichnost')* were linked with conventions of "culturedness" *(kul'turnost')* as indices of modernity and civility (Barker 1999a:26; Boym 1994). By following social norms and mores concerning hygiene, dress, and personal conduct more generally, citizens identified themselves as morally and socially upstanding members of society. These emphases have persisted into the post-Soviet period, and they have found special resonance in public views on welfare. This rhetoric that aid recipients are physically and socially polluting is so embedded in local knowledge that an acquaintance who herself works closely with welfare recipients in her home district nonetheless has asked me if CCM recipients are dirty. Within the CCM soup kitchens, cafeteria workers and recipients monitor the dress and behavior of other recipients. On one occasion, a recipient arrived looking disheveled and reeking of alcohol. Several other recipients immediately confronted her and sharply scolded her for being *neprilichnaia* (indecent) before sending her home. On another occasion, the dictatorial manager of one cafeteria took offense at a young volunteer's skimpy—albeit very trendy—attire and refused to let the young woman stay in the cafeteria, because customers would be offended by her "indecency."

CCM recipients counter these sentiments by paying careful attention to their personal grooming habits and treating the soup kitchens as settings of respectability. Their efforts are mirrored by those of St. Petersburg homeless persons who try to counteract the stigmas of social pollution through discursive strategies that call attention to their cleanliness, helpfulness, and moral decency, as well as through more practical efforts such as trying to keep themselves clean (Höjdestrand 2000). An ethnographic study of begging practices in Moscow reported that pedestrians are more likely to give money to nice-looking elderly people and women with children before giving it to individuals who appear to be alcoholics (Butovskaya, Diakonov, and Salter 2000).[16] Such notions about the appropriateness of aid recipients' behavior—and appearance—accentuate the ways in which local understandings of social assistance are entwined with expectations about responsibility to the community.

This notion of social and personal responsibility is not unilateral, however. Not only do Muscovites depend on potential aid recipients to behave in ways that support the moral social order, but they also expect that persons who have sufficient means will help their fellow members of society. CCM recipients who evaluated the reasons for their participation in the soup kitchen program remarked on Muscovites' changing attitudes about collective assistance. A familiar grievance was that selfish parties—ranging from family members to politicians to the state—were not meeting their obligations to the rest of society. Boris, a sixty-year-old invalid and pensioner, expressed his frustrations by blaming the national gas company and two reform-minded politicians, former finance minister Yegor Gaidar and former prime minister Viktor Chernomyrdin, who had, in his opinion, profited both financially and professionally at the expense of ordinary Russians: "I was in the army for three years. I served at [various fronts] and now cannot afford to feed myself. Gaidar [ruined the economy]. Now you feed us. I cannot buy sausages, meat, bread. Pensioners do not receive much money. It all goes to Gaidar. Chernomyrdin takes it. . . . Gazprom takes it from us. I have no relations with Gazprom."[17] On another occasion Boris pointed out a young woman who was leaning against a Mercedes while talking on her cellular telephone. "Look at the New Russian," he said bitterly. "They don't feed us."

Domestic aid workers contend that Russia's newly emerging cohort of young middle-class professionals have learned the practices of market capitalism and consumerism all too well and are privileging money and status over their responsibilities to other people. Aid workers and recipients also target children and young adults as being too focused on themselves and shirking their responsibilities to other Muscovites. An official with the Russian Red Cross remarked that the second most important group of clients her office serves is composed of people who are not technically alone but have been abandoned by their children. In a separate conversation, a CCM recipient commented that the disappointing behavior of Russia's youth is a manifestation of an exclusionary distinction between "nash" and "ne nash." The woman said that Russia's young people no longer help because they believe that issues such as poverty are "your" (*vasha*) problem and not theirs. These concerns coincide with more widespread fears that young Russians are losing their distinctive Russianness (Zelensky 1999) and, in particular, losing touch with the collectivity of the "nash" by becoming too Americanized.

To support this view, Muscovites criticize American ideology and law that sets emancipation at age eighteen. Citing as evidence the trend in American society for many young people to leave home at this age to attend college or to begin work, respondents conclude that these practices mean that American parents have "kicked" their children out, thereby severing the ties of reciprocal assistance that should connect parents and children. Expressing a sentiment that I heard from several mothers, Irina argued that she would never stop giving her son assistance and that he would always have a place to stay with her. My former landlady Anya succinctly characterized the difference between Russians and Americans in this way: "You Americans are too individualistic. We Russians are collective [my kollektivnye]."

Birthday Parties and Social Capital

In many societies celebrations that mark personal milestones in the company of friends and relatives, such as baptisms, weddings, and funerals, are also important occasions to take stock of one's social assets. Guests are not simply social intimates who are sentimentally linked with the celebrant; they are also social agents with vested interests in the nature and durability of their relations with the subject. Business acquaintances can be recognized and debts can be repaid through invitations to festivities. Personal events are thus opportunities to calculate and display social capital in a public setting. Among Muscovites, birthday parties are particularly compelling indicators of changing social relations in the postsocialist period.[18] Previously, when Muscovites observed personal celebrations such as birthdays they did so in their homes or, more rarely, in restaurants. The celebrant planned the event and provided the food and beverages. Recently, as public dining has become more affordable and more mainstream, birthday parties have become more elaborate and have moved more visibly into the public sphere. Restaurants such as McDonald's offer organized parties for children; adults treat friends and colleagues to more expensive meals, complete with entertainment, served in restaurants or catered in their places of business. Those who have the means can now demonstrate—or even flaunt—both their social and their material status.

Muscovites are also publicly recognized with institutional celebrations. Senior citizens' organizations and veterans' councils send birthday cards and small anniversary presents to elderly clients. At the end of the year, children attend commercial New Year's parties where they play games, eat snacks, watch cultural performances, and receive small gifts of candy and toys. Around March 8, International Women's Day, districts throughout the city invite local women to attend concerts and other performances that honor women and their contributions to the state and society. Typically women receive a box of chocolates afterward. Although recipients of these congratulatory measures can still evaluate their social standing in terms of the quality and type of party they attend and in terms of the gifts they receive, these generalized public events are impersonal and anonymous, as individuals are subsumed within the larger generic population.

More personal events such as birthdays and funerals acquire additional significance as markers of social relations. Particularly for Muscovites with more limited resources, material displays and public festivities are less important than the opportunity to validate one's social worth through companionship with close friends. Veronika, a young woman who had limited finances and few close friends in Moscow, worried that her preschool-age daughter, Ira, spent too much time alone with her elderly grandmother and did not have enough opportunities to interact with other people. Despite the girl's young age, Veronika tried diligently to expose her daughter to public life by scraping together enough money to take Ira to cultural events such as ballets and the opera. For Ira's fourth birthday, Veronika arranged with a friend, an American researcher living in Moscow, to have a party for the little girl. The American woman offered her apartment for the festivities, organized the food, and invited several foreign colleagues who were also friends with Veronika. Veronika brought a cake, some candy, and a bottle of wine. Although Ira was the only person present under the age of twenty-five, and although most of the food was "adult" fare of sandwiches and salads, Veronika conceded that it was a successful celebration, because they were both able to leave their apartment and spend time with friends.

When Aleksandra Petrovna turned seventy-five, she organized two parties for herself. The first event was only for relatives and was observed at her nephew's dacha. For the second affair, Aleksandra Petrovna invited the CCM soup kitchen program director, several coordinators and volunteers, and two neighborhood friends to her apartment for an elaborate dinner party. She spent two days making salads, pastries, boiled chicken, and potatoes, which she served on her nicest tablecloth and with her most elegant china plates and crystal glassware. At the appointed time she sat in her room to wait for her guests. I returned early from a trip outside Moscow to attend the party and was making my way to her apartment from the train station. When I arrived at the metro station nearest her street, I telephoned to tell her that I would be a few minutes late. Over the phone she excitedly told me, "Hurry. We're waiting for you." Embarrassed at the thought of delaying the celebration further, I scurried up the street and arrived ten minutes later, approximately twenty minutes after the set time, only to discover that I was the first to arrive. One hour later, one of the coordinators finally arrived from the soup kitchen and

186 THE MYTHOLOGY OF HUNGER

passed on last-minute regrets from his partner. For another hour the three of us chatted and picked at the salads, as Aleksandra Petrovna did not want to bring out the next course until all the guests had arrived. Every ten minutes or so, Aleksandra Petrovna called round to the other people who had been invited. Evidently no one was home, and she optimistically remarked that they must each be making their way to her home at that very moment. Eventually, the CCM director arrived, bearing a large bouquet of flowers and a bottle of champagne. Resigned to the fact that we were likely to be her only guests, Aleksandra Petrovna asked the men to open the bottles of champagne and wine and then began serving the food. Although she gaily told us stories about her childhood, she periodically stopped to ask us why we thought no one else was coming. It was clear that her happiness at our attendance was overshadowed by her distress at being neglected by her other friends, particularly those she had known for many years (figure 15).[19]

In the soup kitchens, birthday parties are highly visible performances of sociability that serve the additional purpose of demarcating smaller groups of intimates within the larger community. Through these celebrations, one can clearly trace networks and identify subgroups, as well as evaluate one's social standing in the CCM community. The case of Viktor Vladimirovich illustrates this well. Viktor Vladimirovich was the oldest member of the CCM program. He and his wife were among the original recipients and had attended faithfully every day; after his wife died, he continued to come to the soup kitchen by himself almost every day. For his ninety-fifth birthday, several recipients organized a small party for him at the soup kitchen (figure 16). The women had apparently made the plans in advance, because each arrived at the cafeteria with necessary party items: chocolates, homemade pastries, bottles of Sovetskoe champagne, and flowers. They arranged these items, as well as plates, glasses, and silverware, on a table near the desk from which the coordinator dispensed tickets, and then sat down to wait. Usually Viktor Vladimirovich arrived around 11 A.M. On that day, however, he was late, and, in a reversal of the events of Aleksandra Petrovna's party, the women scurried around the room, asking other recipients if they knew where he might be. Finally he arrived and was escorted to his seat of honor at the table. The CCM director and coordinator were invited to join him and the women. Another recipient sat down at the piano and played an assortment of Russian and American songs, including "Happy Birthday," and the party got underway at the table. Other recipients stopped by the table to congratulate Viktor Vladimirovich and to sample the treats. Ever gracious, he thanked

FIGURE 15. Aleksandra Petrovna's birthday party in 2000 was a rousing success, unlike her birthday celebration in 1999.

everyone and kissed the hands of every woman who walked past. Shortly before he left the party, an elderly woman, a usually disagreeable recipient, approached him and shyly offered him a sack of macaroni as a birthday present.

Later that summer, volunteers and recipients organized a joint birthday party for the two coordinators. Two recipients collected money from the other members of the soup kitchen and bought presents for the coordinators. After the serving time had ended, several volunteers and recipients joined the coordinators for a special meal that cafeteria workers had prepared. Over toasts of champagne, the recipients thanked the coordinators for helping "our people" (nashi liudi) and wished them much success and good health in the coming year.

FIGURE 16. CCM coordinators greet Viktor Vladimirovich on his ninety-fifth birthday.

Living Alone

During summer 1999, despite temperatures that soared to record highs, CCM recipients at the fourth soup kitchen turned up regularly every morning. Although most dressed in cooler clothes more appropriate to the weather, one elderly woman steadfastly wore a knitted hat and sweater, despite having to walk almost a mile to the cafeteria. Not surprisingly, she collapsed from heat stroke one morning. While volunteers attempted to make the woman more comfortable, the cafeteria director summoned the physician who was assigned to the building. The doctor examined the woman, gave her some medication, and told her to go home to rest. A volunteer with a car drove the woman back to her apartment, and I escorted the woman to the entryway of her apartment building, where she was met by several neighbors who were sitting on the benches that framed the sidewalk. In response to their concerned questions, she explained what had happened at the soup kitchen. The other women sighed in exasperation and scolded her for going to the soup kitchen in the heat. One woman stated that the older woman should stay home and ask someone to bring her food to her, and her companions nodded their agreement. Later that day, an assistant with the Veterans'

Council was asked by CCM staff about the possibility of finding a volunteer who could collect the woman's meals. The assistant responded pessimistically that because she had been unable to find a volunteer to help the woman in the past, she was doubtful that someone could be located now.

When several weeks had passed and the elderly woman had neither returned to the soup kitchen nor sent someone to collect her food, James, the CCM coordinator, attempted to telephone her at home and ask how she was doing. When James tried the number recorded in the woman's files, he reached a stranger. Afraid that his language ability was preventing him from communicating effectively with the stranger, he asked me to call for him. When I placed the call, the phone was answered by a pleasant-sounding Russian woman. I explained my reason for calling, and she responded, "Yes, a foreign man called the other day. I told him that this was the wrong number, but I don't think he understood. I am sorry that I cannot help you. This is the right address [apartment block], but I don't know that woman." When I apologized for bothering her, the woman quickly replied, "No, thank you for caring about that woman."

The possibility of being cut off from other people is a common fear among pensioners and other people with limited resources. As a United Way official stated, an important component of the agency's mission was to keep clients from feeling "alone" (odinokie). Vera and her nephew Dmitrii acknowledged that they were fortunate because their apartments were located on the ground floor of their respective buildings. Continuing on this topic, they reported that they had recently watched a news program on television about Muscovites who were cut off from the rest of society. According to the report, the decrepit state of many apartment buildings in Moscow causes serious problems for elderly and other incapacitated people. Broken elevators prevent many disabled people from leaving their apartments, particularly those individuals who live on higher floors in tall buildings. One woman allegedly had not left her apartment for the three years that the lift in her building had been broken. Similar news stories related the plight of physically disabled residents who were unable to leave their apartments because their buildings were not wheelchair accessible or did not have elevators. Another series of news articles reported on the circumstances of blind Russians. Assistance animals are rare in Russia and cannot be easily replaced. A blind woman who had rejoiced in the freedom and mobility that came with her seeing-eye dog found herself confined to her apartment after the dog died.

Other Muscovites are limited in the scope of their social contacts because they do not have regular access to a telephone. People such as Veronika and several CCM recipients rely on public telephones or the telephones of friends and neighbors to call friends and acquaintances periodically. Owing to continued scarcities of private telephones, messages are routinely passed on through third parties; it is common and acceptable for people to phone the neighbor of a friend and ask either for a message to be passed on or for the neighbor to bring the friend to the phone, or even to ask a friend to place a telephone call on one's behalf. These means underscore the importance of having social connections to stay in touch, and the loss of such contacts has serious consequences. Between 1998 and 1999, my friend Lena lived in an apartment without a telephone. To reach her, I first telephoned the police department where her husband worked and asked the dispatcher to relay a message to her husband via walkie-talkie. Her husband then passed the message to Lena, and she called me later from a telephone at the post office. Similarly, after Veronika lost her job, she was forced to move into a series of communal apartments, most of which were without a telephone. Because her friends were unable to contact her, they waited for her to call them either at home or at work and pass on her new address and phone number (when available) and to set up times to visit. During summer 2000, however, Veronika lost touch with several of her closest friends. While Veronika was moving between apartments, one of her primary contacts suddenly moved to Germany, and another friend unexpectedly changed both apartments and jobs. Neither had any way of passing her new coordinates to Veronika. All they could do was leave messages at the last several places where Veronika had lived and hope that she would eventually contact those places and collect her messages. Although Veronika had used an electronic mail address in the past, her friends feared that without a job and with very limited savings, her access to a computer would be curtailed. By summer 2001, Veronika had reestablished contact with several friends via electronic mail. Nevertheless, her housing and employment had not, as of 2002, stabilized, and she continued to shuttle between apartments and jobs. Fortunately, she stays in touch with her mother in another city; friends have been able to reach her by calling her mother and leaving messages.

Despite the high costs of service, wireless telephones are increasingly valuable tools for keeping people in contact with each other. Similarly, many Internet service providers have entered the Russian market in the last few years, and Muscovites who do not have access to computers at home or work can take advantage of the many Internet cafés that are appearing around the city. People who cannot afford to buy their own computers or pay the service fees at Internet cafés have opened up free e-mail accounts and borrow Internet time from friends and colleagues with computers. CCM recipients ask their grandchildren or volunteers with computer access to pass on messages to former volunteers and other friends who have gone abroad. One woman applied to her local welfare office for a used computer for her disabled son. She wrote in her letter that her son was unable to leave the apartment and would benefit from being able to communicate with people through the computer. At the same time that these technologies facilitate direct and more immediate communication among Muscovites, they also offer people new means of engaging in more familiar methods of social contact—namely, that of passing information through intermediaries, as they have done through phone relays. Muscovites who send electronic mail ask recipients to pass them on to others, and people give out the wireless telephone numbers of friends and colleagues as their own.[20]

In summer 1998, Muscovites were informed that the city would soon begin charging for local telephone service for in-home telephones. Previously local calls had been free, and residents paid only for intercity or international calls. For those people without telephones in their apartments, local calls could be placed at pay telephones on the street or in the post office for a minimal fee. This announcement sparked a firestorm of controversy in the city. Particularly vocal were pensioners, whose monthly pensions barely covered necessities such as rent, utilities, food, and medicine. Pensioners and their advocates expressed fears that people who could not afford to make telephone calls would find themselves cut off from their primary source of communication with relatives and friends. Especially worrisome was the prospect that disabled people would be stranded in their homes with no means to interact with the outside world. In response to these concerns, city authorities backed off in their efforts and announced that special dispensation from toll costs would be granted to pensioners and other needy people. As of spring 2003, the system of charging for local calls had yet to go into effect.

The Shame of Aloneness

The importance of being able to demonstrate and verify one's membership within a community is emphasized by the embarrassment that emerges when people perceive that their connections are flimsy or when they suspect others will interpret their networks as insufficient. Pensioners in the soup kitchen reflected that their participation in the CCM program had resulted from the state's abandonment of its workers. This reflected a sense of betrayal among those who had trusted the Soviet state's promise to reward faithful workers in their old age. One common theme that recipients mentioned was that although they were grateful for the assistance they had received, they were ashamed *(stydno)* to have been put in the position of requiring aid. Recipients were particularly concerned about receiving aid from foreigners. Many drew attention to the irony of their circumstances: they were receiving food from Africans, many of whom had come from countries that were experiencing their own problems with food poverty.[21] Larissa Antonovna commented one morning that she appreciated the meals at the soup kitchen, but then added, "I am ashamed *[mne stydno]* that it is foreigners feeding us." Another recipient, Galina, expressed this sense of disappointment more simply. Through her tears, she reflected, "I have spent my whole life defending Moscow. And for what?"

Soup kitchen recipients articulate their frustrations and anger with each other through accusations of abandonment and disconnection from networks. When the fourth CCM soup kitchen opened, the cafeteria manager became frustrated with the lack of order among potential recipients. One day she was complaining more generally about the number of unregistered people who had shown up at the soup kitchen in the hopes that they could add their names to the roster. As she hustled people out the door, she grumbled that the program could not feed everybody just because their children had "tossed them out" *(deti brosili)*. It was the responsibility of the children to care for their parents, she argued, but these children had thrown out their parents, and now it was charitable organizations that had to care for them. A woman standing nearby scolded the manager and demanded to know how she could say such things. The manager replied that she had seen enough to know. In response, the other woman asked her to stop shouting and swearing. The interaction developed into a loud and prolonged argument until finally the visitor left. On another occasion, a prospective CCM recipient turned down her spot when she was told that she could not take food for several weeks at a time. She explained that she was embarrassed that her neighbors might discover that she was alone and dependent on charitable assistance.

The stigma of being alone is so powerful that rumors in Moscow allege the existence of companies that will, for a fee, call customers on their wireless telephones and engage them in prearranged conversations on particular topics. For instance, a businessman can request a call in which his responses give the appearance that he is negotiating with a client or dealing with investors. Through this service, Muscovites can demonstrate that they are socially connected.

Aid recipients who otherwise might be consigned to the margins of society appreciate the opportunities they are given to be part of a larger social network. Like several activists for pensioners' interests, Valentina Fëdorovna commented that she received many calls from people in her district who wanted to thank her for remembering them with a small gift on a personal holiday. She reflected that although a small box of chocolate was not much in material terms, it carried great symbolic weight as evidence that recipients had not been forgotten. Other activists reported that late at night they often received telephone calls from pensioners they had helped. As one woman described, the callers simply wanted to express their thanks for the assistance they had received and to wish her a "peaceful night" (*spokoinoi nochi*) before retiring to bed.

The Economics of Friendship

In the culture of the CCM soup kitchens, sociability becomes a precious commodity that participants extend, withhold, and trade with each other, a strategy that Robert Desjarlais has also observed in his ethnographic study of a Boston homeless shelter. Desjarlais argues that social relations among these program recipients were marked by a "mercantile spirit" (1996:887), so that participants carefully structured their relationships with each other to circulate social resources that were in short supply. Thus, the very conditionality of interpersonal exchanges fuses the economic and the social (Herrmann 1997; Scharf 1997; Yan 1996; cf. Bourdieu 1984) and makes them mutually convertible.

Because exchange practices are possible once personal relationships have been established, Muscovites' abilities to share information, food, money, concern, and responsibility demonstrate that they are solidly grounded within a viable collectivity. The sustained importance of social connections is further evident in the ways that CCM participants personalize their relations with each other. Owing to the crucial role played by social resources in Muscovites' everyday survival strategies, as well as the larger cultural context that privileges the collective over the individual, the nature of food aid and other forms of assistance needs to be reconsidered. For the case of Russia, despite the aims and opinions voiced by many foreign observers and aid workers, food assistance is not merely a utilitarian solution to a material problem. Rather, it is a form of security that is intrinsically and necessarily social.

CHAPTER 7

Socialism Revisited

During the course of my research, many people have appealed to me to tell "the truth" about what it is like to live in Moscow today. Both inside and outside the soup kitchen community, Muscovites have disagreed strongly with the conclusions about Russian society that have been reached in foreign political and economic analyses and disseminated to a global audience. The disproportionate weight that has been given to macrolevel perspectives on Eastern Europe and the former Soviet Union has eclipsed the complexities and contradictions that appear only with the extreme detail that is the hallmark of ethnography. Too often, ethnography is dismissed as trivial and anecdotal. Statistics, voting patterns, and the opinions of politicians are uncritically preferred over the voices and more mundane—and more complicated—lives of ordinary people. Even more problematic, however, is that these preferences silence the voices and deny the creativity and agency of these ordinary people. When I presented an earlier draft of one of the chapters in this book to an interdisciplinary workshop on postcommunist politics at Harvard University, my nonanthropologist colleagues debated among themselves the merits of ethnographic research versus statistical analyses. My arguments about the cultural construction of hunger provoked a particularly heated discussion, and my colleagues repeatedly asked me for figures about nutrition and consumer spending habits. Apparently unwilling to let go of "hard facts" and unconvinced by my argument for the importance of culture, they concluded the conversation with one person's comment: "Ethnography is interesting, but it doesn't tell us anything."

This is precisely the perspective that many other anthropologists working in postsocialist spaces have criticized and with which I have tried to take issue in this book.[1] The power of ethnography emerges from the connections that are drawn between the most minute and mundane aspects of daily life, what Malinowski has called the "inponderabilia of actual life" (1961:18), and the larger social fabric in which they are embedded. The nation-state does not exist at a distance from its constituents but is always in a dialectical relationship with them. It is through their everyday routines, relationships, and beliefs that people make sense of and experience the world around them. Thus, this text is simultaneously an ethnography of a community whose members employ a specific set of improvisational practices in their everyday lives and a narrative of post-Soviet life as my subjects have comprehended and experienced it. More important, through this text I have tried to restore to the individuals whose stories are told here their voices and the recognition that they are social agents whose lives are meaningful and whose views on their own lives are analytically significant.

I would like to close this account by returning to where everything began: the CCM soup kitchen. Specifically, I am returning to the feud that erupted between Oksana and Aleksandra Petrovna, because the issues involved in its interactions have informed much of the preceding discussion about the connections among material resources, forms of assistance, and social relations. From a personal perspective, this occurrence was an ethnographic turning point for me, because I suddenly found myself caught up in the local politics and emotions of the community I was studying. I discovered that my role as one of several conduits for the enactment of these negotiations meant that the distinctions between "me" and "them," and between objectivity and subjectivity, were blurred.

Almost without being aware of it, I had become so enmeshed in the affairs of the soup kitchen that it became "my" community. Having to watch as people I cared deeply about battled with each other was troubling, as was the fact that certain individuals wanted me to take sides. I was saddened when this disagreement was not resolved by the time I left Moscow. Once I was back home I tried to decode the news I received from Moscow but was unable to determine what shape the aftereffects of the dispute had taken. In particular, I wondered if Aleksandra Petrovna would recover from her heart attack, whether Oksana would be able to retain the small bit of power and influence she had wielded, and, perhaps more important, whether the CCM coordinators and staff would be able to create a semblance of order and sense of community among a group of recipients who had been together for only several weeks before the feud exploded in their midst.

When I returned to Moscow the following year for a conference, I immediately went to the fourth soup kitchen. Because I was unexpected, I was able to walk in and observe for a few moments before I was recognized. Instead of the angry voices, confusion, and subtle discrimination that I had remembered from the registration period a year before, I watched as recipients warmly greeted the coordinators and one another, found seats and initiated conversations with friends, and shared treats they had brought from home. I heard cafeteria workers, volunteers, and recipients addressing each other with the informal "you" and sharing personal information. On their way back out the door, recipients stopped to say good-bye to the coordinators or to offer them a hug and kiss. My sense that a tightly knit community had emerged from what was originally an impersonal list of names was later confirmed in conversations with coordinators, volunteers, and recipients. Participants claimed that the soup kitchen was now running smoothly and that the unpleasantness of the feud was a distant memory.

When I did not immediately see Aleksandra Petrovna, I asked Alan, one of the coordinators, about her. He grinned and told me that she was there and continued to be one of the anchors of the program. I finally caught sight of her when she emerged from the dish room and then managed to catch up with her as she bustled around delivering other recipients' meals and looking like the picture of health, a vast improvement over her appearance when I had last seen her. Several days later we were able to talk at length, and I asked her to fill me in on the aftermath of the feud and her relationship with Oksana. Aleksandra Petrovna reminded me that after her unexpected meeting with Oksana and subsequent heart attack, she had written a long letter of resignation to the CCM ministers and coordinators. Even though she was an unpaid volunteer, she had wanted to explain formally why she could no longer serve the program. She said she explained in the letter that although she had always believed very strongly that she had a duty and desire to help other people, she was unwilling to stay where she was unwelcome. The CCM ministers refused to accept her resignation and reassured her that she was a valued member of the community. To prevent any further troubles, however, they asked Aleksandra Petrovna not to visit the soup kitchen that Oksana attended.

I was surprised, then, when Aleksandra Petrovna said that she and Oksana had taken steps to mend their relationship and were once again on speaking terms. She remarked that she still did not understand what had compelled Oksana to make such accusations and to behave as she had, particularly because they had been friends for a long time and she had helped Oksana in various ways over the years. Nevertheless, she seemed willing to forgive some of Oksana's behavior—and Oksana had apparently forgiven Aleksandra Petrovna's behavior as well. A week later I witnessed for myself the fragile truce the two women had established. At a party hosted by the CCM ministers and coordinators to thank the soup kitchen volunteers, Aleksandra Petrovna and Oksana greeted each other with a kiss and carried on a civil, chatty conversation for several minutes. The same ritual was repeated later at a CCM church service.

That Aleksandra Petrovna and Oksana were able to patch their relationship back together to some degree, even if only for appearance's sake, was important not only for them personally but also for the rest of the soup kitchen community. Although the feud was localized between two small groups of individuals, if it had continued without resolution, its repercussions could have disrupted the fragile social compact that united the soup kitchen. In keeping with the emphasis that CCM recipients have placed on mutual support and collective responsibility, the significance of a social alliance is that it is a process whereby each member "places his person and all his power in common under the supreme direction of the general will; and as one[, all members] receive each member as an indivisible part of the whole" (Rousseau 1987:148). The success of either woman in excluding the other would have threatened the sense of collective well-being, mutual responsibility, and cooperation that characterized social interactions among participants.

In many respects the feud was a critical turning point for the entire soup kitchen community, because it sent a clear message to all participants that their positions within the group were precarious. Moreover, the events that transpired before, during, and after Oksana and Aleksandra Petrovna's disagreement provide a critical commentary on the soup kitchen's precarious position within the larger transformations in Russia today and, in particular, the future of Russian society in the world of global capitalism.

Commercialization and Its Discontents

The recent changes that have taken place in Russia are firmly situated within a series of modernizing projects. The end of the Soviet Union in 1991 signaled to many outsiders, Americans in particular, an end to the era of communism and the beginning of many opportunities to revamp the Soviet system. Janine Wedel (1998a:4) uses the word *frontier* to describe

Western views of the post-Soviet landscape in Eastern Europe and the former Soviet Union. I find this term apt, because not only does it reflect the popular view among foreign donors and advisers that these regions were ripe for economic and political colonization, but it also captures the sense of lawlessness, violence, and uncertainty that these donors and advisers have attributed to the region. "Experts" from such wide-ranging fields as medicine, law, business, and science, as well as educators and native English-speakers, have been drawn to Russia and elsewhere in the region to help the "natives" learn how to navigate the inevitable and necessary transition to democracy and capitalism and to triumph over the "corruption" of a system entrenched in informal networks. The ultimate goal implicit in these ventures has been for formerly communist societies to reach eventually the utopia of democracy and global capitalism. It should not be surprising, then, that many foreign aid projects in Russia have been focused less on issues of humanitarianism and more on issues of economic and political development.

Although plans such as these appealed to the ideals of improvement implied in evolutionary schemas, their practitioners overlooked the inherent contradictions and potential dangers that lurk in modernizing projects. When initial efforts to reform the Russian economy failed to produce an American-style market system, a common response was "What went wrong?"—suggesting that Russia had somehow deviated from its proper path. Although anthropologists have argued for the unique cultural particularities of different societies, even in today's global context (e.g., Bestor 1999; Watson 1997), this perspective was missing in the attitudes of foreign advisers who predicated their actions on the presumption that a model could be removed from its context of origin and applied in its entirety to a completely different society. My informants wondered how outsiders could have missed what seemed to them an obvious fact, and many succinctly explained the "failures" of the democratization efforts with the straightforward comment that Russia was not like the United States.

As Giddens points out, although it is imperative to understand modernity on its institutional level, we must look for its consequences at the local level (1991:1). For the case of Russia, the commercialization and globalization of the market have had a profound impact on the ways in which Muscovites approach both their material and their social provisioning tactics. The move away from an emphasis on production to one that focuses on consumption and the rapid spread of commodity diversity has forced shoppers to rethink the ways in which they deal with the market and with one another. In essence, the provisioning experience has been transformed from one centered around access to one based on selectivity, a change that has neatly shifted the shopping experience from an intrinsically social venture to a more individualized one.

Muscovites recall their frustrations in the early 1990s, when they were suddenly confronted with a variety of seemingly identical but competing products. To encourage and educate Russian consumers, companies have introduced advertisements, product demonstrations in public spaces, and endorsement campaigns, both to acquaint customers with their goods and to teach them how to make knowledgeable and discriminating choices. Other companies focus even more directly on empowering consumers: personal sales ventures like Herbalife and Mary Kay cosmetics offer consumers opportunities to achieve fluency in capitalist-style transactions.

Commercialization is also affecting the most intimate spheres of social life. Family dynamics are changing as children learn—and increasingly command—the knowledge necessary for dealing in today's marketplace. As young people become more conversant with foreign cultural trends and the global market, this fluency gives them authority as culture brokers. Parents and grandparents look to their children to explain technological innovations, to evaluate brands, and, as English creeps into daily usage, to translate for their elders. Accompanying these shifts in power relations are adjustments in the realm of a family's finances: for many pensioners, the discrepancies between their minuscule state pensions and the salaries that many young people earn in private and multinational companies are disgraceful.

As the parameters of daily life change, CCM recipients feel increasingly disconnected from—and oftentimes resentful of—their own society. In practical terms, Russia's new commercial realm is largely beyond the reach of most CCM recipients, because full access requires greater financial resources than are available to the vast majority of CCM recipients. In more symbolic terms, CCM recipients express their concerns that this new world also signals the loss of more traditional Russian values. Mothers and grandmothers fret that as their daughters come to rely on "American-style" prepared foods and one-stop shopping, they will eventually lose their capacity to cook Russian dishes—and more important, to improvise and make do. Even the activities of foreign charities are problematic for Muscovites who see the transnational aspect of assistance as a preview of the diffusion of Russian culture and social networks. Both aid recipients and social workers are apprehensive that the presence of aid programs funded and administered by foreign charities, especially those that do not work within existing local structures and practices, will displace local assistance programs and minimize the importance of cultural traits such as practical sociability and mutual responsibility. CCM recipients know friends and neighbors who have been promised assistance through other programs and then abandoned when the programs have discontinued their services because of a loss of funding or interest from sponsors. The precarious position of foreign aid programs fosters uncertainty within the CCM soup kitchens; recipients worriedly ask coordinators to deny rumors that the CCM program will be the next to close.

Ultimately, the members of the larger CCM community—recipients, their relatives, social workers, welfare officials, and local politicians—are concerned about the loss of interpersonal relations and a move toward individualization and atomization. From the perspective of these individuals, Western economic practices threaten to displace social relations as the channels through which financial assistance circulates. Muscovites are encouraged to place their trust—and their money—in newly formed institutions, not old friends and family. This growing individualization and the modernizing project in which it is embedded also bring about increasing isolation and social fragmentation, a situation that Marx (1978) predicted with his ideas on "alienation," and Durkheim (1979) with his notion of "anomie." Social cohesion breaks down as individuals become distanced from one another and from themselves. As I described in chapter 6, CCM recipients have argued that many of the hardships facing them and other Russians today are due to the breakdown of sociability and increasing selfishness of Russia's political and economic elite. Domestic aid workers lament that members of Russia's upper class are not interested in supporting their programs and, in some cases, actively try to distance themselves from the unpleasantness of poverty associated with soup kitchens and other programs. CCM recipients have suggested that the reason so few Russian young people serve as volunteers is that they are interested in making money and do not want to be confronted with such a vivid image of what their own future might be like.

Nevertheless, there are paradoxes inherent in this perspective. Even as CCM recipients and aid workers grieve over the breakdown of this purportedly universal social cohesion, they are quick to employ the rhetoric of nash and ne nash to create hierarchies of people who are more deserving of assistance than others. And through their extended exchange networks, there are certainly CCM recipients who count among their connections upwardly mobile people who are committed to fulfilling their responsibilities to family and friends.

Perhaps the greatest paradox of the CCM soup kitchen program is that, although the conditions of material poverty that make it necessary are problematic within the aims of democratization and capitalization currently at work in Russia, the program is in fact a safe haven from these processes. Within the soup kitchens, recipients have responded to the threats of individualization, isolation, social fragmentation, and loss of tradition by establishing a vital community in which members care for one another. Through the flexible ideology of "nash," recipients, volunteers, and cafeteria workers can transform potentially dangerous foreign elements and persons into a locally situated and known social and economic network. Recipients who fear being abandoned by their children and grandchildren reframe the parameters of their social groups to include African, North American, and European volunteers. And it is to these persons that recipients choose to pass on their memories, histories, and cultural traditions, as well as the material goods and survival skills that constitute their personal understandings of what it means to be Russian. Moreover, although these Muscovites are recipients of foreign aid, they have reworked assistance transactions in the CCM program so that they are active creators and producers within the system. They maneuver around the regulations and structures of the program to reflect their own assessments of their needs and responsibilities.

The Future of Socialism

So what does an ethnography of a soup kitchen program reveal about the nature of capitalism and its future in Russia today and, by extension, the nature of socialism and its future in Russia today? My friend Olga offered a fable that might be instructive for thinking about this question. Over dinner one night in summer 2000, Olga confided her concerns that the recent installation of Vladimir Putin as Russia's president would mean a return to the old ways. By way of explanation, she asked if I had heard the fable about the crow and the fox and then told me that it had been adapted for Putin. The story goes like this: A crow finds a piece of cheese and picks it up in his beak. A fox comes up to him and asks, "Did you vote for Putin?" The crow remains silent. The fox asks him again, "Did you vote for Putin?" Again the crow remains silent. Finally the fox asks him again, "Tell me, did you vote for Putin?" At last the crow answers,

"Yes." The piece of cheese falls from his beak, and the fox grabs it up and runs off. The crow then asks, "If I had voted no, would that have changed anything?"

As this fable suggests, there is a sense in Russia that the more things change, the more they stay the same. This is especially so for the ways in which Muscovites see the legacy and future of socialism. In many respects the actions of the CCM soup kitchen participants seem to represent a collective strategy to hold on to the past and an effort to preserve, reinvoke, or reinvent a "socialist" way of life that is at odds with the societal changes currently taking place. This supports the conclusions reached by other anthropologists who work in post-Soviet societies and have challenged the notion of a synchronic "postsocialism" (e.g., Ashwin 1999; Creed 1999; Dunn 1999; Humphrey 1999; Lass 1999). In some cases, revisiting the values and practices of socialism, either positively or negatively, is part of a movement to create a national present through revisionist history and nostalgia (Berdahl 1999a; Hayden 1994). In other cases, renewed interest in socialism is not a remnant of the past but is, rather, a new phenomenon that is paradoxically made possible only through the ideals of participatory democracy and civic empowerment (Creed 1999). At the heart of all these perspectives, however, is the sense that there are social forces that might be beyond the control of individual agents. As a result, what we may be witnessing in Russia today is the persistence of a socialist worldview, or habitus, that will continue to color everyday social life into the future.

Certainly the actual and imagined persistence of socialist practices and ideologies into the second decade of post-Soviet life is problematic for the ways in which we approach both the region of Eastern Europe and the former Soviet Union and the notion of "postsocialism" itself. I like Caroline Humphrey's proposition to use the term *neosocialism,* because, as she writes, "socialism (as indigenously defined) is not dead in Russia" (1999:25). This is certainly true within the CCM soup kitchen community, where participants continue to frame their daily lives through the practices and ideologies of making do that were essential for life during the Soviet period, even as they acknowledge that these practices have acquired new forms, meanings, and purposes in today's Russia. For them, these improvisational skills remain necessary for coping with the changing contours of everyday life in Moscow. I disagree, however, with the argument that socialist practices are forms of resistance to the conditions of the post-Soviet period (Creed 1999:225). This perspective resembles the arguments made by de Certeau (1984) and Scott (1985), among others, that individuals can display agency only by confronting and opposing the structures and institutions that shape their worlds.

Muscovites who belong to the CCM soup kitchen community are not relying on past ideals about social networks, collective responsibility, and cooperative action as means to escape from or to revolt against the changes that are taking place in Russia today. Rather, they are using these ideals and practices to make sense of these changes and, more important, to refashion them in ways they see as authentically Russian. Recipients deal with global flows of persons and information, threats of isolation, and the effects of commercialization on a daily basis. But by applying the improvisational strategies that have stood them in good stead throughout their lives—networking, social provisioning, and the flexible philosophy of "nash"—recipients are able to manage the world around them. They do not shy away from change but engage with it directly and efficiently. This ability to make do with whatever life deals one is the essence of po-russki, or the Russian style. And as bricoleurs par excellence, members of the CCM demonstrate that at the same time they embody Russia's past, they also represent its future.

Epilogue

Because I have been fortunate to return to Moscow every summer since my original fieldwork in 1997–1998, I have been able to keep current with the changes that have taken place in my field site and among my friends and acquaintances. In many ways, things have stayed the same. Aleksandra Petrovna's birthday parties in 2000, 2001, and 2002 were well-attended, festive affairs. Veronika was still moving back and forth among apartments and jobs, dropping out of contact for months at a time, only to reappear suddenly via e-mail. Several CCM coordinators had returned home to Africa, while others were still in Moscow, completing their degrees.

In other ways, however, drastic changes had occurred while I was gone. After my trip to Moscow in summer 2000, I had continued to keep in touch with friends from the CCM soup kitchen program via letter and electronic mail. In his letters, Alan, one of the coordinators at the fourth soup kitchen, periodically forwarded copies of the reports he presented at the soup kitchen coordinators' meetings. At the end of May 2001, I contacted Alan and told him that I would be arriving in Moscow in several weeks. In my letter, I asked him to fill me in on the latest news of the soup kitchen and the CCM congregation. When Alan wrote back several days later, he told me that life in the soup kitchen and the church was busy as usual and going well and that Aleksandra Petrovna and other friends were excited about my arrival and had passed on their greetings. Several days after my arrival, after I had satisfied the various bureaucratic requirements to register my visa, I prepared to go to the fourth soup kitchen. I traveled across the city and made my way to the building where the soup kitchen was housed, careful to arrive after the serving time had started so as not to disrupt the activities. On my way in, I passed a number of elderly men and women, also headed to the cafeteria. I noticed that the elderly gentleman who had worked as a "doorman" the year before was in his customary place supervising the entrance. I walked past and into the cafeteria.

Everything looked the same as I remembered it: elderly Muscovites first queued at a table to receive their meal tickets and then seated themselves at tables spread with bowls of soup, glasses of tea, and slices of bread. Yet after a moment, I realized that something was different: I did not recognize any of the recipients or volunteers present. Particularly noticeable was that there were no African volunteers. Thinking that perhaps CCM staff had changed the serving time, I walked back to the man at the entrance and asked him if he could tell me when the soup kitchen run by the Christian church would meet. He replied that that soup kitchen program no longer met at that cafeteria. When I asked if he knew where they had gone, he told me that they were using the facilities at the district sports complex. He gave me vague directions, and I headed out to find the soup kitchen.

After an hour of fruitless searching (and wishing that I had not accidentally left my address book and city map behind), I abandoned my search and went back to the apartment where I was staying and collected my address book. I telephoned the CCM church office and suddenly found myself talking with Nadia, the congregation administrator. After we had spent a few moments chatting with each other, I told Nadia that I had gone looking for the soup kitchen and had been unable to find it in its new location. She gave me directions to the sports complex and explained that continuing troubles with the cafeteria manager had escalated to the point that CCM staff decided it was necessary to relocate. Evidently the relocation had happened between my receipt of Alan's letter and my arrival in Moscow. Then Nadia dropped an even bigger bombshell: the soup kitchen located at the Moscow Scientific Institute had closed completely. She revealed that the move was swift and unexpected: just two weeks earlier, the university administration had suddenly decided to close the cafeteria for renovations to transform much of the space into a food shop. The CCM staff were taken unawares, she said, and were unable to find another location on such short notice. A small group of recipients who were physically able to traverse the city by public transportation were transferred to the three remaining soup kitchens, even though it meant they were forced to spend at least an hour each way, using a variety of modes of transportation, to reach another soup kitchen. The vast majority of recipients, however, were unable to travel such great distances and so had found themselves cut off from the CCM program.

The next day I made my way to the fourth soup kitchen. As I was walking down the corridor, I met Aleksandra Petrovna. We greeted each other joyfully, and then she immediately began introducing me to everyone who walked past. Once inside the cafeteria, I was greeted again by Alan, who had since been promoted to the position of director of soup kitchens (formerly held by Dr. Steve), the other coordinators and volunteers, and several recipients who remembered me from the year before. Aleksandra Petrovna insisted on giving me a tour of the new facilities and walked me down the serving line and around the tables. The cafeteria was located inside a circular, glass-walled room that overlooked the Moscow River, a soccer field, a track, and ski jumps left over from the Moscow Olympics. To one side of the building was a forested park, where recipients could walk after their meals and rest, Aleksandra Petrovna told me.

Back at the registration table, Alan and the two coordinators, Mark and John, detailed the events leading up to the last-minute move. Ever since the soup kitchen had opened two summers earlier, Svetlana Grigorievna, the self-promoting cafeteria manager, had employed various means to maximize her profits from the partnership with the CCM program. At first it had been to find ways to enroll her employees in the program. Later, she began overcharging for the costs of the meals. At approximately the same time, she informed CCM staff that they could no longer send African volunteers to the cafeteria, because she was concerned that their presence would adversely affect business. In response, CCM staff informed Svetlana Grigorievna that they would terminate their contract with her. She had apparently replied that they would be unable to contract with another facility because she would tell her friends in the foodservices industry that they were engaging in illegal activities with their "African American mafia." Undeterred and bolstered by the favorable relations they enjoyed with local officials and businesspeople in the area, CCM staff were quickly able to find suitable accommodations at the sports complex and moved, much to Svetlana Grigorievna's great surprise. According to both coordinators and recipients, the new location was a tremendous improvement over Svetlana Grigorievna's cafeteria in terms of both environment and food quality. I was cheered by the relocation of the fourth soup kitchen. The cafeteria staff in the new location were friendly and compassionate; the food was good, and portions were generous; and many more volunteers were attending than previously.

At the same time, I found this series of events distressing. With the soup kitchen at the Moscow Scientific Institute closed, not only had my primary field site disappeared, but so had many of my contacts. There were many people with whom I could make contact only through the soup kitchen; and now there was no way to reach them. Even more tragic was the realization that many of these recipients would now find themselves isolated from the very support networks on which they had depended so heavily. These changes highlighted ever more clearly just how tenuous and important social relations are in everyday life and how quickly people can be made "invisible."

Additionally, CCM staff stated that as a result of these unforeseen circumstances, they had decided to shift their attention away from an exclusive focus on the soup kitchens and toward expanding services for African members of the church. Following the 1998 financial crisis, the composition of the church membership had changed significantly. Whereas before the population was approximately half Africans and half North Americans and Europeans, now it had become predominantly African. Consequently, the needs and objectives of the church had changed accordingly. Of particular concern was the significant increase in racial attacks during my absence; practically every African volunteer had a personal story of being violently assaulted. Even individuals with official refugee recognition by the United Nations and the Russian government had been physically harassed by local police. In response, CCM members had decided that it was time to make use of their position and contacts within the community to publicize these problems and to hold local authorities accountable for eradicating racial prejudices.

In light of these events, I do not know how much longer the CCM soup kitchen program will continue to exist in its current formulation. Nor is it clear how much longer foreign donors will be willing to support the program financially once the threat of "material scarcity" has been alleviated in the Russian economy. Yet as I have argued in this book, the threat of material scarcity is minor compared with the threat of a loss of social relations. And in this sense, the disappearance of the CCM soup kitchen program would be a tremendous loss for the many recipients whose social worlds are bound up in this community.

Notes

Chapter 1. Transnational Soup

1. To protect the privacy of my informants, and in keeping with standard ethnographic practice, I have given this university a pseudonym.

2. Mark Field notes that A. Zinoviev coined the term *katastroika* to capture this notion (Field 2000:37 fn. 2).

3. Nancy Ries talks specifically about "mystical poverty" as a key trope in Russian discourse (1997).

4. In his 1998 study of the poor and disabled in eighteenth-century Russia, Daniel Kaiser argues that the poor were invisible in the Russian historical record until the institutionalization and classification of poverty in the seventeenth century. Adele Lindenmeyr's 1996 book about poverty and charity in Imperial Russia is probably the most comprehensive study of welfare programs in Russia.

5. See Susan Brownell's 1995 account about the role of socialized feeding programs in China.

6. For a fascinating look at the socialist politics over kitchens in Hungary, see Fehérváry 2002.

7. For more detailed accounts of the social engineering of Soviet food practices, see Borrero 1997 and 2002, Goldstein 1996, and Rothstein and Rothstein 1997.

8. Sheila Fitzpatrick captures the intimate relations that linked Soviet citizens with the state in the 1930s with this comment: "It is one of the particularities of our subject that the state can never be kept out, try though we may. Soviet citizens attempting to live ordinary lives were continually running up against the state in one of its multifarious aspects" (1999:14).

9. For other ethnographies that focus on food aid communities, see Allahyari 2000, Glasser 1988, and Myerhoff 1978. Ethnographies that address issues of so-

cial support and social relations, including those among recipients and volunteers, in other welfare programs include Desjarlais 1997, Dordick 1997, and Stevens 1997.

10. For a more detailed description of the social and physical landscape of today's Moscow, see Khazanov 1998.

11. The Cathedral of Christ the Savior has a long and tormented history in Russia. Originally built during the Imperial period, it was demolished during the Soviet period, and a swimming pool was built in its place. In the 1990s, in an environment of greater religious tolerance, rebuilding of the church began. Although the renovations are not yet complete, they have been lavish, and funding for the church has come from wealthy Russians—including several with Jewish backgrounds, as a CCM recipient pointed out to me. See also Boym 2001.

12. The CCM community is a rich site for exploring a broad range of important topics in today's Russia: the social lives of the elderly, church-state relations in postsocialist society, the experiences of black Africans, transnationalism and the experiences of expatriates, and so on. Unfortunately, an extended treatment of any one of these topics would take this book away from its primary focus on food aid and social networks. I am currently pursuing these themes in other places: Caldwell 2002, and forthcoming.

13. Although overt displays of personal religious beliefs by CCM volunteers, donors, and staff are not permitted in the soup kitchens, the motivation for the program developed from larger social justice movements that have been associated with American Protestant denominations. See Sack's 2000 account of this connection between food and religion in U.S. society.

14. For a brief period of time in 1997–1998, the soup kitchens operated six days a week. Because of budget constraints, the program has been cut back to five days a week.

15. Despite the flux that characterizes the CCM program, the overall membership is neither contingent nor anonymous, unlike the type of aid programs that are more familiar to the North American context. In her study of a soup kitchen program in Connecticut, Irene Glasser noted that the structure of the program was necessarily loose and permeable because it was "one of the few places in modern life where questions [were] not asked, folders and charts [were] not kept, and where there [were] no eligibility requirements" (1988:34). This impersonal, private approach contrasts with the procedures followed in the CCM program, as well as with those in most aid programs in Russia. For practical considerations such as size and available resources, CCM staff serve only Muscovites who have been officially registered with the program.

16. This question about whether face-to-face interactions constitute more viable and authentic communities than do social groups based on more anonymous and intangible relations sparked a passionate and informative debate at the panel "Futuristic Dilemmas" at the American Ethnological Society meetings in Tampa, Florida, on March 23, 2000.

17. I am grateful to Michael Herzfeld for the phrase "observant participation"

and for challenging me before I began my fieldwork to think critically about the methodological and theoretical distinctions between participant-observation and observant participation.

18. I describe these trends more fully in an article on nationalist food practices in Moscow (Caldwell 2002).

19. See Kornblatt 1999 for more information on the politics behind this legislation and the efforts by Orthodox Church leaders to position their denomination as the official state religion of Russia. See Borenstein 1999b about the spread of evangelical and apocalyptic religious groups in Russia.

20. In a similar vein, Svetlana Boym notes that Russian culture is "inventively eclectic" (1994:24).

Chapter 2. Making Do

1. Margaret Paxson (personal communication) reported that she has encountered a perspective among some Russians that it is unproductive for researchers to work with peasants because peasants do not "think."

2. See Stites 1992:135–136 and Talmadge 1943 for further discussion of the place of humor in Soviet life.

3. Similarly, in her work on Soviet consumer practices, Julie Hessler has used the phrase "culture of shortages" (1996). I prefer to use the phrase "society of shortages," however, to emphasize the social relationships that are embedded within these practices.

4. In similar terms, Steven Sampson has likened the shift from socialism to capitalism in Romania as a shift in habitus (1995:165).

5. The best and most extensive works documenting these practices during the Soviet period are the studies by Sheila Fitzpatrick (1999), Julie Hessler (1996, 1998), and Elena Osokina (2001). Additional tactics included "bagging," whereby enterprising citizens bought up goods, put them in bags, and transported them elsewhere to be sold (Hessler 1996:3–42), and the practice of including false names, known as dead souls, on employee lists to receive additional supplies (Osokina 2001:104). This last activity has enjoyed a long history in Russian social practice. In the nineteenth century, Russian writer Nikolai Gogol famously described in his novel *Dead Souls* how estate owners retained the names of dead serfs on their lists.

6. Adele Marie Barker calls the new type of post-Soviet consumer the "post-Soviet *Homo consumptor*" (1999a:14). Olga Shevchenko (2002) suggests that Russians' attitudes toward large household appliances can be read as commentaries on their efforts to understand identity processes in a society undergoing political and economic change. See also Jennifer Patico's study (2001a) of consumption in St. Petersburg in 1998–1999. For additional information about consumption in contemporary Russia, see the collection of essays in Barker 1999c.

7. Likewise, during summer 2000, after I had boarded a bus in Moscow, I approached the driver and asked to buy two tickets. He informed me that he could

not sell any tickets because he had run out. When I asked what I should do, he simply shrugged his shoulders and turned back to the wheel.

8. Practical activity is thus simultaneously "a medium and a message" (Herzfeld 1985:25).

9. I am using *rational* in the Weberian sense of a system that is predictable, regular, normalizing, and operates according to its own internal logic.

10. Binyon (1983:178) notes that the just-in-case string bags are called *avos'ka* from the Russian word *avos'*, meaning "perchance."

11. Olga Shevchenko (2002) notes that Russian consumers rehabilitate old Soviet refrigerators by investing them with new post-Soviet values and assigning them new tasks as storage containers. Svetlana Boym argues (1994:65) that "disposable objects" were previously unknown in Russian social practice.

12. Hoarding tickets is not without its share of risk, however. To discourage recipients from saving their meal tickets, CCM coordinators use five different sets of color-coded tickets that they rotate randomly during the week. CCM staff claim that this practice is both to ensure that recipients eat a good meal every day and to minimize wastage of food in the cafeteria. Because each team of coordinators decides which color they are going to use only moments before the soup kitchen opens, recipients have no advance warning of which color will be chosen on a given day. Nevertheless, I noticed that many recipients tucked away meal tickets and brought them out when especially good meals were served; some recipients even encouraged coordinators to select the color that corresponded to the tickets they had saved. Eventually this ticket hoarding became so severe that CCM coordinators did not have enough tickets to distribute on a daily basis and were forced to make new tickets every few weeks. To counteract these practices, CCM staff have numbered the tickets, and the coordinators monitor who receives which tickets and which ones go missing.

13. Bread hoarding has a long symbolic history in Russia. As Julie Hessler notes, "People stood in line for a great many things in the Soviet period, but the paradigmatic kind of queue was the bread line" (1996:132).

14. See Slavenka Drakulić's description of hoarding practices in Yugoslavia (Drakulić 1992:189). Also compare with Marko Živković's 2000 account about the tactics of everyday life in Yugoslavia.

15. Marko Živković writes that for the case of Serbia, "To trick the system was a matter of honor" (2000:55).

16. See Ries 1997:51–64 for an extended discussion of these narratives and their role in Russian communicative practices.

17. Several secondhand clothing shops have recently appeared in Moscow, and friends have commented favorably on being able to buy quality outfits at affordable prices.

18. For a first-person account of cooperative shopping, stampedes, and consumerism in general in Moscow in the 1970s, see Young 1989:116–142.

19. Journeys on intercity trains are particularly fascinating opportunities to see what people are selling. Enterprising vendors walk through the train cars offering such diverse items as ice cream, fresh pastries, clothing, clocks, batteries, books, and fertilizer.

20. Alena Ledeneva has treated the topic of *blat* extensively in her 1998 book, *Russia's Economy of Favours*.

21. For other accounts of markets in post-Soviet spaces, see Humphrey 1999, Konstantinov 1996, and Dickinson 2002.

22. This honor system is currently changing in Moscow. To recover revenue from lost fares, controllers have stepped up their efforts to check that riders have paid, and many transit lines now have full-time conductors to sell tickets.

23. See Burawoy and Lukacs 1992, chapter 5, for details about labor in Hungary.

24. Compare with Verdery's accounts of the Caritas scheme in Romania (1995, 1996).

25. See also Humphrey 1999, Ries 1999, and Wedel 1998a, 1998b.

Chapter 3. From Hand to Hand

1. Shlapentokh has noted that "with only a few really close friends, it would be impossible to find access to dozens of offices and enterprises, often in different parts of the country" (1989:176).

2. For discussions of these practices in St. Petersburg, see Lonkila 1998 and Patico 2001a.

3. For a fascinating discussion of how Soviet authorities encouraged citizens to inform on their fellow citizens, see Fitzpatrick 1996 and Siegelbaum 1998.

4. Nancy Ries (1997:21) suggests that the constant surveillance by the Soviet state contributed to the "sacralization of private talk" in opposition to officially sanctioned discourses.

5. Michele Rivkin-Fish addresses this component in her research on health care in Russia (2002).

6. As a foreigner I was often unsure when to switch from the formal to the informal, and I usually waited for verbal cues from other people. Finally at dinner one night, the daughter of a close friend became exasperated with my use of *vy*. She scolded me and announced that once one had eaten with people in their homes, one must use *ty*, the informal "you." Although I encountered exceptions to her classification when I asked other people, most supported the distinction.

7. Most African volunteers speak Russian with varying degrees of fluency, because their university courses are taught exclusively in Russian.

8. From both methodological and ethical perspectives, I found my involuntary participation in these machinations unsettling, to say the least. On the one hand, I interpreted the willingness with which Oksana, Elena, and others included me in their conversations and plans as an indicator that I had gained some small degree of trust and intimacy in the community. On the other hand, I recognized the likelihood that they had strategically approached me as a resource to be manipulated in their struggle. Because I was a non-African foreigner who spoke Russian, I could mediate their relations with CCM staff. Nevertheless, because of my close friendship with Aleksandra Petrovna and knowledge of her extensive activist

work, I was uncomfortable with the possibility of being seen as party to these attacks on her character and honest efforts to help others.

Chapter 4. The Forest Feeds Us

1. Cathy Frierson notes that the images of hardship and deprivation that Aleksandr Engelgardt emphasized in his accounts of peasant life in the 1870s "departed dramatically from idealized notions of the countryside as the seedbed of Russian culture and the home place of a bountiful or nurturing Mother Russia" (1997:52).

2. An RFE/RL account from 1977 reported that Soviet authorities relied heavily on the owners of private plots to provide supplemental food assistance (*Radio Liberty Research Bulletin* 1977:1). In a 1980 report, Wädekin writes that "during the past four years, the private sector has contributed 25 percent of Soviet agriculture's total gross production" (1980:1).

3. See Galtz 2000 and Ioffe and Nefedova 1998:1336–1337 for overviews of the history of dachas in Russia.

4. Ioffe and Nefedova note (1998:1328) that 60 percent of Russians use some form of rural dwelling.

5. See also the related article in the *Moscow Times,* July 1, 2002, p. 3. For a more detailed discussion of the symbolic and health aspects of the Chernobyl disaster, see Petryna 2002 and Wanner 1998:27–33.

6. Although accurate figures are not available, popular wisdom in my field site holds that a significant number of vendors pay bribes to policemen or others who manage public sidewalks and other spaces. Although demands for such payments do not appear to be limited strictly to dark-skinned individuals, personal observation and conversations with people from the Caucasus and Africa suggest that they are more susceptible to public mistrust and instances of discrimination. These activities appear to be increasing in the wake of several bombings of subway stations and apartment buildings in Moscow in the past few years, especially because these actions have been attributed to terrorists from the Caucasus—presumably Chechen separatists. Dark-skinned men are the most likely to be stopped by police for random document checks, and light-skinned women are the least likely to be stopped. One afternoon as I stood outside a metro station for approximately thirty minutes, waiting for a friend who had been delayed, I observed two young policemen stop every dark-skinned man who walked past and demand to see his documents. Even when the documents were apparently in order, the policemen argued with the pedestrians about their business.

7. In subsequent trips home from Russia I have had similar experiences, including an instance when an airline ticket agent at Moscow's Sheremetyevo II airport initially questioned my oversized carry-on bag but then let me through when I explained that it contained jars of jam.

8. Ironically, after hearing Larissa Antonovna's story and reading the literature she gave me that outlined the Hare Krishna philosophy about spiritual and physical cleanliness, I was nonetheless surprised by the appearance of the temple toi-

let facilities on my subsequent visit to the feeding program (Larissa Antonovna had badgered me for months before I finally acquiesced to the visit). The women's toilet room contained two filthy stalls with holes in the floor; dirty water streamed over the floor in the tiny area under and in front of the sink, which comprised a single tap for cold water. Although public facilities in Russia are often not for the faint of heart, this particular toilet ranked among the worst I have seen. Yet it was filled with both Hare Krishna believers and visitors, brushing their teeth, washing themselves, and washing out their dishes.

9. Olga and Evgenii's dacha is also located in an area that had been the scene of intense tank warfare during World War II, and a tank monument alongside the highway indicates the entrance to this community. When I asked Olga about the possibility of unexploded munitions in the woods behind her cottage, she laughed and reassured me that the forests and ground there were safe.

10. While I helped Lena prepare dinner, Anton and their teenaged daughter, Masha, entertained my parents. Masha was currently studying English, and her father had studied English in high school. My father told me later how Anton had proudly described to them the marinated mushrooms they were eating by drawing explicitly on the social relations in which they were embedded: "My father picked these; my mother prepared them."

Chapter 5. Strategic Intimacy

1. Henry Morton (1980:240–241) reports that Soviet housing allocations were determined according to this hierarchy of identity. Because available housing was in short supply in the Soviet Union, citizens waited years for their turn. Those individuals who could legally be served out of turn, however, included Heroes of the Soviet Union, Heroes of Socialist Labor and Order of Glory, military officers and enlisted men, members of the KGB, World War II invalids, and tuberculosis patients, among others. Members of certain other categories, such as architects, composers, and writers, were eligible for more space.

2. Sascha Goluboff (2001) reports that Jews in Russia further distinguish themselves according to perceived ethnic differences. For further elaboration of the attributes assigned to Jews in Russia, see also Pesmen 2000 and Kleyman 2002.

3. See Filipov 1999 for a more detailed description of racist police practices in Moscow. See also Lemon 1995 and 2000; and Caldwell, forthcoming.

4. At its most extreme, this correlation of taste and identity played out in a cruel set of racist slurs and jokes about the taste preferences of Africans. African CCM volunteers reported being harassed by hooligans who called them banana-loving monkeys. Similar themes appeared in local newspapers during my fieldwork. In an interesting contrast, Susan Terrio (2000) reports that in the French chocolate industry essentialized representations of Africans are associated with particular types of chocolate and then commercialized for marketing purposes.

5. Nietzsche's genealogy of morals (1964) offers an instructive parallel. In his analysis of concepts of good and evil, Nietzsche notes that there is nothing intrin-

sically natural or original about these categories. Instead it is the values to which these concepts are attached that reflect the interests of the agents who use them; and it is through their continued use that they gain legitimacy and status as reality.

6. In her discussion about the importance of having a passport in Russian society, Caroline Humphrey reports, "A Russian friend once quoted to me a saying he attributed to Dostoevsky, 'A human being consists of three things: a body, a soul, and a passport' *(Chelovek sostoit iz dushi, tela i pasporta)*" (1996/97:75).

7. Officially *bomzh* is an acronym for a person *bez opredelënnogo mesta zhitel'stva*, "without a specific place of residence," but there are negative stigmas associated with this term. Among homeless persons and their advocates there is a movement to replace this term with the word *bezdomnyi*, "homeless."

8. The CHA center is located on a side street near a major train station in central Moscow. Volunteers at the center cook the food in the kitchen of the Orthodox church next door and then set up large ice chests containing the food on tables just off the street. Meanwhile, recipients line up on the street outside the center and wait for center staff to open the gates. A typical meal includes bread, kasha with meat and vegetables, a sticky roll, and a beverage. Staff members never know how many people will show up, but they say there is usually enough for everyone to get one serving and for many to get seconds.

Chapter 6. The Mythology of Hunger

1. After an extended monologue about the absence of hunger in Russia, the man ordered me to leave. When I refused (I had been granted permission by CCM staff), the man eventually threatened me for having an illegal research permit (which I did not need) and hinted that I could find myself in trouble for my investigation. When I ignored him, he turned his attentions to a CCM supervisor, an African student, and continued his harassment.

2. Because of the frequency with which this term appeared in public discourse (see also Littell 2001), I am convinced that it was not coincidental that informants chose *golod* and its derivatives to talk about scarcity and food assistance programs, as some colleagues have suggested. Nor do I believe that Muscovite informants used the term uncritically, as other colleagues have suggested.

3. See Dirks 1980, Pottier 1999, and Scheper-Hughes 1992 for overviews of this literature.

4. De Waal (1989) provides a rich survey of discrepancies between English-language accounts of famine and the accounts of the people who actually experienced those famines. He also offers a thorough discussion of the genealogy of the concept of "famine" in English-language accounts.

5. In his account of the Soviet food supply during World War II, William Moskoff notes, "The abiding, underlying theme of Soviet political economy during its early years was the struggle to feed the population" (1990:1). See also Borrero 2002 and Osokina 2001 on "the politics of scarcity" in the pre–World War II Soviet Union.

6. American citizens and groups, such as church congregations, sent these aid items through remittances that they bought for particular people in the Soviet Union. Fisher notes that food remittances cost ten dollars, and the food packages were to contain the following items or "their equivalent in food or caloric value: Flour—49 pounds; rice—25 pounds; tea—3 pounds; fats—10 pounds; sugar—10 pounds; preserved milk—20 one-pound cans" (1927:405). Frank Alfred Golden and Lincoln Hutchinson were two of the first American Relief Administration personnel to be sent to the "famine front" in the Soviet Union during this period. They chronicled their experiences and observations in *On the Trail of the Russian Famine* (1927). More recently, charities have used the Internet to offer similar remittance programs for sending food packages to Russia.

7. For firsthand details about the deprivations of Leningrad, see William Moskoff's interviews with blockade survivors about their experiences with hunger (1990).

8. This is Johnson's Russia List, a daily list-serve and discussion group posted on the Internet for scholars, businesspeople, journalists, travelers, and others interested in events in Russia.

9. Nancy Ries (1997:36) has described for the perestroika period Muscovite's narratives about shortages and their strategies for dealing with them.

10. Tova Höjdestrand (2000) has observed a similar emphasis on feelings of humanness and dignity among homeless persons in St. Petersburg.

11. From the report by the World Council of Churches and the Russian Orthodox Church (2000), roundtable on "education for change and diaconia," printed on www.rondtb.msk.ru/info/en/food_en.htm (accessed on September 27, 2000).

12. In her study of a welfare community in Japan, Carolyn Stevens makes a similar observation that aloneness qualifies elderly clients for extra benefits (1997:60).

13. Rosaldo's ideas about cultural visibility and invisibility (1993) offer a valuable lens for considering the power relations that support and perpetuate this collective charade.

14. Even my e-mail letters to other volunteers were printed off, brought in, circulated, and translated for those who did not read English.

15. Ironically, although several congregants privately expressed their concerns that Oksana might use the money for her own purposes, CCM staff were more concerned about the church's bookkeeping practices. Specifically, they were worried that Oksana would not collect receipts for her purchases. Because the CCM is an American organization, the congregation's books are balanced according to American accounting standards, which require receipts. In the Russian system of shopping with which Oksana is most familiar, however, customers first pay and receive a receipt that they exchange for the item purchased. Because salesclerks often use these receipts to balance their registers, customers rarely receive a receipt to take with them. In smaller shops and markets, receipts are nonexistent. Even in grocery stores where receipts are automatically given to customers, most people throw them away. Not only was Oksana not accustomed to thinking

about collecting receipts with her purchases, but she also was not likely to shop in places that routinely gave receipts. Not surprisingly, she initially expressed confusion about the stipulation, and CCM staff went to great lengths to impress upon her the need to account for every item purchased.

16. See also Butovskaya, Salter, et al. 2000.

17. Yegor Gaidar was a pro-reform finance minister in the early 1990s, and Viktor Chernomyrdin was a pro-reform prime minister during the 1990s. Gazprom is the national gas company, rumored to have special relations with various oligarchs and politicians.

18. For comparative ethnographic examples of how changing social relations are represented in birthday parties in China, see Jing 2000, Watson 1997, and Yan 2000.

19. On my subsequent trips to Moscow in 2000, 2001, and 2002, I was fortunate to be in town for Aleksandra Petrovna's birthday parties. In contrast to the party in 1999, these later events were well-attended by both friends and CCM staff and volunteers.

20. Not only have recent technologies such as wireless telephones, faxes, and the Internet transformed how local actors construct their social worlds and social relations, but they also have influenced the ways in which researchers interact and communicate with people "in the field." As Daphne Berdahl has pointed out (2000b), telephone ethnography has enabled anthropologists to remain in continuous "real time" contact with informants even after leaving the field, thereby transforming research relationships into social relationships of friendship and further transforming "the field" itself into an atemporal, transnational entity. No longer are our field sites isolated by geography, so that our data become detached from the contexts in which they were collected. With ever-present means of communication, our research continues long after we leave the field.

21. Jennifer Patico notes (2001b:135–136) that St. Petersburg residents are sensitive to comparisons between Russia and Africa, because these suggest that Russia has degenerated to the status of a Third World country.

Chapter 7. Socialism Revisited

1. See Berdahl 2000a and Wedel 1998a for representative views.

Works Cited

Allahyari, Rebecca Anne. 2000. *Visions of Charity: Volunteer Workers and Moral Community*. Berkeley: University of California Press.

Ammons, Sylvia. n.d. Description of Christian Church of Moscow Soup Kitchen Ministry. Church correspondence.

Anderson, Benedict. 1983. *Imagined Communities: Reflections on the Origin and Spread of Nationalism*. London: Verso.

Appadurai, Arjun. 1986. "Introduction: Commodities and the Politics of Value." In *The Social Life of Things: Commodities in Cultural Perspective*, ed. Arjun Appadurai, 3–63. Cambridge: Cambridge University Press.

——. 1996. *Modernity at Large: Cultural Dimensions of Globalization*. Minneapolis: University of Minnesota Press.

Ardener, Edwin. 1975. "The Problem Revisited." In *Perceiving Women*, ed. Shirley Ardener, 19–27. London: J. M. Dent.

Aretxaga, Begoña. 1997. *Shattering Silence: Women, Nationalism, and Political Subjectivity in Northern Ireland*. Princeton, N.J.: Princeton University Press.

Ashwin, Sarah. 1999. "Redefining the Collective: Russian Mineworkers in Transition." In *Uncertain Transition: Ethnographies of Change in the Postsocialist World*, ed. Michael Burawoy and Katherine Verdery, 245–271. Lanham, Md.: Rowman & Littlefield Publishers.

Babakian, Genine. 1999. "Hunger, Bad Health Are Subjects That Russian Children Know Well." *USA Today*, February 4, 10D.

Barker, Adele Marie. 1999a. "The Culture Factory: Theorizing the Popular in the Old and New Russia." In *Consuming Russia: Popular Culture, Sex, and Society since Gorbachev*, ed. Adele Marie Barker, 12–45. Durham, N.C.: Duke University Press.

——. 1999b. "Rereading Russia." In *Consuming Russia: Popular Culture, Sex, and Society since Gorbachev*, ed. Adele Marie Barker, 3–11. Durham, N.C.: Duke University Press.

——, ed. 1999c. *Consuming Russia: Popular Culture, Sex, and Society since Gorbachev*. Durham, N.C.: Duke University Press.

Barsegian, Igor. 2000. "When Text Becomes Field: Fieldwork in 'Transitional' Societies." In *Fieldwork Dilemmas: Anthropologists in Postsocialist States*, ed. Hermine G. DeSoto and Nora Dudwick, 119–129. Madison: University of Wisconsin Press.

Barth, Fredrik. 1969. "Introduction." In *Ethnic Groups and Boundaries: The Social Organization of Culture Difference*, ed. Fredrik Barth, 9–38. Boston: Little, Brown.

Beissinger, Margaret H. 2001. "Occupation and Ethnicity: Constructing Identity among Professional Romani (Gypsy) Musicians in Romania." *Slavic Review* 60(1):24–49.

Berdahl, Daphne. 1999a. " '(N)Ostalgie' for the Present: Memory, Longing, and East German Things." *Ethnos* 64(2):192–211.

——. 1999b. *Where the World Ended: Re-unification and Identity in the German Borderland*. Berkeley: University of California Press.

——. 2000a. "Introduction: An Anthropology of Postsocialism." In *Altering States: Ethnographies of Transition in Eastern Europe and the Former Soviet Union*, ed. Daphne Berdahl, Matti Bunzl, and Martha Lampland, 1–13. Ann Arbor: University of Michigan Press.

——. 2000b. "Mixed Devotions: Religion, Friendship, and Fieldwork in Postsocialist Eastern Germany." In *Fieldwork Dilemmas: Anthropologists in Postsocialist Places*, ed. Hermine G. DeSoto and Nora Dudwick, 172–194. Madison: University of Wisconsin Press.

Berdahl, Daphne, Matti Bunzl, and Martha Lampland, eds. 2000. *Altering States: Ethnographies of Transition in Eastern Europe and the Former Soviet Union*. Ann Arbor: University of Michigan Press.

Bershidsky, Leonid. 1998. Personal correspondence to list-serve members. Johnson's Russia List #2316, August 28, 1998, available at www.cdi.org/russia/johnson/archives.cfm.

Bestor, Theodore C. 1999. "Wholesale Sushi: Culture and Commodity in Tokyo's Tsukiji Market." In *Theorizing the City: The New Urban Anthropology Reader*, ed. Setha M. Low, 201–242. New Brunswick, N.J.: Rutgers University Press.

Binyon, Michael. 1983. *Life in Russia*. New York: Berkeley Books.

Bobroff-Hajal, Anne. 1994. *Working Women in Russia under the Hunger Tsars: Political Activism and Daily Life*. New York: Carlson Publishing.

Bordo, Susan. 1997. "Anorexia Nervosa: Psychopathology as the Crystallization of Culture." In *Food and Culture: A Reader*, ed. Carole Counihan and Penny Van Esterik, 226–250. New York: Routledge.

Borenstein, Eliot. 1999a. "Public Offerings: MMM and the Marketing of Melodrama." In *Consuming Russia: Popular Culture, Sex, and Society since Gorbachev*, ed. Adele Marie Barker, 49–75. Durham, N.C.: Duke University Press.

——. 1999b. "Suspending Disbelief: 'Cults' and Postmodernism in Post-Soviet Russia." In *Consuming Russia: Popular Culture, Sex, and Society since Gorbachev*, ed. Adele Marie Barker, 437–462. Durham, N.C.: Duke University Press.

Borrero, Mauricio. 1997. "Communal Dining and State Cafeterias in Moscow and Petrograd, 1917–1921." In *Food in Russian History and Culture*, ed. Musya Glants and Joyce Toomre, 162–176. Bloomington: Indiana University Press.

——. 2002. "Food and the Politics of Scarcity in Urban Soviet Russia, 1917–1941." In *Food Nations: Selling Taste in Consumer Societies*, ed. Warren Belasco and Philip Scranton, 258–276. New York: Routledge.

Bourdieu, Pierre. 1977. *Outline of a Theory of Practice*. Trans. Richard Nice. Cambridge: Cambridge University Press.

——. 1980. *The Logic of Practice*. Trans. Richard Nice. Stanford, Calif.: Stanford University Press.

——. 1984. *Distinction: A Social Critique of the Judgement of Taste*. Trans. Richard Nice. Cambridge, Mass.: Harvard University Press.

Boym, Svetlana. 1994. *Common Places: Mythologies of Everyday Life in Russia*. Cambridge, Mass.: Harvard University Press.

——. 2001. *The Future of Nostalgia*. New York: Basic Books.

Brady, Rose. 1992. "The Great Russian Depression of 1992?" *Business Week* 3262:47–48.

Bromley, Yurii, ed. 1974. *Soviet Ethnology and Anthropology Today*. The Hague: Mouton.

Brownell, Susan. 1995. *Training the Body for China: Sports in the Moral Order of the People's Republic*. Chicago: University of Chicago Press.

Bruno, Marta. 1998. "Playing the Co-operation Game: Strategies around International Aid in Post-Socialist Russia." In *Surviving Post-Socialism: Local Strategies and Regional Responses in Eastern Europe and the Former Soviet Union*, ed. Sue Bridger and Frances Pine, 170–187. London: Routledge.

Burawoy, Michael. 1999. "Afterword." In *Uncertain Transition: Ethnographies of Change in the Postsocialist World*, ed. Michael Burawoy and Katherine Verdery, 301–311. Lanham, Md.: Rowman & Littlefield Publishers.

Burawoy, Michael, and Janos Lukacs. 1992. *The Radiant Past: Ideology and Reality in Hungary's Road to Capitalism*. Chicago: University of Chicago Press.

Burawoy, Michael, Pavel Krotov, and Tatyana Lytkina. 2000. "Involution and Destitution in Capitalist Russia." *Ethnography* 1(1):43–65.

Butovskaya, Marina L., Ivan Diakonov, and Frank Salter. 2000. "Social Status and Probability of Alms Giving: A Questionnaire Study of Moscow Students." Paper presented at conference "Hierarchy and Power in the History of Civilizations." Moscow, Russia, June 15–18.

Butovskaya, M., Frank Salter, I. Diakonov, and A. Smirnov. 2000. "Urban Begging and Ethnic Nepotism in Russia: An Ethological Pilot Study." *Human Nature* 11(2):157–182.

Bynum, Caroline Walker. 1997. "Fast, Feast, and Flesh: The Religious Significance of Food to Medieval Women." In *Food and Culture: A Reader*, ed. Carole Counihan and Penny Van Esterik, 138–158. New York: Routledge.

Caldwell, Melissa L. 1998. "Pepsi, Pensioners, and Peter the Great: Performing Temporality in Russia." *Anthropology of East Europe Review* 16(2):19–25.

———. 1999. "Where There Is No Hunger: Food, Time, and Community in Moscow." Ph.D. dissertation, Harvard University.

———. 2002. "The Taste of Nationalism: Food Politics in Postsocialist Russia." *Ethnos* 67(3):295–319.

———. Forthcoming. "Race and Social Relations: Crossing Borders in a Moscow Food Aid Program." In *Social Networks in Movement: Time, Interaction and Interethnic Spaces in Central Eastern Eurasia,* ed. D. Torsello and M. Pappová, Lilium Aurum: Dunajská Streda (SK).

Carrier, James. 1990. "Gifts in a World of Commodities: The Ideology of the Perfect Gift in American Society." *Social Analysis: Journal of Cultural and Social Practice* 29:19–37.

Cheal, David. 1988. *The Gift Economy.* London: Routledge.

Clarke, Nigel, and Sergey Koptev. 1992. "The Russian Consumer: A Demographic Profile of a New Consumer Market." *Journal of European Business* 4(1):23–31.

Clinton, William J. 1998. Statement on the Russia–United States Agreement to Provide Food Aid to Russia. *Weekly Compilation of Presidential Documents* 34(35, November 9):2250.

Cohen, Stephen. 1998. "Why Call It Reform?" *Nation,* September 1. Cited in Johnson's Russia List #2316, August 20, 1998, available at www.cdi.org/russia/johnson/archives.cfm.

Coleman, Fred. 1998. "Russia's Future Looks Bleak: Food Shortages, Unrest Not Far Off." *USA Today,* November 10, 1B.

Conquest, Robert. 1986. *The Famine of Sorrow: Soviet Collectivization and the Terror-Famine.* New York: Oxford University Press.

Creed, Gerald W. 1997. *Domesticating Revolution: From Socialist Reform to Ambivalent Transition in a Bulgarian Village.* University Park: Pennsylvania State University Press.

———. 1999. "Deconstructing Socialism in Bulgaria." In *Uncertain Transition: Ethnographies of Change in the Postsocialist World,* ed. Michael Burawoy and Katherine Verdery, 223–243. Lanham, Md.: Rowman & Littlefield Publishers.

Creed, Gerald W., and Janine R. Wedel. 1997. "Second Thoughts from the Second World: Interpreting Aid in Post-Communist Eastern Europe." *Human Organization* 56(3):253–264.

Crowley, David, and Susan E. Reid. 2000. "Style and Socialism: Modernity and Material Culture in Post-War Eastern Europe." In *Style and Socialism: Modernity and Material Culture in Post-War Eastern Europe,* ed. Susan E. Reid and David Crowley, 1–24. Oxford: Berg.

Cushman, Thomas. 1995. *Notes from Underground: Rock Music Counterculture in Russia.* Albany: State University of New York Press.

Davis, Deborah S., ed. 2000. *The Consumer Revolution in Urban China.* Berkeley: University of California Press.

Davydov, M. I. 1971. *Bor'ba za khleb* (Fight for bread). Moscow: Mysl'.

de Certeau, Michel. 1984. *The Practice of Everyday Life.* Trans. Steven Rendell. Berkeley: University of California Press.

Desjarlais, Robert. 1996. "The Office of Reason: On the Politics of Language and Agency in a Shelter for 'The Homeless Mentally Ill.' " *American Ethnologist* 23(4):880–900.

———. 1997. *Shelter Blues: Sanity and Selfhood among the Homeless.* Philadelphia: University of Pennsylvania Press.

de Waal, Alexander. 1989. *Famine That Kills: Darfu, Sudan, 1984–1985.* Oxford: Clarendon Press.

Dickinson, J. 2002. "A Full-Time Job, but Still Not Work: Occupational Identity in Ukrainian Market Workers' Narratives." Paper presented at Soyuz Symposium, University of Michigan, February 22.

Dirks, Robert. 1980. "Social Responses During Severe Food Shortages and Famine." *Current Anthropology* 21(1):21–44.

Dolot, Miron. 1985. *Execution by Hunger: The Hidden Holocaust.* New York: W. W. Norton.

Dordick, Gwendolyn A. 1997. *Something Left to Lose: Personal Relations and Survival among New York's Homeless.* Philadelphia: Temple University Press.

Douglas, Mary. 1990. "Foreword: No Free Gifts." In *The Gift: The Form and Reason for Exchange in Archaic Societies,* by Marcel Mauss, vii–xviii. Trans. W. D. Halls. London: Routledge.

———. 1994. *Purity and Danger: An Analysis of the Concepts of Pollution and Taboo.* London: Routledge.

Douglas, Mary, and John Isherwood. 1979. *The World of Goods: Towards an Anthropology of Consumption.* New York: Basic Books.

Dragadze, Tamara. 1988. *Rural Families in Soviet Georgia: A Case Study in Ratcha Province.* London: Routledge.

Drakulić, Slavenka. 1992. *How We Survived Communism and Even Laughed.* London: Hutchinson.

Drèze, Jean, and Amartya Sen. 1989. *Hunger and Public Action.* Oxford: Clarendon Press.

Dudwick, Nora, and Hermine G. DeSoto. 2000. "Introduction." In *Fieldwork Dilemmas: Anthropologists in Postsocialist States,* ed. Hermine G. DeSoto and Nora Dudwick, 3–8. Madison: University of Wisconsin Press.

Dumont, Louis. 1970. *Homo Hierarchicus: The Caste System and Its Implications.* Trans. Mark Sainsbury. Chicago: University of Chicago Press.

Dunn, Elizabeth. 1999. "Slick Salesmen and Simple People: Negotiated Capitalism in a Privatized Polish Firm." In *Uncertain Transition: Ethnographies of Change in the Postsocialist World,* ed. Michael Burawoy and Katherine Verdery, 125–150. Lanham, Md.: Rowman & Littlefield Publishers.

Durkheim, Émile. 1979. *Suicide: A Study in Sociology.* Trans. John A. Spaulding and George Simpson. New York: Free Press.

Economist. 1998. "Europe: But Will It Help?" 349 (November 14):54–55.

Ericson, Richard E. 1995. "The Russian Economy since Independence." In *The New Russia: Troubled Transformation,* ed. Gail Lapidus, 37–77. Boulder, Colo.: Westview Press.

Erwin, Kathleen. 2000. "Heart-to-Heart, Phone-to-Phone: Family Values, Sexuality, and the Politics of Shanghai's Advice Hotlines." In *The Consumer Revolution in Urban China,* ed. Deborah S. Davis, 145–170. Berkeley: University of California Press.

Evans-Pritchard, E. E. 1940. *The Nuer.* New York: Oxford University Press.

Fabian, Johannes. 1983. *Time and the Other: How Anthropology Makes Its Object.* New York: Columbia University Press.

Fehérváry, Krisztina E. 2002. "American Kitchens, Luxury Bathrooms, and the Search for a 'Normal' Life in Post-Socialist Hungary." *Ethnos* 67(3):369–400.

Field, Mark G. 2000. "The Health and Demographic Crisis in Post-Soviet Russia: A Two-Phase Development." In *Russia's Torn Safety Nets: Health and Social Welfare during the Transition,* ed. Mark G. Field and Judyth L. Twigg, 11–42. New York: St. Martin's Press.

Field, Mark G., David M. Kotz, and Gene Bukhman. 2000. "Neoliberal Economic Policy, 'State Desertion,' and the Russian Health Crisis." In *Dying for Growth: Global Inequality and the Health of the Poor,* ed. Jim Yong Kim, Joyce V. Millen, Alec Irwin, and John Gershman, 154–173. Monroe, Me.: Common Courage Press.

Filipov, David. 1999. "Eyeing Chechnya, Moscow Police Wage Racist War." *Boston Globe,* October 6, A1, A14.

Fisher, H. H. 1927. *The Famine in Soviet Russia, 1919–1923: The Operation of the American Relief Administration.* Hoover War Library Publications, 9. Stanford, Calif.: Stanford University Press.

Fitchen, Janet M. 1997. "Hunger, Malnutrition, and Poverty in the Contemporary United States." In *Food and Culture: A Reader,* ed. Carole Counihan and Penny Van Esterik, 384–401. New York: Routledge.

Fitzpatrick, Sheila. 1996. "Signals from Below: Soviet Letters of Denunciation of the 1930s." *Journal of Modern History* 68(4):831–866.

———. 1999. *Everyday Stalinism: Ordinary Life in Extraordinary Times: Soviet Russia in the 1930s.* New York: Oxford University Press.

Frierson, Cathy A. 1997. "Forced Hunger and Rational Restraint in the Russian Peasant Diet: One Populist's Vision." In *Food in Russian History and Culture,* ed. Musya Glants and Joyce Toomre, 49–66. Bloomington: Indiana University Press.

Frisby, Tanya. 1998. "The Rise of Organised Crime in Russia: Its Roots and Social Significance." *Europe-Asia Studies* 50(1):27–49.

Gal, Susan. 1991. "Gender in the Post-Socialist Transition: The Abortion Debate in Hungary." *East European Politics and Societies* 8(2):256–286.

Galtz, Naomi Roslyn. 2000. "Space and the Everyday: An Historical Sociology of the Moscow Dacha." Ph.D. dissertation, University of Michigan.

Gellner, Ernest. 1983. *Nations and Nationalism.* Ithaca, N.Y.: Cornell University Press.

Giddens, Anthony. 1991. *Modernity and Self-Identity: Self and Society in the Late Modern Age.* Stanford, Calif.: Stanford University Press.

Giroux, Alain. 2001. "Is Food Aid to Russia Necessary?" In *The Geopolitics of Hunger, 2000–2001: Hunger and Power,* ed. Action Against Hunger, 275–281. Boulder, Colo.: Lynne Reinner Publishers.

Glants, Musya, and Joyce Toomre. 1997. "Introduction." In *Food in Russian History and Culture*, ed. Musya Glants and Joyce Toomre, xi–xxvii. Bloomington: Indiana University Press.

Glasser, Irene. 1988. *More Than Bread: Ethnography of a Soup Kitchen*. Tuscaloosa: University of Alabama Press.

Golden, Frank Alfred, and Lincoln Hutchinson. 1927. *On the Trail of the Russian Famine*. Stanford, Calif.: Stanford University Press.

Goldstein, Darra. 1996. "Domestic Porkbarreling in Nineteenth-Century Russia, or Who Holds the Keys to the Larder?" In *Russia, Women, Culture*, ed. Helena Goscilo and Beth Holmgren, 125–151. Bloomington: Indiana University Press.

Goluboff, Sascha. 2001. "Fist Fights at the Moscow Choral Synagogue: Ritual and Ethnicity in Post-Soviet Russia." *Anthropological Quarterly* 74(2):55–71.

Goskomstat Rossii. 1999. *Sotsial'noe polozhenie i uroven' zhizni naseleniia Rossii: 1999* (Social position and standard of living of the population of Russia: 1999). Moscow: Gosudarstvennyi Komitet Rossiiskoe Federatsii po Statistike.

Grant, Bruce. 1995. *In the Soviet House of Culture: A Century of Perestroikas*. Princeton, N.J.: Princeton University Press.

Habermas, Jürgen. 1987. *The Theory of Communicative Action*, vol. 2: *Lifeworld and System: A Critique of Functionalist Reason*. Trans. Thomas McCarthy. Boston: Beacon Press.

Handler, Richard. 1988. *Nationalism and the Politics of Culture in Quebec*. Madison: University of Wisconsin Press.

Haney, Lynne. 1999. " 'But We Are Still Mothers': Gender, the State, and the Construction of Need in Postsocialist Hungary." In *Uncertain Transition: Ethnographies of Change in the Postsocialist World*, ed. Michael Burawoy and Katherine Verdery, 151–187. Lanham, Md.: Rowman & Littlefield Publishers.

Hastrup, Kirsten. 1993. "Hunger and the Hardness of Facts." *Man* 28(4):727–739.

Hayden, Robert M. 1994. "Recounting the Dead: The Rediscovery and Redefinition of Wartime Massacres in Late- and Post-Communist Yugoslavia." In *Memory, History, and Opposition under State Socialism*, ed. Rubie S. Watson, 167–184. Santa Fe, N.M.: School of American Research.

———. 1996. "Imagined Communities and Real Victims: Self-Determination and Ethnic Cleansing in Yugoslavia." *American Ethnologist* 23(4):783–801.

Hayek, Friedrich August von. 1984. *The Essence of Hayek*. Ed. Chiaki Nishiyama and Kurt R. Leube. Stanford, Calif.: Hoover Institution Press.

Herrmann, Gretchen. 1997. "Gift or Commodity: What Changes Hands in the U.S. Garage Sale?" *American Ethnologist* 24(4):910–930.

Herzfeld, Michael. 1985. *The Poetics of Manhood: Contest and Identity in a Cretan Village*. Princeton, N.J.: Princeton University Press.

———. 1987a. *Anthropology through the Looking-Glass: Critical Ethnography in the Margins of Europe*. Cambridge: Cambridge University Press.

———. 1987b. " 'As In Your Own House': Hospitality, Ethnography, and the Stereotype of Mediterranean Society." In *Honor and Shame and the Unity of the Mediterranean*, ed. David D. Gilmore, 75–89. Special Publication No. 22. Washington, D.C.: American Anthropological Association.

———. 1990. "Pride and Perjury: Time and the Oath in the Mountain Villages of Crete." *Man*, n.s., 25(2):305–322.

———. 1991. *A Place in History: Social and Monumental Time in a Cretan Town.* Princeton, N.J.: Princeton University Press.

———. 1992. *The Social Production of Indifference: Exploring the Symbolic Roots of Western Democracy.* Chicago: University of Chicago Press.

———. 1993. "In Defiance of Destiny: The Management of Time and Gender at a Cretan Funeral." *American Ethnologist* 20(2):241–255.

———. 1997. *Cultural Intimacy: Social Poetics in the Nation-State.* New York: Routledge.

———. 2000. "Afterword: Intimations from an Uncertain Place." In *Fieldwork Dilemmas: Anthropologists in Postsocialist States,* ed. Hermine G. DeSoto and Nora Dudwick, 219–235. Madison: University of Wisconsin Press.

Hessler, Julie M. 1996. "Culture of Shortages: A Social History of Soviet Trade." Ph.D. dissertation, University of Chicago.

———. 1998. "A Postwar Perestroika? Toward a History of Private Enterprise in the USSR." *Slavic Review* 57(3):516–542.

Hirsch, Francine. 1997. "The Soviet Union as a Work-in-Progress: Ethnographers and the Category *Nationality* in the 1926, 1937, and 1939 Censuses." *Slavic Review* 56(2):251–278.

Höjdestrand, Tova. 2000. "We Are People Too: Notions of Humanness among Homeless Russians." Paper presented at Sixth Biennial Meeting of European Association of Social Anthropologists, Krakow, Poland, July.

Hollander, Paul. 1991. "Politics and Social Problems." In *Soviet Social Problems,* ed. Anthony Jones, Walter D. Connor, and David E. Powell, 9–23. John M. Olin Critical Issues Series. Boulder, Colo.: Westview Press.

Humphrey, Caroline. 1983. *Karl Marx Collective: Economy, Society, and Religion in a Siberian Collective Farm.* Cambridge: Cambridge University Press.

———. 1995. "Creating a Culture of Disillusionment: Consumption in Moscow, a Chronicle of Changing Times." In *Worlds Apart: Modernity through the Prism of the Local,* ed. Daniel Miller, 43–68. London: Routledge.

———. 1996/97. "Myth-Making, Narratives, and the Dispossessed in Russia." *Cambridge Anthropology* 19(2):70–92.

———. 1999. "Traders, 'Disorder,' and Citizenship Regimes in Provincial Russia." In *Uncertain Transition: Ethnographies of Change in the Postsocialist World,* ed. Michael Burawoy and Katherine Verdery, 19–52. Lanham, Md.: Rowman & Littlefield Publishers.

Ioffe, Grigory, and Tatyana Nefedova. 1998. "Environs of Russian Cities: A Case Study of Moscow." *Europe-Asia Studies* 50(8):1325–1356.

Jackson, Jean E. 2000. *"Camp Pain": Talking with Chronic Pain Patients.* Philadelphia: University of Pennsylvania Press.

Jing, Jun, ed. 2000. *Feeding China's Little Emperors: Food, Children, and Social Change.* Stanford, Calif.: Stanford University Press.

Kaiser, Daniel H. 1998. "The Poor and Disabled in Early Eighteenth-Century Russian Towns." *Journal of Social History* 32(1):125–155.

Kates, Robert W. 1995. "Times of Hunger." In *Person, Place and Thing: Interpre-*

tive and Empirical Essays in Cultural Geography. Baton Rouge: Geosciences Publications, Louisiana State University.

Katseneliboigen, A. 1978. *Studies in Soviet Planning*. White Plains, N.Y.: M. E. Sharpe.

Khazanov, Anatoly M. 1998. "Whose City Is Moscow Today?" *Anthropology of East Europe Review* 16(1):15–26.

Khrushchev, N. S. 1964. Report to the USSR Supreme Soviet on Measures for Fulfilling the CPSU Program for Raising the Living Standards of the People. July 13, 1964. *Soviet Documents* 2(33–34):3–58.

Kideckel, David A. 1993. *The Solitude of Collectivism: Romanian Villagers to the Revolution and Beyond*. Ithaca, N.Y.: Cornell University Press.

Kingsbury, Susan M., and Mildred Fairchild. 1935. *Factory, Family, and Woman in the Soviet Union*. New York: G. P. Putnam's Sons.

Kitanina, T. M. 1985. *Voina, khleb i revoliutsiia* (War, bread and revolution). Leningrad: Nauka.

Kleyman, Vladimir. 2002. "After the Exodus: Soviet-Jewish Émigrés and Their Interaction with the American-Jewish Community." Senior thesis, Harvard University.

Kondo, Dorinne K. 1990. *Crafting Selves: Power, Gender, and Discourses of Identity in a Japanese Workplace*. Chicago: University of Chicago Press.

Konstantinov, Yulian. 1996. "Patterns of Reinterpretation: Trader-Tourism in the Balkans (Bulgaria) as a Picaresque Metaphorical Enactment of Post-Totalitarianism." *American Ethnologist* 23(4):762–782.

Kornai, János. 1997. *Struggle and Hope: Essays on Stabilization and Reform in a Post-Socialist Economy*. Northhampton, Mass.: Edward Elgar.

———. 2001. "The Borderline between the Spheres of Authority of the Citizen and the State: Recommendations for the Hungarian Health Reform." In *Reforming the State: Fiscal and Welfare Reform in Post-Socialist Countries*, ed. János Kornai, Stephan Haggard, and Robert R. Kaufman, 181–209. Cambridge: Cambridge University Press.

Kornai, János, and Karen Eggleston. 2001. *Welfare, Choice and Solidarity in Transition: Reforming the Health Care Sector in Eastern Europe*. Cambridge: Cambridge University Press.

Kornai, János, Stephan Haggard, and Robert R. Kaufman, eds. 2001. *Reforming the State: Fiscal and Welfare Reform in Post-Socialist Countries*. Cambridge: Cambridge University Press.

Kornblatt, Judith Deutsch. 1999. " 'Christianity, Antisemitism, Nationalism': Russian Orthodoxy in a Reborn Orthodox Russia." In *Consuming Russia: Popular Culture, Sex, and Society since Gorbachev*, ed. Adele Marie Barker, 414–436. Durham, N.C.: Duke University Press.

Kotkin, Stephen. 1995. *Magnetic Mountain: Stalinism as a Civilization*. Berkeley: University of California Press.

Kroncher, Allan. 1979. "The Economic and Political Aspects of Combatting Grain Losses in the USSR." *Radio Liberty Research Bulletin, RFE/RL* 55(70):1–2.

Krylova, Anna. 1999. "Saying 'Lenin' and Meaning 'Party': Subversion and

Laughter in Soviet and Post-Soviet Society." In *Consuming Russia: Popular Culture, Sex, and Society since Gorbachev,* ed. Adele Marie Baker, 243–265. Durham, N.C.: Duke University Press.

Lappé, Frances Moore, and Joseph Collins. 1997. "Beyond the Myths of Hunger: What Can We Do?" In *Food and Culture: A Reader,* ed. Carole Counihan and Penny Van Esterik, 402–411. New York: Routledge.

Lass, Andrew. 1999. "Portable Worlds: On the Limits of Replication in the Czech and Slovak Republics." In *Uncertain Transition: Ethnographies of Change in the Postsocialist World,* ed. Michael Burawoy and Katherine Verdery, 273–300. Lanham, Md.: Rowman & Littlefield Publishers.

Ledeneva, Alena V. 1996/97. "Between Gift and Commodity: The Phenomenon of *Blat.*" *Cambridge Anthropology* 19(3):43–66.

———. 1998. *Russia's Economy of Favours:* Blat, *Networking and Informal Exchange.* Cambridge: Cambridge University Press.

Leites, K. 1922. *Recent Economic Developments in Russia.* Oxford: Clarendon Press.

Lemon, Alaina. 1995. " 'What Are They Writing about Us Blacks'? Roma and Race in Russia." *Anthropology of East Europe Review* 13(2):34–40.

———. 1998. " 'Your Eyes Are Green Like Dollars': Counterfeit Cash, National Substance, and Currency Apartheid in 1990s Russia." *Cultural Anthropology* 13(1):22–55.

———. 2000. "Talking Transit and Spectating Transition: The Moscow Metro." In *Altering States: Ethnographies of Transition in Eastern Europe and the Former Soviet Union,* ed. Daphne Berdahl, Matti Bunzl, and Martha Lampland, 14–39. Ann Arbor: University of Michigan Press.

Lih, Lars T. 1990. *Bread and Authority in Russia, 1914–1921.* Berkeley: University of California Press.

Lindenmeyr, Adele. 1996. *Poverty Is Not a Vice: Charity, Society, and the State in Imperial Russia.* Princeton, N.J.: Princeton University Press.

Littell, Jonathan. 2001. "Food Aid to Russia: Welcome or Unwelcome?" In *The Geopolitics of Hunger, 2000–2001: Hunger and Power,* ed. Action Against Hunger, 283–301. Boulder, Colo.: Lynne Reinner Publishers.

Lonkila, Markku. 1998. "The Social Meaning of Work: Aspects of the Teaching Profession in Post-Soviet Russia." *Europe-Asia Studies* 50(4):699–712.

Lotman, Yu. M. 1994. *Besedy o russkoi kul'ture: Byt i traditsii russkogo dvorianstva (XVIII–nachalo XIX veka)* (Discussions about Russian culture: Daily life and the traditions of Russian nobility [18th–beginning of 19th century]). Saint Petersburg: "Isskustvo–SPB."

McAuley, Mary. 1991. *Bread and Justice: State and Society in Petrograd, 1917–1922.* Oxford: Clarendon Press.

McGuire, Michael. 1998. "Living on $10 a Month: Plunged into Poverty, Pensioners Try to Survive." *Chicago Tribune,* December 24, 1, 9.

McMahon, Colin. 1999. "Blood Shed over Theft of Produce." *Gazette,* September 27, A1.

McNabb, John. 1997. "Russians Face Food Shortages." *Chattanooga Times,* April 25, A2.

Malaby, Thomas. 2003. *Gambling Life: Dealing in Contingency in a Greek City*. Urbana: University of Illinois Press.

Malinowski, Bronislaw. 1961. *Argonauts of the Western Pacific*. New York: E. P. Dutton.

Marx, Karl. 1978. "The German Ideology: Part I." In *The Marx-Engels Reader*, ed. Robert C. Tucker, 146–200. New York: W. W. Norton.

Mauss, Marcel. 1990. *The Gift: The Form and Reason for Exchange in Archaic Societies*. Trans. W. D. Halls. London: Routledge.

Moine, Nathalie. 2000. "Are There Deserving Poor in the Country of Socialism? Some Examples of Social Work in Moscow during the 1930s." Paper presented at the Davis Center for Russian Studies, Harvard University, November.

Morton, Henry N. 1980. "Who Gets What, When, and How? Housing in the Soviet Union." *Soviet Studies* 32(2):235–259.

Moscow Times. 2002. "200 Kilograms of Radioactive Berries Seized." July 1, no. 2468:3.

Moskoff, William. 1990. *The Bread of Affliction: The Food Supply in the USSR during World War II*. Cambridge: Cambridge University Press.

Myerhoff, Barbara. 1978. *Number Our Days*. New York: Simon and Schuster.

Newman, Katherine S. 1999. *No Shame in My Game: The Working Poor in the Inner City*. New York: Vintage Books.

Nietzsche, Friedrich. 1964. *The Genealogy of Morals*. New York: Russell and Russell.

Noonan, John T. 1984. *Bribes*. Berkeley: University of California Press.

Okely, Judith. 1996. *Own or Other Culture*. London: Routledge.

Osokina, Elena. 2001. *Our Daily Bread: Socialist Distribution and the Art of Survival in Stalin's Russia, 1927–1941*. Armonk, N.Y.: M. E. Sharpe.

Patico, Jennifer. 2001a. "Consumption and Logics of Social Difference in Post-Soviet Russia." Ph.D. dissertation, New York University.

———. 2001b. "Globalization in the Postsocialist Marketplace: Consumer Readings of Difference and Development in Urban Russia." *Kroeber Anthropological Society Papers* 86:127–142.

Patico, Jennifer, and Melissa L. Caldwell. 2002. "Consumers Exiting Socialism: Ethnographic Perspectives on Daily Life in Post-Communist Europe." *Ethnos* 67(3):285–294.

Pesmen, Dale. 2000. *Russia and Soul: An Exploration*. Ithaca, N.Y.: Cornell University Press.

Petryna, Adriana. 2002. *Life Exposed: Biological Citizens after Chernobyl*. Princeton, N.J.: Princeton University Press.

Pine, Frances, and Sue Bridger. 1998. "Introduction: Transitions to Post-Socialism and Cultures of Survival." In *Surviving Post-Socialism: Local Strategies and Regional Responses in Eastern Europe and the Former Soviet Union*. ed. Sue Bridger and Frances Pine, 1–15. London: Routledge.

Pipes, Richard. 1984. *Survival Is Not Enough: Soviet Realities and America's Future*. New York: Simon and Schuster.

Platz, Stephanie. 2000. "The Shape of National Time: Daily Life, History, and

Identity during Armenia's Transition to Independence, 1991–1994." In *Altering States: Ethnographies of Transition in Eastern Europe and the Former Soviet Union,* ed. Daphne Berdahl, Matti Bunzl, and Martha Lampland, 114–138. Ann Arbor: University of Michigan Press.

Poppendieck, Janet. 1998. *Sweet Charity? Emergency Food and the End of Entitlement.* New York: Penguin Books.

Pottier, Johan. 1999. *The Anthropology of Food: The Social Dynamics of Food Security.* Cambridge: Polity Press.

Prindle, Peter H. 1979. "Peasant Society and Famine: A Nepalese Example." *Ethnology* 18(1):49–60.

Radio Liberty Research Bulletin, RFE/RL. 1977. "Critical Situation in the Food Sector." 105(77):1–2.

Reed-Danahay, Deborah. 1996. *Education and Identity in Rural France: The Politics of Schooling.* Cambridge: Cambridge University Press.

Riches, Graham, ed. 1997. *First World Hunger: Food Security and Welfare Politics.* New York: St. Martin's Press.

Ries, Nancy. 1997. *Russian Talk: Culture and Conversation during Perestroika.* Ithaca, N.Y.: Cornell University Press.

———. 1999. "Business, Taxes, and Corruption in Russia." *Anthropology of East Europe Review* 17(1):59–62.

———. 2000. "Foreword: Anthropology and Postsocialism." In *Fieldwork Dilemmas: Anthropologists in Postsocialist States,* ed. Hermine G. DeSoto and Nora Dudwick, ix–xi. Madison: University of Wisconsin Press.

———. n.d. "Surviving Economic Hardship in Russia." Unpublished manuscript.

Riskin, Carl. 1991. "Feeding China: The Experience since 1949." In *The Political Economy of Hunger,* vol. 3, ed. Jean Drèze and Amartya Sen, 15–53. Oxford: Clarendon Press.

Rivkin-Fish, Michele. 2002. "Gifts, Bribes, and Unofficial Payments: Towards an Anthropology of 'Corruption' in Russia." Paper presented at Seventh Biennial Meetings of the European Association of Social Anthropologists, Copenhagen, Denmark, August.

Rosaldo, Renato. 1993. *Culture and Truth: The Remaking of Social Analysis.* Boston: Beacon Press.

Rotenberg, Robert. 1999. "Landscape and Power in Vienna: Gardens of Discovery." In *Theorizing the City: The New Urban Anthropology Reader,* ed. Setha Low, 138–165. New Brunswick, N.J.: Rutgers University Press.

Rothstein, Halina, and Robert A. Rothstein. 1997. "The Beginnings of Soviet Culinary Arts." In *Food in Russian History and Culture,* ed. Musya Glants and Joyce Toomre, 177–194. Bloomington: Indiana University Press.

Rousseau, Jean-Jacques. 1987. *The Basic Political Writings,* ed. and trans. Donald A. Cress. Indianapolis: Hackett Publishing Company.

Royce, Anya. 1982. *Ethnic Identity: Strategies of Diversity.* Bloomington: Indiana University Press.

Ruby, Walter. 1999. "Moscow Soup Kitchen Nourishes Pensioners' Spirit As Well As Body." *New Jersey Jewish News.* April 1. www.njjewishnews.com/issues/4_1_99/mw/feature/text/story1.html. Accessed on April 4, 2003.

Russian Information and Review. 1921. "Famine Notes." 1 (4, November 15):77–80.

Russian Red Cross Society Central Committee. 1998. Belarus, Moldova, Russian Federation, Ukraine: Winter Emergency 1998–1999. Appeal No. 30/98. September 30, 1998.

Sachs, Ignacy. 1991. "Growth and Poverty: Some Lessons from Brazil." In *The Political Economy of Hunger,* vol. 3, ed. Jean Drèze and Amartya Sen, 93–118. Oxford: Clarendon Press.

Sack, Daniel. 2000. *Whitebread Protestants: Food and Religion in American Culture.* New York: St. Martin's Press.

Sahlins, Marshall. 1972. *Stone Age Economics.* Chicago: Aldine Atherton.

Said, Edward W. 1978. *Orientalism.* New York: Vintage Books.

Sampson, Steven. 1995. "All Is Possible, Nothing Is Certain: The Horizons of Transition in a Romanian Village." In *East European Communities: The Struggle for Balance in Turbulent Times,* ed. David A. Kideckel, 159–176. Boulder, Colo.: Westview Press.

Schama, Simon. 1995. *Landscape and Memory.* New York: Vintage Books.

Scharf, Thomas. 1997. "Informal Support for Older People in Post-Unification East Germany: Stability and Change." *Journal of Cross-Cultural Gerontology* 12:61–72.

Scheper-Hughes, Nancy. 1992. *Death without Weeping: The Violence of Everyday Life in Brazil.* Berkeley: University of California Press.

Scott, James C. 1985. *Weapons of the Weak: Everyday Forms of Peasant Resistance.* New Haven, Conn.: Yale University Press.

Shack, William A. 1997. "Hunger, Anxiety, and Ritual: Deprivation and Spirit Possession among the Gurage of Ethiopia." In *Food and Culture: A Reader,* ed. Carole Counihan and Penny Van Esterik, 125–137. New York: Routledge.

Shekshnia, Stanislav V., Sheila M. Puffer, and Daniel J. McCarthy. 2002. "To Russia with Big Macs: Labour Relations in the Russian Fast-Food Industry." In *Labour Relations in the Global Fast-Food Industry,* ed. Tony Royle and Brian Towers, 117–135. London: Routledge.

Shevchenko, Olga. 2002. " 'In Case of Emergency': Consumption, Security, and the Meaning of Durables in a Transforming Society." *Journal of Consumer Culture* 2(2):147–170.

Shkolnikov, Vladimir M., Mark G. Field, and Evgueniy M. Andreev. 2001. "Russia: Socioeconomic Dimensions of the Gender Gap in Mortality." In *Challenging Inequities in Health: From Ethics to Action,* ed. Timothy Evans, Margaret Whitehead, Finn Diderichsen, Abbas Bhuiya, and Meg Wirth, 138–155. Oxford: Oxford University Press.

Shlapentokh, Vladimir. 1989. *Public and Private Life of the Soviet People: Changing Values in Post-Stalin Russia.* New York: Oxford University Press.

Siegelbaum, Lewis H. 1998. " 'Dear Comrade, You Ask What We Need': Socialist Paternalism and Soviet Rural 'Notables' in the Mid-1930s." *Slavic Review* 57(1): 107–132.

Silverman, Carol. 2000. "Researcher, Advocate, Friend: An American Fieldworker among Balkan Roma, 1980–1996." In *Fieldwork Dilemmas: Anthropol-*

ogists in Postsocialist States, ed. Hermine G. DeSoto and Nora Dudwick, 195–217. Madison: University of Wisconsin Press.

Simonsen, Sven Gunnar. 1999. "Inheriting the Soviet Policy Toolbox: Russia's Dilemma over Ascriptive Identity." *Europe-Asia Studies* 51(6):1069–1087.

Slavin, Barbara. 1998. "Distribution Dispute Tangles Relief Package for Russia: U.S. Wants to Ensure $885 Million Worth of Food Gets to Needy." *USA Today,* December 23, 8A.

Smith, Adam. 1981. *An Inquiry into the Nature and Causes of the Wealth of Nations.* Vols. 1 and 2. Ed. R. H. Campbell and A. S. Skinner. Indianapolis: Liberty Fund.

Steele, Jonathan. 1998. "Russia's Abnormal Economy." *Journal of Commerce,* August 14. Cited in Johnson's Russia List #2307, August 14, 1998, available at www.cdi.org/russia/johnson/archives.cfm.

Stepanov, Yu. S. 1997. *Konstanty: Slovar' russkoi kul'tury* (Constants: Dictionary of Russian culture). Moscow: Shkola "Iazyki Russkoi Kul'tury."

Stevens, Carolyn S. 1997. *On the Margins of Japanese Society: Volunteers and the Welfare of the Urban Underclass.* London: Routledge.

Stites, Richard. 1992. *Russian Popular Culture: Entertainment and Society since 1900.* Cambridge: Cambridge University Press.

Szemere, Anna. 2000. " 'We've Kicked the Habit': (Anti)Politics of Art's Autonomy and Transition in Hungary." In *Altering States: Ethnographies of Transition in Eastern Europe and the Former Soviet Union,* ed. Daphne Berdahl, Matti Bunzl, and Martha Lampland, 158–180. Ann Arbor: University of Michigan Press.

Talmadge, I. D. W. 1943. "The Enjoyment of Laughter in Russia." *Russian Review* 2(2):45–51.

Tapper, Richard, and Nancy Tapper. 1986. " 'Eat This, It'll Do You a Power of Good': Food and Commensality among Durrani Pashtuns." *American Ethnologist* 13(1):62–79.

Terrio, Susan J. 2000. *Crafting the Culture and History of French Chocolate.* Berkeley: University of California Press.

Turnbull, Colin M. 1972. *The Mountain People.* New York: Simon and Schuster.

Turner, Victor. 1967. *The Forest of Symbols: Aspects of Ndembu Ritual.* Ithaca, N.Y.: Cornell University Press.

Twigg, Judyth L. 2000. "Unfulfilled Hopes: The Struggle to Reform Russian Health Care and Its Financing." In *Russia's Torn Safety Nets: Health and Social Welfare during the Transition,* ed. Mark G. Field and Judyth L. Twigg, 43–64. New York: St. Martin's Press.

U.S. Senate. 1999. Committee on Foreign Relations. *Corruption in Russia: Hearing before the Committee on Foreign Relations.* 106th Cong., 1st sess., September 30.

Verdery, Katherine. 1983. *Transylvanian Villagers: Three Centuries of Political, Economic, and Ethnic Change.* Berkeley: University of California Press.

———. 1995. "Faith, Hope, and *Caritas* in the Land of the Pyramids: Romania, 1990 to 1994." *Comparative Studies in Society and History* 37(4):625–669.

———. 1996. *What Was Socialism and What Comes Next?* Princeton, N.J.: Princeton University Press.

———. 1999. "Fuzzy Property: Rights, Power, and Identity in Transylvania's Decollectivization." In *Uncertain Transition: Ethnographies of Change in the Postsocialist World,* ed. Michael Burawoy and Katherine Verdery, 53–81. Lanham, Md.: Rowman & Littlefield Publishers.

Wädekin, Karl-Eugen. 1980. "Round-Table Discussion on Private Food Production and Marketing." *Radio Liberty Research Bulletin, RFE/RL* 449(80):1–4.

Walker, Michael. 1998. "Survival Strategies in an Industrial Town in East Ukraine." In *Surviving Post-Socialism: Local Strategies and Regional Responses in Eastern Europe and the Former Soviet Union,* ed. Sue Bridger and Frances Pine, 188–202. London: Routledge.

Wanner, Catherine. 1998. *Burden of Dreams: History and Identity in Post-Soviet Ukraine.* University Park: Pennsylvania State University Press.

Watson, James L. 1997. "Introduction: Transnationalism, Localization, and Fast Foods in East Asia." In *Golden Arches East: McDonald's in East Asia,* ed. James L. Watson, 1–38. Stanford, Calif.: Stanford University Press.

Wedel, Janine R. 1986. *The Private Poland.* New York: Facts on File.

———. 1998a. *Collision and Collusion: The Strange Case of Western Aid to Eastern Europe, 1989–1998.* New York: St. Martin's Press.

———. 1998b. "Informal Relations and Institutional Change: How Eastern European Cliques and States Mutually Respond." *Anthropology of East Europe Review* 16(1):4–13.

Weissman, Benjamin M. 1974. *Herbert Hoover and Famine Relief to Soviet Russia: 1921–1923.* Hoover Institution Publications, 134. Stanford, Calif.: Stanford University Press.

Wheeler, Marcus. 1984. *The Oxford Russian-English Dictionary.* Oxford: Clarendon Press.

Womack, Helen. 1998. "A Rotten, Decaying Nation." *Independent,* August 17. Cited in Johnson's Russia List #2311, August 17, 1998, available at www.cdi.org/russia/johnson/archives.cfm.

Woodruff, David. 1999. "Barter of the Bankrupt: The Politics of Demonetization in Russia's Federal State." In *Uncertain Transition: Ethnographies of Change in the Postsocialist World,* ed. Michael Burawoy and Katherine Verdery, 83–124. Lanham, Md.: Rowman & Littlefield Publishers.

World Council of Churches and Russian Orthodox Church. 2000. "The Problems of Food Aid to the Poor in Russia Today." *Round Table "Education for Change and Diaconia."* www.rondtb.msk.ru/info/en/food_en.htm. Accessed on September 27, 2000.

Yan, Yunxiang. 1996. *The Flow of Gifts: Reciprocity and Social Networks in a Chinese Village.* Stanford, Calif.: Stanford University Press.

———. 2000. "Of Hamburger and Social Space: Consuming McDonald's in Beijing." In *The Consumer Revolution in Urban China,* ed. Deborah S. Davis, 201–225. Berkeley: University of California Press.

Yang, Mayfair. 1989. "The Gift Economy and State Power in China." *Comparative Studies in Society and History* 31(1):25–54.

Young, Cathy. 1989. *Growing Up in Moscow: Memories of a Soviet Girlhood.* New York: Ticknor & Fields.

Zabusky, Stacia E. 1995. *Launching Europe: An Ethnography of European Conversation in Space Science.* Princeton, N.J.: Princeton University Press.

Zelensky, Elizabeth Kristofovich. 1999. "Popular Children's Culture in Post-Perestroika Russia: Songs of Innocence and Experience Revisited." In *Consuming Russia: Popular Culture, Sex, and Society since Gorbachev,* ed. Adele Marie Barker, 138–160. Durham, N.C.: Duke University Press.

Zhukov, V. P. 1998. *Slovar' russkikh poslovits i pogovorok* (Dictionary of Russian proverbs and sayings). Moscow: Izdatel'stvo "Russkii Iazyk."

Zinoviev, Aleksandr. 1985. *Homo Sovieticus.* Trans. Charles Janson. Boston: Atlantic Monthly Press.

Živković, Marko. 2000. "Telling Stories of Serbia: Native and Other Dilemmas on the Edge of Chaos." In *Fieldwork Dilemmas: Anthropologists in Postsocialist Places,* ed. Hermine G. DeSoto and Nora Dudwick, 73–99. Madison: University of Wisconsin Press.

Index

Italicized page numbers indicate illustrations.

Compositor:	Binghamton Valley Composition
Text:	10/13 Galliard
Display:	Galliard
Printer and binder:	Maple-Vail Manufacturing Group